I0879003

The Famous Speeches of the Eight Chicago Anarchists

WORKING CLASSICS

The Working Classics series grounds us in lineages of radical thought. We find writers throughout our movement's history grappling with many of the same questions we struggle to answer today, while facing similar opponents. These anarchist lineages offer strength for the road ahead by providing a map of where we've been.

Also in the series:

The Conquest of Bread, by Peter Kropotkin
Now and After, by Alexander Berkman
Anarchism and Other Essays, by Emma Goldman (annotated edition)

The Famous Speeches of the Eight Chicago Anarchists

When Asked if They Had Anything to Say Why Sentence of Death Should Not Be Passed Upon Them, Oct. 7, 8, and 9, 1886.

Edited by Lucy E. Parsons

Foreword by David R. Roediger

Appendix includes an essay by Voltairine de Cleyre

AK PRESS

The Famous Speeches of the Eight Chicago Anarchists
Edited by Lucy E. Parsons
Working Classics series
This edition © 2025 AK Press
Foreword © 2025 David R. Roediger

ISBN 9781849356305
E-ISBN 9781849356312
Library of Congress Number: 2025936925

AK Press
370 Ryan Avenue #100
Chico, CA 95973
www.akpress.org
akpress@akpress.org
510.208.1700

AK Press
33 Tower St.
Edinburgh EH6 7BN
Scotland
www.akuk.com
akuk@akpress.org

Cover design by Suzanne Shaffer
Cover illustration by Dante Aguilera Benitez
Interior illustrations from William D. Bancroft's *McKinley, Garfield, Lincoln : Their Lives, Their deeds, Their Deaths, with a Record of Notable Assassinations and a History of Anarchy* and *Washington Progress*.
Printed in the USA on acid-free paper

Their Last Words on the Scaffold

There will come a time when our silence will be more powerful than the voices you strangle today. —August Spies.

Hurrah for Anarchy! —George Engel.

Hurrah for Anarchy! This is the happiest moment of my life. —Adolph Fischer.

Let me speak, oh men of America! Will you let me speak, Sheriff Matson! Let the voice of the people be heard! Oh— —Albert R. Parsons.

Contents

Foreword by David R. Roediger 1

Introduction by Lucy Parsons. 9

Speeches:

August Spies. 19

Michael Schwab. 43

Oscar Neebe 49

Adolph Fischer 57

Louis Lingg. 61

George Engel 67

Samuel Fielden 73

Albert Parsons. 115

Appendix: "The Eleventh of November 1887"
by Voltairine de Cleyre 213

Foreword

Haymarket was not that long ago. In my longest stretch of living in Chicago, from the mid-1970s till the mid-1990s, the artist O. William Neebe was very much alive. Known as Bill, he was the grandson of Oscar Neebe, one the eight Haymarket bombing defendants whose final words to the court that convicted them are republished in this book. The granddad was the only one not originally sentenced to death, though two others later saw their sentences reduced and then, like Neebe, received pardons from the governor of Illinois. Bill Neebe would get to know his grandfather. Eventually, but only by leaving the United States, Bill also came to know Oscar's fame in the wider world.

Those of us working to build on the heritage of Haymarket in Chicago cherished but also were challenged by the story Bill Neebe told of visiting Mexico City in 1939 as a fifteen-year-old. There he encountered Oscar's image in both May Day demonstrations and in the celebrated Unity House murals of Diego Rivera, where the Haymarket defendants stood alongside Karl Marx. If this was heady stuff for a teenager reimagining his grandfather it was also sobering for us who regarded Chicago as the logical place for such learning to occur. Franklin Rosemont and I knew the story as we assembled *Haymarket Scrapbook* in the mid-1980s. It both inspired and burdened us.

The tragedy of how little Haymarket occupies historical imagination in the US reflects the ability of rulers to portray May Day, a world labor holiday whose roots lie in the Haymarket mass strikes and their repression, as if it were an enemy invention. In the US May Day is officially Law Day, in a crude disavowal of the anarchists who put it on the calendar. Academic historians have tried to tell a different story, with three major studies of the Haymarket events (by Henry David, Paul Avrich, and James Green) appearing over the years along with Bruce Nelson's magnificent history from below of the anarchist movement. Work on the brilliant anarchist troublemaker Lucy Parsons, the editor of this book of speeches, has proceeded as well.

Public history in Chicago has not made the Haymarket martyrs well-known but has ensured that they not be fully forgotten. The high point came early with the 1893 dedication of the Forest Home Cemetery monument to those executed. The graves of later radicals bunch now around the monument. Visitors arrive regularly and crowds occasionally. Often though they are international tourists a little deflated that there's not more going on, especially if their visits deliberately coincide with May Day.

Another statue, constructed in 1889 as a memorial to the police, originally stood at the site of the bombing and police riot itself. Thrice destroyed, it is banished to the relative privacy of Chicago's Police Training Center. Labor, public historians, and municipal authorities joined forces to produce what is now an official Haymarket monument, unveiled in 2004. It sits near where the police statue had been, reproducing the wagon from which protesters had spoken, a well-meaning piece of public art but one rightly described by the *New York Times* as "ambiguous" in its political meaning. If my email inbox is a guide, Haymarket is a mass strike that has launched a thousand high-school History Day projects. There are now apartment buildings named for Lucy Parsons.

But we remain very far from realizing the dream of the great Chicago writer Nelson Algren regarding how the Haymarket martyrs ought to be remembered in public. Algren urged, in an interview with Rosemont, that the Haymarket site be marked by a statue of Albert Parsons. He further proposed that the words of the youngest and most vilified—and by some of us understandably romanticized—of the martyrs, Louis Lingg, appear on its base: "I despise your order, your laws, your force-propped authority. Hang me for it."

What we sadly lack are US cultural productions telling the story of Haymarket. Where is the US equivalent of Rivera's Unity House murals, for example? In theatre, there are US plays about Haymarket, including the recent, award-winning *Haymarket: A New Folk Musical*. But the cultural front of the 1930s and 40s notwithstanding, no Haymarket drama foundational to US theatre or to proletarian literature exists. An embarrassing comparison is with Germany, where

Erwin Piscator's 1924 staging of Alfons Paquet's *Flags*, a play bringing Haymarket to life, is plausibly claimed—including by Piscator himself—as the "first Marxist drama." US commercial culture, including especially Hollywood, has remained spectacularly indifferent to the dramas of the Haymarket events.

And yet dramas of love, transformation, and solidarity run through Haymarket and its cast of characters. Hollywood ignores the incredible love story of Albert Parsons, the longest speaking of the defendants in this book, and his partner Lucy. She was born a slave and he, as a teenager, soldiered for the Confederacy in the Civil War. Liberated by the example of what W.E.B. Du Bois called the "general strike of the slaves," and the self-emancipation it produced, Lucy and Albert both embraced freedom dreams. He printed a pro-Reconstruction newspaper and worked for the Republican party, which Parsons and Du Bois both regarded as a "labor party" at that time. The newly free air of Texas made it possible for Lucy and Albert to become both comrades and a couple. But with the forces of counter-revolution gathering, and Albert already wounded in the attending terror, they moved to Chicago and new kinds of working-class radicalism.

Even the romance of August Spies and Nina Van Zandt Spies, much more suited to Hollywood formulae, went unfilmed. He was a handsome German immigrant upholsterer and anarchist leader, just turned thirty, and the first named when the state indicted the Haymarket Eight. She, described as beautiful, descended from colonial elites in the US and reputedly from Stuart dynasty in Britain. Nina had attended Vassar College and a finishing school in Chicago. The notorious judge in the Haymarket trial arranged for Nina and her mother to attend its proceedings. Nina, fascinated with the defendants and with the new worlds opened to her by the issues in the case, snatched moments to be with Spies particularly, and the two fell in love. They married, in a proxy ceremony, not long before his hanging ended the "jailhouse romance."

The dramas of solidarity were as arresting as those involving romance. Albert Parsons, who went underground in the anti-anarchist, anti-immigrant hysteria after the Haymarket bombing, was successfully hiding and working in the building trades in Wisconsin as the defendants were about face trial for their lives. Never apprehended by the authorities, he simply walked into the court as the trial started, asking to be tried with his comrades. Neebe received the news that the court had spared him from a death sentence by declaring that he wished all the accused had been treated alike.

The speeches of the Haymarket defendants reproduced below carry their own dramas, framed by the circumstances of their delivery. The police riot and bombing occurred on May 4, 1886. By October the court had pronounced death sentences on seven of the eight. After the verdict theirs was an opportunity to speak, whether in mitigation, in an argument for a new trial, or in defiance, to a court that had already validated their views regarding how the state treats those demanding a new society.

They spoke for their lives, for their dignity as truth tellers, for the possibility of building a popular movement against their own hangings, and for the future of the "Chicago idea's" combination of anarchism and socialism. The defendants emphasized that the court had allowed that only a loose conspiracy defined by talking about self-defense and revolutionary violence needed to proven, not actual involvement in the particular bombing on May 4, subverting the possibility of a fair trial.

Condemned in effect for anarchy, the accused disavowed it neither as a philosophy nor as a political project. In particular they defended the idea that force shaped society as a commonsense proposition and as a historical truth forwarded not just or first by revolutionaries but by class society. They wrote after all as men shaped by the striking combination of carnage and liberation attending the US Civil War, by the anti-Indian wars that followed, by the German wars of unification, by the beginning of the obscene European "scramble" for African colonies, and by the heartless repression of the Paris Commune. George Engel emphasized, refusing to soft-pedal political views before a hostile court, that he and fellow members of the International Working People's Association (IWPA) "have the firm conviction that the workingman can free himself from the tyranny of capitalism only through force."

Moreover, and this is better seen in that other volume of Haymarket eight *testimonios*, *The Autobiographies of the Haymarket Martyrs*, the migrations and work lives of the defendants reflected forced choices, driven by want. As the Haymarket defendant Michael Schwab told the court, the worker "acts under compulsion, and they call it a free contract." Such structured oppression, the convicted militants stressed, and not the calls of anarchists, predicted violence.

The labor struggles workers mounted in response, fighting as Radical Republicans, Socialists, Knights of Labor, or anarchists, were met with rifle and cannon fire. Attacks came whether in Texas, Michigan, Pennsylvania, Chicago, or East St. Louis and whether at the hands of police, company guards, the Ku Klux Klan, federal troops, or conservative citizens constituted as private anti-labor militias. Engel's insistence that "when workingmen ask an increase in their wages, the militia and the police are sent out to shoot them down" was not theorizing on his part but reporting based on bitter experience. Certainly, as the speeches establish, the bloodlust toward socialists and the poor expressed by capitalist leaders and their press far outmatched that of the anarchists. The early publication of the defendants' words by the Socialistic Publishing Society featured *Famous Speeches* not as title but as subtitle. Above was the title: *THE ACCUSED THE ACCUSERS.*

At first the remedy seemed obvious. Anarchists and others formed study-and-rifle clubs, drilling to fight against those who would shoot them. They were invited into the coalition supporting May 1, 1886, campaigns for the eight-hour working day by the relatively conservative Federation of Organized Trades and Labor Unions in part because their armed organization could reassure workers that a mass strike would not necessarily lead, as it had in the past, to strikers being butchered.

When just such violence did unfold, outside the McCormick farm equipment factory on May 3, the IWPA had to show the ability to insist on rights in the face of terror. Thus the May 4 protest. Some of the accused, and here again there was no shrinking from conviction, allowed that some organizing for that demonstration mentioned the possibility of resistance in self-defense if there were police attacks. The speeches showed the defendants' remarkable ability, as Lucy Parsons put it in a different context, to be "firm without bravado" when they confidently asserted armed self-defense as a right established constitutionally and at law.

But by the time of the May 1, 1886 mass strikes a sharp question had arisen as to whether study-and-rifle clubs could compete with the armed might of governments and other representatives of endless counterrevolutions of property. The hard fact that revolutionaries faced was that, in the words of Albert Parsons, "A Winchester rifle cost $18." The intimidating street-riot drills with which the state aimed to terrify workers underlined, in Parsons' view, the fact the authorities possessed vast resources for studying war and securing weapons that workers could not equal.

The cheapness and destructive power of dynamite therefore exercised considerable appeal. Parsons turned from gloom over capital's funding of repressive firepower to the observation that "the dynamite bomb . . . costs six cents." Lingg's defiant speech reasserted what he had long told authorities: "If you cannonade us, we shall dynamite you." Parsons extravagantly hoped that "dynamite comes as the emancipator of man from the domination and enslavement of his fellowman."

And yet in closing it seems necessary to stress—as it would have seemed unnecessary to do even twenty years ago—that for all their candid, courageous speaking their movement's truths to power, the Haymarket Eight unanimously and vigorously declared in their speeches that they were absolutely innocent of the Haymarket bombing. They held that they were victims of a wild, nativist, and capitalist miscarriage of justice. They excoriated the state's and the press' resort to anti-immigrant hatred and the prosecution's bait-and-switch dodge from promising at the start to prove that August Spies led a conspiracy to kill police at Haymarket to securing a conviction instead based in large measure merely on what the radical writer Floyd Dell would later call "bomb-talking" by the IWPA. They pointed out that many defendants were absent from Haymarket when the bomb exploded and that they did not meet to conspire—indeed did not have regular, or in some cases any, contact with each other.

Whether from an academic desire for new narratives or from a wish to remember that the oppressed have sometimes managed to give as good as it got where violence is concerned, the ideas that the Haymarket defendants were guilty and, more outrageously, that they received a fair trial have gained a little toehold in the history business. Such arguments may have already outlived their vogue, or they may continue. In any case we should remember that these were decidedly not the arguments of the Haymarket martyrs themselves.

David R. Roediger

INTRODUCTION

The Eleventh of November, 1887

As included in the eighth edition of *The Famous Speeches of the Eight Chicago Anarchists*, edited by Lucy E. Parsons

The Eleventh of November has become a day of international importance, cherished in the hearts of all true lovers of liberty as a day of martyrdom. On this day was offered upon the cruel gallows tree, martyrs as true to their high ideals as were ever sacrificed in any age.

The writer will assume that the present generation is but superficially informed regarding the details that led up to the eleventh of November, for in this busy age, twenty-five years is a long time to remember the details of any event, however important.

In 1886 the working class of America, for the first time, struck for the reduction of the hours of daily toil to eight per day. It was a great strike. Chicago was the storm center of that strike, because of the activities of the martyrs of the eleventh of November, 1887.

The working class practically tied up the city of Chicago, Illinois, for three days. On the afternoon of the third, of that year, the police shot several strikers and clubbed many more brutally. The next evening, May the fourth, the now historic Haymarket meeting was held. The Haymarket meeting is referred to historically as the "Haymarket Riot." This Haymarket meeting was absolutely peaceable and quiet. The Mayor of Chicago attended the meeting, and, subsequently, took the stand as the first witness for the defense at the Anarchist Trial, so called. Following is the mayor's testimony in part:

"I went to the meeting for the purpose of dispersing it, in case I should feel it necessary for the safety of the city. There was no suggestion made by either of the speakers looking toward calling for immediate use of force or violence towards any persons that night; if there had been, I should have dispersed them at once. I went to the police station during Parsons' speech and I stated to Captain Bonfield that I thought the speeches were about over; that nothing had occurred or looked likely to occur to require interference, and that he had better issue orders to his reserves at the stations to go home. Bonfield replied that he had reached the same conclusion from reports brought to him. . . . During my attendance I saw no weapons at all upon any person. . . . In listening to the speeches, I concluded that it was not an organization to destroy property. After listening a little longer, I went home." This extract is here given from the Mayor's testimony, because this meeting is referred to very often, even by radicals, as the "Haymarket Riot." Had the inspector of police obeyed the Mayor's orders and not rushed a company of police upon that peaceful meeting, there would have been no trouble. Instead, as soon as the Mayor left, the inspector rushed a company of bluecoats to the meeting; they began clubbing the men and women and scattered them in every direction. Upon this onrush of the police, someone threw a bomb. Who threw that bomb, no one to this day knows, except he who threw it.

He has never been identified, never been arrested, consequently could never have been tried, but my husband and his comrades were put to death on November 11th as co-conspirators with the bomb-thrower, but he is unknown!

Our comrades were not murdered by the state because they had any connection with the bomb-throwing, but because they had been active in organizing the wage-slaves of America thirty years ago.

The capitalistic class didn't want to find the bomb-thrower; they foolishly believed that by putting to death the active spirits of the labor movement of that time they could frighten the working class back into slavery.

The so-called trial was the greatest travesty upon justice of modern times. The bailiff who was selecting the jury, a creature named Ryce, boasted thus: "I am managing this case and I know what I am about. Those fellows [our comrades] are going to hang as certain as death. I am calling such men as the defendants will have to challenge peremptorily and waste their time and challenges. Then they will have to take such jurymen as the prosecution wants."

The jury that did try the case was out less than three hours. They left the court room after four o'clock on August 23 and before seven o'clock the self—same afternoon had reached the astounding verdict, sending seven men to the gallows and the eighth man to the penitentiary for the term of fifteen years. The trial had lasted some sixty-three days. Think of the mass of testimony that the jury would have had to go over in order to give them even the semblance of a fair trial! Then think of the audacity of a jury being out less than three hours, and of the brutality of a community putting men to death under such a verdict and never allowing them a new trial!

Albert R. Parsons, my husband, never was arrested. On May 5, the day after the Haymarket meeting, when he saw the men with whom he had been organizing labor for the past ten years of his life, being arrested and thrown into prison and treated generally as criminals, he left Chicago. On June 21, the day the trial began, he walked into the court room, unrecognized by the police and detectives, and surrendered himself, he having been indicted during his absence and a reward of $5,000 having been offered for his arrest. He asked the court to grant him a fair trial that he might prove his absolute innocence. He was never granted the shadow of a fair and impartial trial and was put to death with the rest of his comrades on November 11, 1887!

The men were asked if they had anything to say as to why sentence of death should not be passed upon them. They arose in the court room on the days of October 7, 8 and 9, 1886, and delivered their now so "Famous Speeches," giving their reasons why the sentence of death should be suspended and they be given a new trial. They called the judge's attention to the fact that the leading capitalistic paper in Chicago had opened up its columns to receive subscriptions to a fund of $100,000.00, to be paid to the jury as a present for the verdict it had rendered against them. But they were never granted a new trial. They were, instead, railroaded to the gallows at the command of the money power!

For the past two years I have devoted myself to selling their speeches. The Seventh Edition, of 14,000, will be out in a few weeks' time, being now in press.* These copies of the Speeches have been practically all sold amongst the members of the conservative organized labor unions.

Verily, their "SILENCE IS MORE POWERFUL THAN THE VOICES THAT WERE STRANGLED" that dark November day!

There could be no other results in a matter that had already been fixed in advance, except such as came on October 10, when the infamous Judge "Jeffries" gave out his reasons for denying a new trial, and afterwards sentenced them to death. No more remarkable scene than that could well be imagined. The hot, stifling courtroom, crammed to its utmost capacity by an eager crowd, quite in sympathy with the capitalistic ideas and breaking at times into clapping, which was illy and hypocritically repressed by the only too gratified court—the little, ugly, hard-visaged judge, with a nutcracker bald head and cunning eyes. One could fancy his tender mercies—if ever they existed—as dried up and long since fallen to dust. Then the coarse, brutal state's attorney, with the ferocious howl of an infuriated, blood-hungry wild beast, who continually bellowed for the lives of these men before him. And the little cunning, red-headed lawyer who made the most telling speech that the State gave out, a cruel, crafty effort that misrepresented everything, absolutely, and did it so foxily that each point drew blood like the slash of a claw.

Forever will live in the minds' eyes of those who had the sad privilege of seeing this strange and terrible scene, the calm and noble countenances of the accused, who showed no feeling except

* The Jewish comrades now have a movement started to have these Speeches translated and published in the Yiddish language.

when an occasional flicker of fine scorn passed over their refined countenances, as they sat and heard their every act, deed, thought, meaning, however innocent, misrepresented, twisted and their lives going to certain destruction at the hands of their enemies' tools and minions. All the way through and especially noticeable the last day, detectives and police, plain-clothes men, and others of that ilk, filled the court room. When the sentence of death was being pronounced, these fellows stood up and pointed their revolvers right into the faces of our comrades, evidently fearing—scoundrels are ever cowards—an attempt at rescue on the part of friends, on this, the last appearance of the prisoners outside of the jail. But no such attempt was made and sentence was passed, the date of the execution being set for December 3. One instant to give a passing hand-shake to sorrowing relatives and indignant friends and they were marched back again to their dungeons.

Then began the long, tedious period that lasted for over a year, our comrades languishing in their living tombs. The attorneys for the defense began occupying themselves with their preparations for taking the case to the Illinois Supreme Court and accordingly an appeal was made to a judge of that body, on November 25, who granted a supersedeas and admitted that error had been made. Many friends believed that this meant that our comrades would evidently walk out free men, but those who had seen the working of the trial knew better. They knew that the supersedeas as well as every other step of the proceedings, was carefully taken with a view to giving the world an idea of the "impartiality" of the absolutely hellish conspiracy, the animus of which was to do away with certain labor leaders whose intelligence, honesty and fearlessness had made them objects of the fear and hatred of the capitalistic "Robber-Baron" element. This supersedes, therefore, merely gave a breathing spell for the lawyers to get ready their briefs for a hearing of the plea for a new trial before the Illinois Supreme Court. The friends and many persons indignant at the monstrousness of proceedings they had only supposed possible under the reign of the "Little Father" of all the Russians, were firmly determined to try every court available, in order to prove and make the point that the courts were not impartial but, instead, the ready tools of the moneyed power. Our comrades themselves always believed this, that no justice would ever be done them by any court, and, indeed, that the whole affair was to be regarded in the light of a howling farce, were not murder, of the most revolting and cold-blooded sort, the evident intention.

This appeal went to the Illinois Supreme Court on March 18, had the same hypocritical examination, the honorable judges deciding that no errors had been made of any gravity,—when, as a matter of fact, they were there thick—and the decision of the lower court was sustained, the day of execution being again set, this time for November 11, 1887.

So month after month dragged along for our comrades, suffering acutely for want of exercise and fresh air—when this old jail was subsequently torn down to make way for the new one, a black lake of putrid filth was found, fully explaining why our comrades had their teeth decay and fall out—and in the frantic efforts of friends, sympathizers and enlightened persons generally, to show the mass of the people what was being done, all in the name of law and order. The relatives, friends, the Defense Committee and many persons of recognized positions, writers, lecturers, poets, held meetings, distributed circulars, brochures and wrote articles for the radical press—the capitalistic press was solidly closed against one word of the truth—and the public would have finally seen at least something of what was being done, had not the police, ever vigilant in their hate, counteracted it all by "finding" bombs at regular intervals, under sidewalks, in alleys, etc. Made by the police themselves, placed there in the night, these bombs were solemnly "found" in the morning and served as the subject of blazing editorials and solemn, life-sized pictures in the leading capitalistic papers. The public, which does not go below the surface, believed what it was told. The old, wicked Judge "Jeffries," the state's attorney, and other tools of the money-power, all whined about threats on their lives and so on, and so the public was kept at that excited and ugly temper that was wanted of them—as when, two thousand years ago they shouted "Let loose to us Barabbas"—for the hirelings of the high and mighty scoundrels who were putting through this judicial murder fully meant to so befuddle the public on the facts as to get its backing and consent.

So the time wore away through the hot summer to autumn, when the attorneys for the defense took the case to the U. S. Supreme Court. These scoundrelly bigwigs, in solemn conclave, decided that no Constitutional Right had been violated, although two of the main points in the Constitution had been grossly trodden under foot, namely, the right of free speech and free assembly at the Haymarket meeting, and the right to free and impartial trial at the hands of the law, which was absolutely wanting. It is a matter of conjecture as to how many millions of capitalistic gold went to animate that decision!

So we are brought down to the last days when the friends and sympathizers circulated petitions for executive clemency by the thousands and the police, no less active, "found" bombs and even one of the Supreme Court judges got an infernal machine (which turned out to be a box of papers about some other case!). The only serene people were our condemned comrades. Finally, the last hours, an appeal was to be made to the governor for executive clemency. This meant a sort of pilgrimage to the City of Springfield by hundreds of persons, including scores of friends and some of the relatives. Thousands of others wrote letters, our comrades themselves, except in the cases of Fielden and Schwab, positively refusing to admit that they had committed any misdemeanor or to ask for any mercy. They protested that they wished merely justice. The city was, at this point, in a perfect state of martial law. Several regiments were camped, with cannon, close to the city hall and sleuths, armed police and such wretches were everywhere. One wondered why the plutocrats were so afraid of their bad consciences which, doubtless, raised avenging hands from every shadow!

Our comrades, in the meantime, were subjected to every outrage and humiliation. Their clothing and even their persons were continually searched, the daily papers were denied them, they were no longer allowed the freedom of the corridors for a moment's exercise, relatives and friends no longer admitted to see them. They were even forced to the horrid task of willing their bodies, each separately to their families, to keep them from being desecrated by the police, after death.

The weather had turned very cold and those of the members of the families who had not gone to Springfield to see the governor, gathered in a pitiful group in the corridor of the jail vestibule, really then the court house, and beginning in the early morning, begged for a last word of farewell with their loved ones. This was flatly denied. All the livelong, terrible day these people, mostly women, had to stand on their feet in the bitter cold and witness the preparations for the execution—they had seen the coffins carried in the evening before!—without either food or water, hour after hour, with a brutal crowd of police and their friends crowding about to the extent of hundreds, staring and commenting. At midnight, a very few of the relatives were taken in, one at a time, by a turnkey, with a lantern in his left hand and a revolver in the other. The inside of the jail buzzed like a hive, so full was it with reporters, police, sleuths, and other tools of the moneyed class.

After a few seconds of agonized parting, each poor woman was marched back and left in the dark corridor. After midnight, the "decision" of the governor was not announced in order to keep down any attempt at rescue by friends and sympathizers. The governor simply refused interference, except in the cases of Schwab and Fielden, who received life-sentences in the penitentiary (afterwards these were pardoned by Governor Altgeld).

The morning of the eleventh found our dear comrades composed, smiling, firm without bravado. I, who had been denied admission on Thursday evening, went again in the morning, accompanied by a woman friend and comrade and our two children, to say a last farewell to my beloved husband and that the children might have their father's blessing and last remembrance. A cordon of police armed with Winchesters surrounded the jail. Pressing against this was a crowd of thousands of persons. To one policeman after another I appealed without effect, until one told us to come around the corner and he would "let us in," which he proceeded to do by hustling us into a patrol wagon and taking us to the station house, where we were stripped naked, searched and locked up all day, until three in the afternoon, that is three hours after the execution. The city was in the hands of the people and drunken police. The rich, to a man, had gone away for a few days' vacation, terrorized by their own black consciences.

The execution itself was put through as swiftly as possible. Our comrades were not to be permitted the usual speech, always accorded to doomed men. They had, however, foreseen this and each had prepared a sentence to express his last feelings. This they said just as the caps were being adjusted that forever shut the light from their eyes. Their clear voices rang out in those sentences now become classics. Let us pass over the agonizing scenes at the homes of the men, when wives, children, mothers, sisters, brothers, friends, received back the bodies of their dear ones, from whom life had been crushed out and all only because they had dared to tell the workers the simple truth!

On Sunday morning, November 14, the funeral took place, and no more remarkable sight will ever be witnessed than that procession of countless thousands that filed past the dead as they lay in their homes, and then the procession of five black hearses that passed through the city, accompanied by bands playing dirges and carriages bearing the friends and sympathizers, the mourners directly behind the hearses. Past the offices of the newspapers that Parsons and Spies had edited to the North Western train in waiting, passed the cortege which bore them to Waldheim Cemetery. The streets along which this remarkable procession wended its way were solidly packed with human faces and as the hearses passed, hats were taken off by thousands, instinctively, as it were. They did not know it, but they somehow *felt* that they were in the presence of great dead who had died nobly!

At the cemetery, a way had to be cleared through the dense throng for the procession. Four addresses were made in English and German, the most notable being the oration pronounced by Captain Black, leading attorney for the defense. And so, beneath mountains of floral offerings, before sorrowing relatives and friends, all that was left of our beloved comrades was consigned to their last resting place, on the banks of the Desplaines River.

But only their ashes, for their noble, true souls, animated by an undying faith in and love of humanity, will never die and their last words will continue to echo in the hearts of people, down through the ages of men, who still believe in right and the brotherhood of man. That the present generation thinks this, may be gathered by the fact that on every Decoration Day, or day set apart for the decoration of the graves of soldiers that died in our wars, thousands pass around the Anarchist Monument in silent homage or grave thoughtfulness, as if weighing the question of these men "who were not as other men."

REPORT FROM CAPITALIST PAPER

"When the march was begun to the gallows, all the men showed remarkable courage, without the slightest hint of bravado.

"Parsons was wonderfully composed.

"The moment his feet touched the scaffold, Parsons seemed to completely lose his identity and feel that his spirit was no longer a part of his body. He stood like one transfigured. Only he—the one American—seemed to realize the full extent that he must die in a manner to impress, if possible, on all future generations the thought that he was a martyr. No tragedian that has placed a stage in America ever made a more marvelous presentation of a self-chosen part, perfect in every detail.

"The upward turn of his eyes, his distant, far-away look, and, above all, the attitude of apparent complete resignation that every fold of the awkward shroud only served to make more distinct, was by far the most striking feature of the gallows picture. When the halter was placed about his neck he never faltered. He stood erect, looking earnestly yet reproachfully at the people before him. The nooses were quickly adjusted, the caps pulled down, and a hasty movement made for the straps. Then from beneath the hoods came these words:

"Spies:—'There will come a time when our silence will be more powerful than the voices you are strangling today!'

"Engel:—'Hurrah for Anarchy!'

"Fischer:—'This is the happiest moment of my life!'

"Parsons:—'Will I be allowed to speak, Oh men of America, let me speak, Sheriff Matson! Let the voice of the people be heard! Oh—.' But the signal had been given, and the foul murder was over."

ADDRESS OF AUGUST SPIES

YOUR HONOR: In addressing this court I speak as the representative of one class to the representative of another. I will begin with the words uttered five hundred years ago on a similar occasion, by the Venetian Doge Faheri, who, addressing the court, said: "*My defense is your accusation; the causes of my alleged crime your history!*" I have been indicted on the charge of murder, as an accomplice or accessory. Upon this indictment I have been convicted. There was no evidence produced by the State to show or even indicate that I had any knowledge of the man who threw the bomb, or that I myself had anything to do with the throwing of the missile, unless, of course, you weigh the testimony of the accomplices of the State's Attorney and Bonfield, the testimony of Thompson and Gilmer, by the price they were paid for it. If there was no evidence to show that I was legally responsible for the deed, then my conviction and the execution of the sentence is nothing less than willful, malicious, and deliberate murder, as foul a murder as may be found in the annals of religious, political, or any other sort of persecution. There have been many judicial murders committed where the representatives of the State were acting in good faith, believing their victims to be guilty of the charge accused of. In this case the representatives of the State cannot shield themselves with a similar excuse. For they themselves have fabricated most of the testimony which was used as a pretense to convict us; to convict us by a jury picked out to convict! Before this court, and before the public, which is supposed to be the State, I charge the State's Attorney and Bonfield with the heinous conspiracy to commit murder.

I will state a little incident which may throw light upon this charge. On the evening on which the Praetorian Guards of the Citizen's Association, the Bankers' Association, the Association of the Board of Trade men, and the railroad princes, attacked the meeting of workingmen on the Haymarket, with murderous intent—on that evening, about 8 o'clock I met a young man, Legner by name, who is a member of the Aurora Turn-Verein. He accompanied me, and never left me on that evening until I jumped from the wagon, a few seconds before the explosion occurred. He knew that I had not seen Schwab on that evening. He knew that I had no such conversation with anybody as Mr. Marshal Field's protege, Thompson, testified to. He knew that I did not jump from the wagon to strike the match and hand it to the man who threw the bomb. He is not a Socialist. Why did we not bring him on the stand? Because the honorable representatives of the State, Grinnell and Bonfield, spirited him away. These honorable gentlemen knew everything about Legner. They knew that his testimony would prove the perjury of Thompson and Gilmer beyond any reasonable doubt. Legner's name was on the list of witnesses for the State. He was not called, however, for obvious reasons. Aye, he stated to a number of friends that he had been offered $500 if he would leave the city, and threatened with direful things if he remained here and appeared as a witness for the defense. He replied that he could neither be bought nor bulldozed to serve such a damnable and dastardly plot. When we wanted Legner, he could not be found; Mr. Grinnell said—and Mr. Grinnell is an honorable man!—that he had himself been searching for the young man, but had not been able to find him. About three weeks later I learned that the very same young man had been kidnapped and taken to Buffalo, N. Y., by two of the illustrious guardians of "Law and Order," two Chicago detectives. Let Mr. Grinnell, let the Citizens' Association, his employer, let them answer for this! And let the public sit in judgment upon the would-be assassins.

No, I repeat, the prosecution has not established our legal guilt, notwithstanding the purchased and perjured testimony of some, and notwithstanding the originality of the proceedings of this trial. And as long as this has not been done, and you pronounce upon us the sentence of an appointed vigilance committee, acting as a jury, I say, you, the alleged representatives and high priests of "Law and Order," are the real and only law breakers, and in this case to the extent of murder. It is well that the people know this. And when I speak of the people I don't mean the few co-conspirators of Grinnell, the noble patricians who thrive upon the misery of the multitudes. These drones may constitute the State, they may control the State, they may have their Grinnells, their Bonfields and other hirelings! No, when I speak of the people I speak of the great mass of human bees, the working people, who unfortunately are not yet conscious of the rascalities that are perpetrated in the "name of the people,"—in their name.

The contemplated murder of eight men, whose only crime is that they have dared to speak the truth, may open the eyes of these suffering millions; may wake them up. Indeed, I have noticed that our conviction has worked miracles in this direction already. The class that clamors for our lives, the good, devout Christians, have attempted in every way, through their newspapers and otherwise, to conceal the true and only issue in this case. By simply designating the defendants as Anarchists, and picturing them as a newly discovered tribe or species of cannibals, and by inventing shocking and horrifying stories of dark conspiracies said to be planned by them—these good Christians zealously sought to keep the naked fact from the working people and other righteous parties, namely: That on the evening of May 4, two hundred armed men, under the command of a notorious ruffian, attacked a meeting of peaceable citizens! With what intention? With the intention of murdering them, or as many of them as they could. I refer to the testimony given by two of our witnesses. The wage workers of this city began to object to being fleeced too much—they began to say some very true things, but they were highly disagreeable to our patrician class; they put forth—well, some very modest demands. They thought eight hours hard toil a day for scarcely two hours' pay was enough. This lawless rabble had to be silenced! The only way to silence them was to frighten them, and murder those whom they looked up to as their "leaders." Yes, these "foreign dogs" had to be taught a lesson, so that they might never again interfere with the high-handed exploitation of their benevolent and Christian masters. Bonfield, the man who would bring a blush of shame to the managers of the St. Bartholomew night—Bonfield, the illustrious gentleman with a visage that would have done excellent service to Dore in portraying Dante's fiends of hell—Bonfield was the man best fitted to consummate the conspiracy of the Citizens' Association, of our patricians. If I had thrown that bomb, or had caused it to be thrown, or had known of it, I would not hesitate a moment to say so. It is true a number of lives were lost—many were wounded. But hundreds of lives were thereby saved! But for that bomb, there would have been a hundred widows and hundreds of orphans where now there are few. These facts have been carefully suppressed, and we were accused and convicted of conspiracy by the real conspirators and their agents. This, your honor, is one reason why sentence should not be passed by a court of justice—if that name has any significance at all.

"But," says the State, "you have published articles on the manufacture of dynamite and bombs." Show me a daily paper in this city that has not published similar articles! I remember very distinctly a long article in the Chicago *Tribune* of February 23, 1885. The paper contained a description and drawings of different kinds of infernal machines and bombs. I remember this one especially, because I bought the paper on a railroad train, and had ample time to read it. But since that time the *Times* has often published similar articles on the subject, and some of the dynamite articles found in the *Arbeiter-Zeitung* were translated articles from the *Times*, written by Generals Molineux and Fitz John Porter, in which the use of dynamite bombs against striking workmen is advocated as the most effective weapon against them. May I learn why the editors of these papers have not been indicted and convicted for murder? Is it because they have advocated the use of this destructive agent only against the common rabble? I seek information. Why was Mr. Stone of the *News* not made a defendant in this case? In his possession was found a bomb. Besides that Mr. Stone published an article in January which gave full information regarding the manufacture of bombs. Upon this information any man could prepare a bomb ready for use at the expense of not more than ten cents. The *News* probably has ten times the circulation of the *Arbeiter-Zeitung*. Is it not likely that the bomb used on May 4th was one made after the *News'* pattern? As long as these men are not charged with murder and convicted, I insist, your honor, that such discrimination in favor of capital is incompatible with justice, and sentence should therefore not be passed.

Grinnell's main argument against the defendants was "they were foreigners. They are not citizens." I cannot speak for the others. I will only speak for myself. I have been a resident of this State fully as long as Grinnell, and probably have been as good a citizen—at least, I should not wish to be compared with him. Grinnell has incessantly appealed to the patriotism of the jury. To that I reply in the language of Johnson, the English literateur, "an appeal to patriotism is the last resort of a scoundrel."

My efforts in behalf of the disinherited and disfranchised millions, my agitation in this direction, the popularization of economic teachings—in short, the education of the wage workers, is declared "a conspiracy against society." The word "society" is here wisely substituted for "the State," as represented by the Patricians of today. It has always been the opinion of the ruling classes that the people must be kept in ignorance, for they lose their servility, their modesty and their obedience to the powers that be, as their intelligence increases. The education of a black slave a quarter of a century ago was a criminal offense. Why? Because the intelligent slave would throw off his shackles at whatever cost. Why is the education of the working people of today looked upon by a certain class as an offense against the State? For the same reason! The State, however, wisely avoided this point in the prosecution of this case. From their testimony one is forced to conclude that we had, in our speeches and publications, preached nothing else but destruction and dynamite. The court has this morning stated that there is no case in history like this. I have noticed, during this trial, that the gentlemen of the legal profession are not well versed in history. In all historical cases of this kind truth had to be perverted by the priests of the established power that was nearing its end.

What have we said in our speeches and publications?

We have interpreted to the people their conditions and relations in society. We have explained to them the different social phenomena and the social laws and circumstances under which they occur. We have, by way of scientific investigation, incontrovertibly proved and brought to their knowledge that the system of wages is the root of the present social iniquities—iniquities so monstrous that they cry to Heaven. We have further said that the wage system, as a specific form of social development, would, by the necessity of logic, have to make room for higher forms of civilization; that the wage system must furnish the foundation for a social system of co-operation—that is, Socialism. That whether this or that theory, this or that scheme regarding future arrangements were accepted was not a matter of choice, but one of historical necessity, and that to us the tendency of progress seemed to be Anarchism—that is, a free society without kings or classes—a society of sovereigns in which the liberty and economic equality of all would furnish an unshakable equilibrium as a foundation for natural order.

It is not likely that the honorable Bonfield and Grinnell can conceive of a social order not held intact by the policeman's club and pistol, nor of a free society without prisons, gallows, and State's attorneys. In such a society they probably fail to find a place for themselves. And is this the reason why Anarchism is such a "pernicious and damnable doctrine?"

Grinnell has intimated to us that Anarchism was on trial. The theory of Anarchism belongs to the realm of speculative philosophy. There was not a syllable said about Anarchism at the Haymarket meeting. At that meeting the very popular theme of reducing the hours of toil was discussed. But, "Anarchism is on trial!" foams Mr. Grinnell. If that is the case, your honor, very well; you may sentence me, for I am an Anarchist. I believe with Buckle, with Paine,

Jefferson, Emerson, and Spencer, and many other great thinkers of this century, that the state of castes and classes—the state where one class dominates over and lives upon the labor of another class, and calls this order—yes, I believe that this barbaric form of social organization, with its legalized plunder and murder, is doomed to die, and make room for a free society, voluntary association, or universal brotherhood, if you like. You may pronounce the sentence upon me, honorable judge, but let the world know that in A. D. 1886, in the State of Illinois eight men were sentenced to death, because they believed in a better future; because they had not lost their faith in the ultimate victory of liberty and justice!

"You have taught the destruction of society and civilization," says the tool and agent of the Bankers' and Citizens' Association, Grinnell. That man has yet to learn what civilization is. It is the old, old argument against human progress. Read the history of Greece, of Rome; read that of Venice; look over the dark pages of the church and follow the thorny path of science. "No change! No change! You would destroy society and civilization!" has ever been the cry of the ruling classes. They are so comfortably situated under the prevailing system that they naturally abhor and fear even the slightest change. Their privileges are as dear to them as life itself, and every change threatens these privileges. But civilization is a ladder whose steps are monuments of such changes! Without these social changes—all brought about against the will and the force of the ruling classes—there would be no civilization. As to the destruction of society which we have been accused of seeking, sounds this not like one of Æsop's fables—like the cunning of the fox? We, who have jeopardized our lives to save society from the fiend—the fiend who has grasped her by the throat; who sucks her life-blood, who devours her children—we, who would heal her bleeding wounds, who would free her from the fetters you have wrought around her; from the misery you have brought upon her—we her enemies!! Honorable Judge, the demons of hell will join in the laughter this irony provokes!

"We have preached dynamite!" Yes, we have predicted from the lessons history teaches, that the ruling classes of today would no more listen to the voice of reason than their predecessors; that they would attempt by brute force to stay the wheel of progress. Is it a lie, or was it the truth we told? Are not already the large industries of this once free country conducted under the surveillance of the police, the detectives, the military, and the sheriffs—and is this return to militancy not developing from day to day? American sovereigns—think of it—working like galley convicts under military guards! We have predicted this, and predict that soon these conditions will grow unbearable. What then? The mandate of the feudal lords of our time is slavery, starvation, and death! This has been their program for years. We have said to the toilers, that science had penetrated the mystery of nature—that from Jove's head once more has sprung a Minerva—dynamite! If this declaration is synonymous with murder, why not charge those with the crime to whom we owe the invention?

To charge us with an attempt to overthrow the present system on or about May 4th, by force, and then establish Anarchy, is too absurd a statement, I think, even for a political office holder to make. If Grinnell believed that we attempted such a thing, why did he not have Dr. Bluthardt make an inquiry as to our sanity? Only mad men could have planned such a brilliant scheme, and mad people cannot be indicted or convicted of murder. If there had existed anything like a conspiracy or a pre-arrangement, does your honor believe that events would not have taken a different course than they did on that evening and later? This "conspiracy" nonsense is based upon an oration I delivered on the anniversary of Washington's birthday at Grand Rapids, Mich., more than a year and a half ago. I had been invited by the Knights of Labor for that purpose. I dwelt upon the fact that our country was far from being what the great revolutionists of the last century had intended it to be. I said that those men if they lived today would clean the Augean Stables with iron brooms, and that they, too, would undoubtedly be characterized as "wild Socialists." It is not unlikely that I said Washington would have been hanged for treason if the revolution had failed. Grinnell made this "sacrilegious remark" his main arrow against me. Why? Because he intended to inveigh the know-nothing spirit against us. But who will deny the correctness of the statement? That I should have compared myself with Washington, is a base lie. But if I had, would that be murder? I may have told that individual who appeared here as a witness that the workingmen should procure arms, as force would in all probability be the *ultima ratio regum*; and that in Chicago there were so and so many armed, but I certainly did not say that we proposed to "inaugurate the social revolution." And let me say here: Revolutions are no more made than earthquakes and cyclones. Revolutions are the effect of certain causes and conditions. I have made social philosophy a specific study for more than ten years, and I could not have given vent to such nonsense! I do believe, however, that the revolution is near at hand—in fact, that it is upon us. But is the physician responsible for the death of the patient because he foretold that death? If any one is to be blamed for the coming revolution it is the ruling class who steadily refused to make concessions as reforms became necessary; who maintain that they can call a halt to progress, and dictate a standstill to the eternal forces, of which they themselves are but the whimsical creation.

The position generally taken in this case is that we are morally responsible for the police riot on May 4th. Four or five years ago I sat in this very court room as a witness. The workingmen had been trying to obtain redress in a lawful manner. They had voted, and among others, had elected their aldermanic candidate from the fourteenth ward. But the street car company did not like the man. And two of the three election judges of one precinct, knowing this, took the ballot box to their home and "corrected" the election returns, so as to cheat the constituents of the elected candidate of their rightful representative, and give the representation to the benevolent street car monopoly. The workingmen spent $1,500 in the prosecution of the perpetrators of this crime. The proof against them was so overwhelming that they confessed to having falsified the returns and forged the official documents. Judge Gardner, who was presiding in this court, acquitted them, stating that "that act had apparently not been prompted by criminal intent." I will make no comment. But when we approach the field of moral responsibility, it has an immense scope! Every man who has in the past assisted in thwarting the efforts of those seeking reform is responsible for the existence of the revolutionists in this city today! Those, however, who have sought to bring about reforms must be exempted from the responsibility—and to these I belong.

If the verdict is based upon the assumption of moral responsibility, your honor, I give this as a reason why sentence should not be passed.

If the opinion of the court given this morning is good law, then there is no person in this country who could not lawfully be hanged. I vouch that, upon the very laws you have read, there is no person in this courtroom now who could not be "fairly, impartially and lawfully" hanged! Fouche, Napoleon's right bower, once said to his master: "Give me a line that any one man has ever written, and I will bring him to the scaffold." And this court has done essentially the same. Upon that law every person in this country can be indicted for conspiracy, and, as the case may be, for murder. Every member of a trade union, of the Knights of Labor, or any other labor organization, can then be convicted of conspiracy, and in cases of violence, for which they may not be responsible at all, of murder, as we have been. This precedent once established, and you force the masses who are now agitating in a peaceable way into open rebellion! You thereby shut off the last safety valve—and the blood which will be shed, the blood of the innocent—it will come upon your heads!

"Seven policemen have died," said Grinnell, suggestively winking at the jury. You want a life for a life, and have convicted an equal number of men, of whom it cannot be truthfully said that they had anything whatsoever to do with the killing of Bonfield's victims. The very same principle of jurisprudence we find among various savage tribes. Injuries among them are equalized, so to speak. The Chinooks and the Arabs, for instance, would demand the life of an enemy for every death that they had suffered at their enemy's hands. They were not particular in regard to the persons, just so long as they had a life for a life. This principle also prevails today among the natives of the Sandwich Islands. If we are to be hanged on this principle, then let us know it, and let the world know what a civilized and Christian country it is in which the Goulds, the Vanderbilts, the Stanfords, the Fields, Armours, and other local money *hamsters* have come to the rescue of liberty and justice!

Grinnell has repeatedly stated that our country is an enlightened country. The verdict fully corroborates the assertion! This verdict against us is the anathema of the wealthy classes over their despoiled victims—the vast army of wage workers and farmers. If your honor would not have these people believe this; if you would not have them believe that we have once more arrived at the Spartan Senate, the Athenian Areopagus, the Venetian Council of Ten, etc., then sentence should not be pronounced. But, if you think that by hanging us, you can stamp out the labor movement—the movement from which the downtrodden millions, the millions who toil and live in want and misery, the wage slaves, expect salvation—if this is your opinion, then hang us! Here you will tread upon a spark, but here, and there, and behind you and in front of you, and everywhere, flames will blaze up. It is a subterranean fire. You cannot put it out. The ground is on fire upon which you stand. You can't understand it. You don't believe in magical arts, as your grandfathers did, who burned witches at the stake, but you do believe in conspiracies; you believe that all these occurrences of late are the work of conspirators! You resemble the child that is looking for his picture behind the mirror. What you see, and what you try to grasp is nothing but the deceptive reflex of the stings of your bad conscience. You want to "stamp out the conspirators"—the "agitators?" Ah, stamp out every factory lord who has grown wealthy upon the unpaid labor of his employees. Stamp out every landlord who has amassed fortunes from the rent of overburdened workingmen and farmers. Stamp out every machine that is revolutionizing industry and agriculture, that intensifies the production, ruins the producer, that increases the national wealth, while the creator of all these things stands amidst them tantalized with hunger! Stamp out the railroads, the telegraph, the telephone, steam and yourselves—for everything breathes the revolutionary spirit.

You, gentlemen, are the revolutionists! You rebel against the effects of social conditions which have tossed you, by the fair hand of Fortune, into a magnificent paradise. Without inquiring, you imagine that no one else has a right in that place. You insist that you are the chosen ones, the sole proprietors. The forces that tossed you into the paradise, the industrial forces, are still at work. They are growing more active and intense from day to day. Their tendency is to elevate all mankind to the same level, to have all humanity share in the paradise you now monopolize. You, in your blindness, think you can stop the tidal wave of civilization and human emancipation by placing a few policemen, a few Gatling guns, and some regiments of militia on the shore—you think you can frighten the rising waves back into the unfathomable depths, whence they have arisen, by erecting a few gallows in the perspective. You, who oppose the natural course of things, you are the real revolutionists. You and you alone are the conspirators and destructionists!

Said the court yesterday, in referring to the Board of Trade demonstration: "These men started out with the express purpose of sacking the Board of Trade building." While I can't see what sense there would have been in such an undertaking, and while I know that the said demonstration was arranged simply as a means of propaganda against the system that legalizes the respectable business carried on there, I will assume that the three thousand workingmen who marched in that procession really intended to sack the building. In this case they would have differed from the respectable Board of Trade men only in this—that they sought to recover property in an unlawful way, while the others sack the entire country lawfully and unlawfully—this being their highly respectable profession. This court of "justice and equity" proclaims the principle that when two persons do the same thing, it is not the same thing. I thank the court for this confession. It contains all that we have taught and for which we are to be hanged, in a nutshell! Theft is a respectable profession when practiced by the privileged class. It is a felony when resorted to in self preservation by the other class. Rapine and pillage are the order of a certain class of gentlemen who find this mode of earning a livelihood easier and preferable to honest labor—this is the kind of order we have attempted, and are now trying, and will try as long as we live to do away with. Look upon the economic battle fields! Behold the carnage and plunder of the Christian patricians! Accompany me to the quarters of the wealth-creators in this city. Go with me to the half-starved miners of the Hocking Valley. Look at the pariahs in the Monongahela Valley, and many other mining districts in this country, or pass along the railroads of that great and most orderly and law-abiding citizen, Jay Gould. And then tell me whether this order has in it any moral principle for which it should be preserved.

I say that the preservation of such an order is criminal—is murderous. It means the preservation of the systematic destruction of children and women in factories. It means the preservation of enforced idleness of large armies of men, and their degradation. It means the preservation of intemperance, and sexual as well as intellectual prostitution. It means the preservation of misery, want, and servility on one hand, and the dangerous accumulation of spoils, idleness, voluptuousness and tyranny on the other. It means the preservation of vice in every form. And last but not least, it means the preservation of the class struggle, of strikes, riots and bloodshed. That is your "order," gentlemen. Yes, and it is worthy of you to be the champions of such an order. You are eminently fitted for that role. You have my compliments!

Grinnell spoke of Victor Hugo. I need not repeat what he said, but will answer him in the language of one of our German philosophers*: "Our Bourgeoisie erects monuments in honor of the memory of the classics. If they had read them they would burn them!" Why, amongst the articles read here from the *Arbeiter-Zeitung*, put in evidence by the State, by which they intend to convince the jury of the dangerous character of the accused anarchists, is an extract from Goethe's Faust,

"Es erben sich Gesetz und Rechte,
We eine ew'ge Krankheit fort," etc.

("Laws and class privileges are transmitted like an hereditary disease.") And Mr. Ingham in his speech told the Christian jurors that our comrades, the Paris Communists, had in 1871, dethroned God, the Almighty, and had put up in his place a low prostitute. The effect was marvelous! The good Christians were shocked. I wish your honor would inform the learned gentlemen that the episode related occurred in Paris nearly a century ago, and that the sacrilegious perpetrators were the co-temporaries of the founders of the Republic—and among them was Thomas Paine. Nor was the woman a prostitute, but a good *citoyenne de Paris*, who served on that occasion simply as an allegory of the goddess of reason.

* He asserted that Victor Hugo's writings (of which he knows no more than the average policeman) were not revolutionary.

Referring to Most's letter, read here, Mr. Ingham said: "They," meaning Most and myself, "they might have destroyed thousands of innocent lives in the Hocking Valley with that dynamite." I have said all I know about the letter on the witness stand, but will add that two years ago I went through the Hocking Valley as a correspondent. While there I saw hundreds of lives in the process of slow destruction, gradual destruction. There was no dynamite, nor were they Anarchists who did that diabolical work. It was the work of a party of highly respectable monopolists, law-abiding citizens, if you please. It is needless to say the murderers were never indicted. The press had little to say, and the State of Ohio assisted them. What a terror it would have created if the victims of this diabolical plot had resented and blown some of those respectable cut-throats to atoms! When, in East St. Louis, Jay Gould's hirelings, "the men of grit," shot down in cold blood and killed six inoffensive workingmen and women, there was very little said, and the grand jury refused to indict the gentlemen. It was the same way in Chicago, Milwaukee and other places. A Chicago furniture manufacturer shot down and seriously wounded two striking workingmen last spring. He was held over to the grand jury. The grand jury refused to indict the gentleman. But when, on one occasion, a workingman in self-defense resisted the murderous attempt of the police and threw a bomb, and for once blood flowed on the other side, then a terrific howl went up from the land: "Conspiracy has attacked vested rights!" And eight victims are demanded for it. There has been much said about the public sentiment. There has been much said about the public clamor. Why, it is a fact, that no citizen dared express another opinion than that prescribed by the authorities of the State, for if one had done otherwise, he would have been locked up; he might have been sent to the gallows to swing, as they will have the pleasure of doing with us, if the decree of our "honorable court" is consummated.

"These men," Grinnell said repeatedly, "have no principles; they are common murderers, assassins, robbers," etc. I admit that our aspirations and objects are incomprehensible to unprincipled ruffians, but surely for this we are not to be blamed. The assertion, if I mistake not, was based upon the ground that we sought to destroy property. Whether this perversion of facts was intentional, I know not. But in justification of our doctrines I will say that the assertion is an infamous falsehood. Articles have been read here from the *Arbeiter-Zeitung* and *Alarm* to show the dangerous characters of the defendants. The files of the *Arbeiter-Zeitung* and *Alarm* have been searched for the past years. Those articles which generally commented upon some atrocity committed by the authorities upon striking workingmen were picked out and read to you. Other articles were not read to the court. Other articles were not what was wanted. The State's Attorney (who well knows that he tells a falsehood when he says it), upon those articles asserts that "these men have no principles."

A few weeks before I was arrested and charged with the crime for which I have been convicted, I was invited by the clergymen of the Congregational Church to lecture upon the subject of socialism, and debate with them. This took place at the Grand Pacific Hotel. And so that it cannot be said that after I have been arrested, after I have been indicted, and after I have been convicted, I have put together some principles to justify my action, I will read what I said then—

Capt. Black: Give the date of the paper.

Mr. Spies: January 9, 1886.

Capt. Black: What paper, the *Alarm*?

Mr. Spies: The *Alarm*. When I was asked upon that occasion what Socialism was, I said this:

"Socialism is simply a resume of the phenomena of the social life of the past and present traced to their fundamental causes, and brought into logical connection with one another. It rests upon the established fact that the economic conditions and institutions of a people from the ground work of all their social conditions, of their ideas—aye, even of their religion, and further, that all changes of economic conditions, every step in advance, arises from the struggles between the dominating and dominated class in different ages. You, gentlemen, cannot place yourselves at this standpoint of speculative science; your profession demands that you occupy the opposite position, that which professes acquaintance with things as they actually exist, but which presumes a thorough understanding of matters which to ordinary mortals are entirely incomprehensible.

It is for this reason that you cannot become Socialists. (Cries of "Oh! oh!") Lest you should be unable to exactly grasp my meaning, however, I will now state the matter a little more plainly. It cannot be unknown to you that in the course of this century there have appeared an infinite number of inventions and discoveries, which have brought about great, aye, astonishing changes in the production of the necessities and comforts of life. The work of machines has, to a great extent, replaced that of men.

"Machinery involves a great accumulation of power, and always a greater division of labor in consequence.

"The advantages resulting from this centralization of production were of such a nature as to cause its still further extension, and from this concentration of the means of labor and of the operations of laborers, while the old system of distribution was (and is) retained, arose those improper conditions which ail society today.

"The means of production thus came into the hands of an ever decreasing number, while the actual producers, through the introduction of machinery, deprived of the opportunity to toil, and being at the same time disinherited of the bounties of nature, were consigned to pauperism, vagabondage—the so-called crime and prostitution—all these evils which you gentlemen would like to exorcise with your little prayer book.

"The Socialists award your efforts a jocular rather than a serious attention (symptoms of uneasiness) otherwise, pray, let us know how much you have accomplished so far by your moral lecturing toward ameliorating the condition of those wretched beings who through bitter want have been driven to crime and desperation? (Here several gentlemen sprang to their feet, exclaiming, 'We have done a great deal in some directions!') Aye, in some cases you have perhaps given a few alms; but what influence has this, if I may ask, had upon societary conditions, or in affecting any change in the same? Nothing; absolutely nothing. You may as well admit it, gentlemen, for you cannot point me out a single instance.

"Very well. Those proletarians doomed to misery and hunger through the labor-saving of our centralized production, whose number in this country we estimate at about a million and a half, is it likely that they and the thousands who are daily joining their ranks, and the millions who are toiling for a miserable pittance, will suffer peacefully and with Christian resignation their destruction at the hand of their thievish and murderous, albeit very Christian wage masters? They will defend themselves. It will come to a fight.

"The necessity of common ownership in the means of toil will be realized, and the era of socialism, of universal co-operation begins. The dispossessing of the usurping classes—the socialization of these possessions—and the universal co-operation of toil, not for speculative purposes, but for the satisfaction of the demands which we make upon life; in short co-operative labor for the purpose of continuing life and of enjoying it—this in general outlines, is Socialism. This is not, however, as you might suppose, a mere 'beautifully conceived plan,' the realization of which would be well worth striving for if it could only be brought about. No; this socialization of the means of production, of the machinery of commerce, of the land and earth, etc., is not only something desirable, but has become an imperative necessity, and wherever we find in history that something has once become a necessity there we always find that the next step was the doing away with that necessity by the supplying of the logical want.

"Our large factories and mines, and the machinery of exchange and transportation, apart from every other consideration, have become too vast for private control. Individuals can no longer monopolize them.

"Everywhere, wherever we cast our eyes, we find forced upon our attention the unnatural and injurious effects of unregulated private production. We see how one man, or a number of men, have not only brought into the embrace of their private ownership a few inventions in technical lines, but have also confiscated for their exclusive advantage all natural powers, such as water, steam, and electricity. Every fresh invention, every discovery belongs to them. The world exists for them only. That they destroy their fellow-beings right and left they little care. That, by their machinery, they even work the bodies of little children into gold pieces, they hold to be an especially good work and a genuine Christian act. They murder, as we have said, little children and women by hard labor, while they let strong men go hungry for lack of work.

"People ask themselves how such things are possible, and the answer is that the competitive system is the cause of it. The thought of a co-operative, social, rational, and well-regulated system of management irresistibly impresses the observer. The advantages of such a system are of such a convincing kind, so patent to observation—and where could there be any other way out of it? According to physical laws a body always moves itself, consciously or unconsciously, along the line of least resistance. So does society as a whole. The path of co-operative labor and distribution is leveled by the concentration of the means of labor under the private capitalistic system. We are already moving right in that track. We cannot retreat even if we would. The force of circumstances drives us on to Socialism.

"'And now, Mr. Spies, won't you tell us how you are going to carry out the expropriation of the possessing classes?' asked Rev. Dr. Scudder.

"'The answer is in the thing itself. The key is furnished by the storms raging through the industrial life of the present. You see how penuriously the owners of the factories, of the mines, cling to their privileges, and will not yield the breadth of an inch. On the other hand, you see the half-starved proletarians driven to the verge of violence.'

"'So your remedy would be violence?'

"'Remedy? Well, I should like it better if it could be done without violence, but you, gentlemen, and the class you represent, take care that it cannot be accomplished otherwise. Let us suppose that the workingmen of today go to their employers, and say to them: 'Listen! Your administration of affairs don't suit us any more; it leads to disastrous consequences. While one part of us are worked to death, the others, out of employment, are starved to death; little children are ground to death in the factories, while strong, vigorous men remain idle; the masses live in misery while a small class of respectables enjoy luxury and wealth; all this is the result of your maladministration, which will bring misfortune even to yourselves; step down and out now; let us have your property, which is nothing but unpaid labor; we shall take this thing in our hands; we shall administrate matters satisfactorily, and regulate the institutions of society; voluntarily we shall pay you a life-long pension.' Now, do you think the 'bosses' would accept this proposition? You certainly don't believe it. Therefore force will have to decide—or do you know of any other way?'

"'So you are organizing a revolution?'

"It was shortly before my arrest, and I answered: 'Such things are hard to organize. A revolution is a sudden upwelling—a convulsion of the fevered masses of society.'

"We are preparing society for that, and insist upon it that workingmen should arm themselves and keep ready for the struggle. The better they are armed the easier will the battle be, and the less the bloodshed.

"'What would be the order of things in the new society?'

"'I must decline to answer this question, as it is, till now, a mere matter of speculation. The organization of labor on a co-operative basis offers no difficulties. The large establishments of today might be used as patterns. Those who will have to solve these questions will expediently do it, instead of working according to our prescriptions—if we should make anything of the kind; they will be directed by the circumstances and conditions of the time, and these are beyond our horizon. About this you needn't trouble yourselves.'

"'But, friend, don't you think that about a week after the division, the provident will have all, while the spendthrift will have nothing?'

"'The question is out of order,' interfered the Chairman; 'there was not said anything about division.'

"Prof. Wilcox: 'Don't you think the introduction of Socialism will destroy all individuality?'

"'How can anything be destroyed which does not exist? In our times there is no individuality; that only can be developed under Socialism, when mankind will be independent economically. Where do you meet today with real individuality? Look at yourselves, gentlemen! You don't dare to give utterance to any subjective opinion which might not suit the feelings of your bread-givers and customers. You are hypocrites (murmurs of indignation); every business man is a hypocrite. Everywhere is mockery, servility, lies and fraud. And the laborers! You feign anxiety about their individuality; about the individuality of a class that has been degraded to machines—used each day for ten or twelve hours as appendages of the lifeless machines! About their individuality you are anxious!'

Does that sound as though I had at that time, as has been imputed to me, organized a revolution—a so-called social revolution, which was to occur on or about the 1st of May to establish Anarchy in place of our present "ideal order?" I guess not.

So Socialism does not mean the destruction of society. Socialism is a constructive and not a destructive science. While capitalism expropriates the masses for the benefit of the privileged class; while capitalism is that school of economics which teaches how one can live upon the labor (i.e., property) of others; Socialism teaches how all may possess property, and further teaches that every man must work honestly for his own living, and not be playing the "respectable board of trade man," or any other highly (?) respectable business man or banker, such as appeared here as talesmen in the jurors' box, with the fixed opinion that we ought to be hanged. Indeed, I believe they have that opinion! Socialism, in short, seeks to establish a universal system of co-operation, and to render accessible to each and every member of the human family the achievements and benefits of civilization, which, under capitalism, are being monopolized by a privileged class and employed, not as they should be, for the common good of all, but for the brutish gratification of an avaricious class. Under capitalism the great inventions of the past, far from being a blessing for mankind, have been turned into a curse! Under Socialism the prophecy of the Greek poet, Antiporas, would be fulfilled, who, at the invention of the first water mill, exclaimed: "This is the emancipator of male and female slaves"; and likewise the prediction of Aristotle, who said: "When, at some future age, every tool, upon command or by predestination, will perform its work as the art works of Daedalus did, which moved by themselves, or like the three feet of Hephaestus, which went to their sacred work instinctively, when thus the weaver shuttles will weave by themselves, then we shall no longer have masters and slaves." Socialism says this time has come, and can you deny it? You say: "Oh, these heathens, what did they know?" True! They knew nothing of political economy; they knew nothing of Christendom. They failed to conceive how nicely these man-emancipating machines could be employed to lengthen the hours of toil and to intensify the burdens of the slaves. These heathens, yes, they excused the slavery of one on the ground that thereby another would be afforded the opportunity of human development. But to preach the slavery of the masses in order that a few rude and arrogant parvenues might become "eminent manufacturers," "extensive packing house owners," or "influential shoe black dealers," to do this they lacked that specific Christian organ.

Socialism teaches that the machines, the means of transportation and communication are the result of the combined efforts of society, past and present, and that they are therefore rightfully the indivisible property of society, just the same as the soil and the mines and all natural gifts should be. This declaration implies that those who have appropriated this wealth wrongfully, though lawfully, shall be expropriated by society. The expropriation of the masses by the monopolists has reached such a degree that the expropriation of the expropriators has become an imperative necessity, an act of social self-preservation. Society will reclaim its own, even though you erect a gibbet on every street corner. And Anarchism, this terrible "ism," deduces that under a co-operative organization of society, under economic equality and individual independence, the State—the political State—will pass into barbaric antiquity. And we will be where all are free, where there are no longer masters and servants, where intellect stands for brute force; there will no longer be any use for the policemen and militia to preserve the so-called "peace and order"—the order that the Russian general speaks of when he telegraphed to the Czar after he had massacred half of Warsaw, "Peace reigns in Warsaw!"

Anarchism does not mean bloodshed; does not mean robbery, arson, etc. These monstrosities are, on the contrary, the characteristic features of capitalism. Anarchism means peace and tranquility to all. Anarchism, or Socialism, means the re-organization of society upon scientific principles and the abolition of causes which produce vice and crime. Capitalism first produces these social diseases and then seeks to cure them by punishment.

The court has had a great deal to say about the incendiary character of the articles read from the *Arbeiter-Zeitung*. Let me read to you an editorial which appeared in the Fond du Lac *Commonwealth*, in October, 1886, a Republican paper. If I am not mistaken the court is Republican, too.

"To arms, Republicans! Work in every town in Wisconsin for men not afraid of firearms, blood or dead bodies, to preserve peace (that is the 'peace' I have been speaking of) and quiet; avoid a conflict of parties to prevent the administration of public affairs from falling into the hands of such obnoxious men as James G. Jenkins. Every Republican in Wisconsin should go armed to the polls on next election day. The grain stacks, houses and barns of active Democrats should be burned; their children burned and their wives outraged, that they may understand that the Republican party is the one which is bound to rule, and the one which they should vote for, or keep their vile carcasses away from the polls. If they still persist in going to the polls, and persist in voting for Jenkins, meet them on the road, in the bush, on the hill, or anywhere, and shoot every one of these base cowards and agitators. If they are too strong in any locality, and succeed in putting their opposition votes into the ballot box, break open the box and tear in shreds their discord-breathing ballots. Burn them. This is the time for effective work. Yellow fever will not catch among Morrison Democrats; so we must use less noisy and more effective means. The agitators must be put down, and whoever opposes us does so at his peril. Republicans, be at the polls in accordance with the above directions, and don't stop for a little blood. That which make the solid South will make a solid North!"

What does your honor say to these utterances of a "law and order" organ—a Republican organ? How does the *Arbeiter-Zeitung* compare with this?

The book of John Most, which was introduced in court, I have never read, and I admit that passages were read here that are repulsive—that must be repulsive to any person who has a heart. But I call your attention to the fact that these passages have been translated from a publication of Andrieux, the ex-prefect of police, Paris, by an exponent of your order! Have the representatives of your order ever stopped at the sacrifice of human blood? Never!

It has been charged that we (the eight here) constituted a conspiracy. I would reply to that that my friend Lingg I had seen but twice at meetings of the Central Labor Union, where I went as a reporter, before I was arrested. I had never spoken to him. Engel I have not been on speaking terms with for at least a year. And Fischer, my lieutenant (?), used to go round and make speeches against me. So much for that.

You honor has said this morning, "we must learn their objects from what they have said and written," and in pursuance thereof the court has read a number of articles.

Now, if I had as much power as the court, and were a law abiding citizen, I would certainly have the court indicted for some remarks made during this trial. I will say that if I had not been an anarchist at the beginning of this trial I would be one now. I quote the exact language of the court on one occasion: "It does not necessarily follow that all laws are foolish and bad because a good many of them are so." That is treason, sir! if we are to believe the court and the State's Attorney. But, aside from that, I cannot see how we shall distinguish the good from the bad laws. Am I to judge of that? No; I am not. But if I disobey a bad law, and am brought before a bad judge, I undoubtedly would be convicted.

In regard to a report in the *Arbeiter-Zeitung*, also read this morning, the report of the Board of Trade demonstration, I would say (and this is the only defense, the only word I have to say in my own defense) that I did not know of that article until I saw it in the paper, and the man who wrote it, wrote it rather as a reply to some slurs in the morning papers. He was discharged. The language used in that article would never have been tolerated if I had seen it.

Now, if we cannot be directly implicated with this affair, connected with the throwing of the bomb, where is the law that says, these men shall be picked out to suffer? Show me that law if you have it! If the position of the court is correct, then half of the population of this city ought to be hanged, because they are responsible the same as we are for that act on May 4th. And if half of the population of Chicago is not hanged, then show me the law that says, "eight men shall be picked out and hanged as scapegoats!" You have no good law. Your decision, your verdict, our conviction is nothing but an arbitrary will of this lawless court. It is true there is no precedent in jurisprudence in this case! It is true we have called upon the people to arm themselves. It is true that we have told them time and again that the great day of change was coming. It was not our desire to have bloodshed. We are not beasts. We would not be socialists if we were beasts. It is because of our sensitiveness that we have gone into this movement for the emancipation of the oppressed and suffering. It is true we have called upon the people to arm and prepare for the stormy times before us.

This seems to be the ground upon which the verdict is to be sustained. "But when a long train of abuses and usurpations pursuing invariably the same object evinces a design to reduce the people under absolute despotism, it is their right, it is their duty, to throw off such government and provide new guards for their future safety." This is a quotation from the Declaration of Independence. Have we broken any laws by showing to the people how these abuses, that have occurred for the last twenty years, are invariably pursuing one object, viz: to establish an oligarchy in this country as strong and powerful and monstrous as never before has existed in any country? I can well understand why that man Grinnell did not urge upon the grand jury to charge us with treason. I can well understand it. You cannot try and convict a man for treason who has upheld the constitution against those who try to trample it under their feet. It would not have been as easy a job to do that, Mr. Grinnell, as to charge these men with murder.

Now, these are my ideas. They constitute a part of myself. I cannot divest myself of them, nor would I, if I could. And if you think that you can crush out these ideas that are gaining ground more and more every day; if you think you can crush them out by sending us to the gallows; if you would once more have people suffer the penalty of death because they have dared to tell the truth—and I defy you to show us where we have told a lie—I say, if death is the penalty for proclaiming the truth, then I will proudly and defiantly pay the costly price! Call your hangman! Truth crucified in Socrates, in Christ, in Giordano Bruno, in Huss, Gallileo, still lives—they and others whose number is legion have preceded us on this path. We are ready to follow!

ADDRESS OF MICHAEL SCHWAB

It is not much I have to say. And I would say nothing at all if keeping silent did not look like a cowardly approval of what has been done here. To term the proceedings during the trial justice, would be a sneer. Justice has not been done, more than this, could not be done. If one class is arrayed against the other, it is idle and hypocritical to think about justice. Anarchy was on trial, as the State's attorney put it in his closing speech, a doctrine, an opinion, hostile to brute force, hostile to our present murderous system of production and distribution. I am condemned to die for writing newspaper articles and making speeches. The State's attorney knows as well as I do that that alleged conversation between Mr. Spies and myself never took place. He knows a good deal more than that. He knows of all the beautiful work of his organizer, Furthman. When I was before the Coroner's jury, two or three detectives swore very positive of having seen me at the Haymarket when Mr. Parsons finished his speech. I suppose they wanted at that time to fix the bomb throwing on me; for the first dispatches to Europe said that M. Schwab had thrown several bombs at the police. Later on they sent detectives to Lake View, and found that would not do. And then Schnaubelt was the man.

Anarchy was on trial. Little did it matter who the persons were to be honored by the prosecution. It was the movement the blow was aimed at. It was directed against the labor movement, against Socialism, for today every labor movement must, of necessity, be socialistic.

Talk about a gigantic conspiracy! A movement is not a conspiracy. All we did was done in open daylight.

There were no secrets. We prophesied in word and writing the coming of a great revolution, a change in the system of production in all industrial countries of the globe. And the change will come, and must come. Is it not absurd to suppose, as the State's attorney and his associates have supposed, that this social revolution—a change of such immense proportions—was to be inaugurated on or about the first of May in the city of Chicago by making war on the police? The organizer Furthman searched hundreds of numbers of the *Arbeiter-Zeitung* and the *Alarm*, and so the prosecution must have known very well what we understood when we talked about the coming revolution. But the prosecuting attorneys preferred to ignore these explanatory articles.

The articles in evidence were carefully selected and paraded as samples of violent language, but the language used in them was just the same as newspapers used in general against us and their enemies. Even against the police and their practices they used words of the same kind as we did.

The president of the citizens' association, Edwin Lee Brown, after the last election of Mayor Harrison, made a speech in North Side Turner Hall in which he called on all good citizens to take possession of the courthouse by force, even if they had to wade in blood. It seems to me that the most violent speakers are not to be found in the ranks of the Anarchists.

It is not violence in word or action the attorneys of the State and their urgers-on are waging war against; it is our doctrine—Anarchy.

We contend for communism and Anarchy—why? If we had kept silent, stones would have cried out. Murder was committed day by day. Children were slain, women worked to death, men killed inch by inch, and these crimes are never punished by law. The great principle underlying the present system is unpaid labor. Those who amass fortunes, build palaces, and live in luxury, are doing these things by virtue of unpaid labor. Being directly or indirectly the possessors of land and machinery, they dictate their terms to the workingman. He is compelled to sell his labor cheap, or to starve. The price paid him is always far below the real value. He acts under compulsion, and they call it a free contract. This infernal state of affairs keeps him poor and ignorant; an easy prey for exploitation.

I know what life has in store for the masses. I was one of them. I slept in their garrets, and lived in their cellars. I saw them work and die. I worked with girls in the same factory—prostitutes they were, because they could not earn enough wages for their living. I saw females sick from overwork; sick in body and mind on account of the lives they were forced to lead. I saw girls from ten to fourteen years of age working for a mere pittance. I heard how their morals were killed by the foul and vile language and the bad example of their ignorant fellow-workers, leading them on the same road of misery, and as an individual I could do nothing. I saw families starving and able-bodied men worked to death. That was in Europe. When I came to the United States, I found that there were classes of workingmen who were better paid than the European workmen, but I perceived that the state of things in a great number of industries was even worse, and that the so-called better paid skilled laborers were degrading rapidly into mere automatic parts of machinery. I found that the proletariat of the great industrial cities was in a condition that could not be worse. Thousands of laborers in the city of Chicago live in rooms without sufficient protection from the weather, without proper ventilation, in which never a stream of sunlight flows. There are hovels where two, three and four families live in one room. How these conditions influence the health and the morals of these unfortunate sufferers, it is needless to say. And how do they live? From the ash barrels they gather half rotten vegetables, in the butcher shops they buy for some cents offal of meat, and these precious morsels they carry home to prepare from them their meals. The dilapidated houses in which this class of laborers live need repairs very badly, but the greedy landlord waits in most cases till he is compelled by the city to have them done. Is it a wonder that diseases of all kind kill men, women and children in such places by wholesale, especially children? Is this not horrible in a so-called civilized land where there is plenty of food and riches? Some years ago a committee of the citizen's association, or league, made an investigation of these matters, and I was one of the reporters that went with them.

What these common laborers are today, the skilled laborers will be tomorrow. Improved machinery that ought to be a blessing for the workingman, under the existing conditions becomes for him a curse. Machinery multiplies the army of unskilled laborers, makes the laborer more dependent upon the men who own the land and machines. And that is the reason that Socialism and Communism got a foothold in this country. The outcry that Socialism, Communism and Anarchism are the creed of foreigners, is a big mistake. There are more Socialists of American birth in this country than foreigners, and that is much, if we consider that nearly half of all industrial workingmen are not native Americans. There are Socialistic papers in a great many States edited by Americans for Americans. The capitalistic newspapers conceal that fact very carefully.

Socialism, as we understand it, means that land and machinery shall be held in common by the people. The production of goods shall be carried on by productive groups which shall supply the demands of the people. Under such a system every human being would have an opportunity to do useful work, and no doubt would work. Some hours' work every day would suffice to produce all that, according to statistics, that is necessary for a comfortable living. Time would be left to cultivate the mind, and to further science and art.

That is what the Socialists propose. Some say it is un-American! Well, then, is it American to let people starve and die in ignorance? Is exploitation and robbery of the poor, American? What have the great political parties done for the poor? Promised much; done nothing, except corrupting them by buying their votes on election day. A poverty-stricken man has no interest in the welfare of the community. It is only natural that in a society where women are driven to sell their honor, men should sell their votes.

But we were not only "Socialists and Communists"; we were "Anarchists."

What is Anarchy?

Is it not strange that when Anarchy was tried nobody ever told what Anarchy was? Even when I was on the witness stand, and asked the State's attorney for a definition of Anarchy, he declined to give it. But in their speeches he and his associates spoke very frequently about Anarchy, and it appeared that they understood it to be something horrible—arson, rapine, murder. In so speaking, Mr. Grinnell and his associates did not speak the truth. They searched the *Alarm* and the *Arbeiter-Zeitung*, and hunted up articles written years before the month of May, 1886. In the columns of these papers it is very often stated what we, the Anarchists, understood by the term Anarchy. And we are the only competent judges in this matter. As soon as the word is applied to us and our doctrine, it carries with it the meaning which we, the Anarchists, saw fit to give to it. "Anarchy" is Greek, and means, verbatim: without rulership; not being ruled. According to our vocabulary, Anarchy is a state of society, in which the only government is reason; a state of society in which all human beings do right for the simple reason that it is right, and hate wrong because it is wrong. In such a society, no laws, no compulsion will be necessary. The attorney of the State was wrong when he said: "Anarchy is dead." Anarchy, up to the present day, has existed only as a doctrine, and Mr. Grinnell has not the power to kill any doctrine whatever. You may call Anarchy, as defined by us, an idle dream, but that dream was dreamed by Gotthold Ephraim Lessing, one of the three great German poets and the most celebrated German critic of the last century. If anarchy were the thing the State's attorney makes it out to be, how could it be that such eminent scholars as Prince Kropotkin and the greatest living geographer, Élisée Reclus, were avowed Anarchists, even editors of Anarchistic newspapers? Anarchy is a dream, but only in the present. It will be realized. Reason will grow in spite of all obstacles. Who is the man that has the cheek to tell us that human development has already reached its culminating point? I know that our ideal will not be accomplished this or next year, but I know that it will be accomplished as near as possible, some day, in the future. It is entirely wrong to use the word Anarchy as synonymous with violence. Violence is one thing and Anarchy another. In the present state of society violence is used on all sides, and, therefore, we advocated the use of violence against violence, but against violence only, as a necessary means of defense. I never read Mr. Most's book, simply because I did not find time to read it. And if I had, what of it? I am an agnostic, but I like to read the Bible nevertheless. I have not the slightest idea who threw the bomb on the Haymarket, and had no knowledge of any conspiracy to use violence on that or any other night.

ADDRESS OF OSCAR NEEBE

YOUR HONOR: I have found out during the last few days what law is. Before I didn't know. I did not know before that I was convicted because I knew Spies and Fielden and Parsons. I have met these gentlemen. I have presided in a mass-meeting, as the evidence against me shows, held in the Turner Hall, at which meeting your honor was invited to appear. The judges, the preachers, the newspaper men, and everybody in fact, were invited to appear at that meeting for the purpose of discussing Anarchism and Socialism. I was at that hall. I am well known among the workingmen of this city, and I was elected chairman of that meeting. None of the representatives of the capitalistic system came forward to speak, to discuss the questions of Labor and Anarchism or Socialism with laboring men. No; they couldn't stand it. I was chairman of that meeting. I don't deny it.

I also on one occasion had the honor to be marshal of a labor demonstration in this city, and I never saw a more respectable lot of men than I saw on that day. They marched like soldiers, and I am proud that I was marshal of those men. They were the toilers and the workingmen of this city. The men marched through the streets to protest against the wrongs of society, and I was marshal of them. If that is a crime, then I have found out, as a native, free-born American, of what I have been guilty. I always supposed I had a right to express my opinion as the chairman of a peaceable meeting, and to be marshal of a labor demonstration. Was it a crime to be marshal of that demonstration? I am convicted for that.

On the morning of the fifth of May, your honor, on the road to my business, I heard that August Spies and Michael Schwab were arrested. I was in the yeast business. I peddled my yeast through the southern part of the city. I was informed that they were arrested. That was the first time I learned that there had been a mass meeting held at the Haymarket the day before. After I was done with my business and drove home, I stopped at the *Arbeiter-Zeitung* to see what was going on, and I met there Mrs. Parsons and Mrs. Holmes and a couple of boys of the *Arbeiter-Zeitung*. They explained to me that the men were arrested. Just as I was going to speak to Mrs. Parsons about it, up rushed a lot of pirates, called detectives, of Chicago; men—you could see the rum and ignorance in their faces—mostly picked up from the ruffians of the streets of Chicago. I never saw a rougher set. Well, I don't wish to make any further remarks about these honorable pirates. Mayor Harrison was with these pirates. He came in and he says: "Who is the manager of this paper here?" The two boys couldn't speak English, and I knew Harrison, so I said: "Harrison, what is it?" "Well," he says, "I want to have this thing stopped. There won't be any more inflammable articles allowed in this paper." Said I: "Mr. Harrison, I will sit here and read the articles, and see that there won't be anything inflammatory in this day's issue." Our compositors were not arrested at that time. So Harrison said to me, "I will go to the house and send Mr. Hand over here." I know him, and both of us together revised all the articles printed in the paper that day. A few minutes later Harrison went out, and our whole set of compositors were coming down the stairs, and another lot of ruffians came up the steps, and Mrs. Holmes and Mrs. Parsons were sitting at the desk writing, and a man whom you could see was a noble Democratic officer, said: "What are you doing there?" Mrs. Holmes is a lady in my eyes, and she said: "I am corresponding with my brother. He is the editor of a labor paper." As she said that he snatched the lady, and she protested as an American woman, and as she protested he said: "Shut up, you bitch, or I will knock you down." I repeat the same words here, and I have a right to, as the noble officers of Chicago have used this language. That is one of your men, Mr. Grinnell—just like you. You have insulted ladies when you have not dared to insult gentlemen. Mrs. Parsons was called the same name by the officers. They called her a black bitch, and wanted to knock her down; and they said they would not let us publish any paper; they would take the types and material and throw them out of the window. We are a stock company, a company chartered by the State of Illinois for the publication of a labor paper and labor literature. Our charter states it. When I heard they wanted to destroy the property of the laboring men of the city of Chicago, who have collected money by paying dollars and cents to publish it, I said: "As long as I stand I shall publish that paper," and I took charge of the paper. I suppose Grinnell thought after Oscar Neebe was indicted for murder the *Arbeiter-Zeitung* would go down. But it didn't happen that way. And Mr. Furthman, too (pointing to the Assistant State's attorney)—he is a scoundrel, and I can tell it to you to your face. There is only one man that acted as a gentleman, and he is Mr. Ingham; but you three have not. Inside of two weeks I had enough money from the toilers, from hired girls, and from men who would take their last cent out of their pockets to re-establish the paper and to buy a press of our own. I could not publish the paper sooner because the honorable detectives and Mr. Grinnell followed us up, and no printing house would print our paper, because of the threats of these men, and we had to have our own press. We published our own paper after we had a press purchased by the money of the workingmen of the city.

That is the crime I have committed, getting men to try and establish a workingman's paper that stands today; and I am proud of it. They have not got one press simply—they have two presses today, and they belong to the workingmen of this city. From the date of the first issue to the present day, your honor, we have gained four thousand subscribers to our daily paper. There are the gentlemen sitting over there from the *Freie Presse* and *Staats-Zeitung*—they know it. The Germans of this city are condemning these actions. I say that it is a verdict against Germans, and I, as an American, must say that I never saw anything like that.

These are the crimes I have committed after the fourth of May. Before the fourth of May I committed some other crimes. My business brought me in connection with the bakers. I saw that the bakers in this city were treated like dogs. The baker bosses treated their dogs better than they treated their men. I said to myself: "These men have to be organized; in organization there is strength"; and I helped to organize them. That is a great crime. The men are now working ten hours a day, instead of fourteen and sixteen hours, and instead of being compelled to eat slops like the dogs, and sleep on the stairways or in the barn, they can sleep and work whenever they please. I have helped to establish that, your honor. That is another crime. And I committed a greater crime than that. I saw in the morning when I drove away with my team that the beer brewers of the city of Chicago went to work at four o'clock in the morning. They came home at seven and eight o'clock at night. They never saw their families or their children by daylight. I said to myself: "If you organize these men they can live like men. You can help to make good citizens out of them." And everybody said: "They are down low; they are drunkards." I went to work and organized them. I rented a hall and issued an appeal for them, and got them to come, and I organized the men. On Saturday, May 1 or May 2, I was conferring with the beer brewer bosses of Chicago and we had a meeting. I was the chairman of the committee, and I asked the beer brewer bosses to reduce the hours of labor down to ten hours a day, and they did it. On the Monday after I committed that great crime—that was Saturday—I was in session with the beer brewers the whole day. In the evening I took my supper and went to the North Side Turner Hall, where the union men, over eight hundred strong, were, and I don't know anything about McCormick's or what Spies had done or said. I entered the hall. I went on the platform and I presented the union with a document signed by every beer brewer of Chicago, guaranteeing ten hours labor and

$sixty-five wages—$fifteen more wages per month, and no Sunday work, to give the men a chance to go to church, as many of them are good Christians. There are a good many Christians among them. So, in that way, I was aiding Christianity—helping the men to go to church.

After the meeting I left the hall, and stepped into the front saloon, and there were circulars lying there called the "revenge" circular. I picked up a couple of them from a table and folded them together and put them in my pocket, not having a chance to read them, because everybody wanted to treat me. They all thought it was by my efforts that they got $fifteen a month more wages and ten hours a day. Why, I didn't have a chance to read the circulars. From there I went to another saloon across the street, and the president of the Beer Brewers' Union was there; he asked me to walk with him, and on the way home we went into Heine's saloon. He was talking to Heine about the McCormick affair, and I picked up a circular and read it, and Heine asked me: "Can you give me one?" I gave him one and he laid it back on his counter.

That is my statement. You can believe it or not; but Heine didn't testify any other way. Mr. Grinnell indicted me for murder. That is the whole story in short of what I had to do with this Haymarket affair. So you see I had nothing to do with it, and didn't know anything about it. The next day I read in the paper that Attorney Walker—certainly an honorable man—was in the saloon. It was kind of dangerous for him evidently, for he subsequently denied being there. However that may have been, I was there.

And your honor, I committed another crime. I saw that the grocery clerks and the other clerks of this city worked until ten and eleven o'clock in the evening. I issued a call and rented a hall, and paid for the hand-bills, and called them together, and today they are working only until seven o'clock in the evening, and no Sunday work. That is a great crime I have committed, in your sight. I saved for the men from four to five hours a day. I have saved the bakers from six to eight hours work a day, and that gives them time for education. We Socialists are great believers that the laboring men should educate themselves, not to be ignoramuses, as some people express themselves, "as the ignorant anarchists are." We are great friends of education and a reduction of the hours of labor. A reduction of the hours of labor was my principal aim, and I have done some good work to bring it about.

I have been in the labor movement since 1865. I have seen how the police have trodden on the Constitution of this country, and crushed the labor organizations. I have seen from year to year how they were trodden down, where they were shot down, where they were "driven into their holes like rats," as Mr. Grinnell said to the jury. But they will come out! Remember that within three years before the beginning of the French Revolution, when laws had been stretched like rubber, that the rubber stretched too long, and broke—a result which cost a good many State's attorneys and a good many honorable men their necks.

We Socialists hope such times may never come again; we do everything in our power to prevent it, such as reducing the hours of labor and increasing wages. But you capitalists won't allow this to be done. You use your power to perpetuate a system by which you make your money for yourselves and keep the wage-workers poor. You make them ignorant and miserable, and you are responsible for it. You won't let the toilers live a decent life.

We want to educate the masses and keep them back from destroying life and property, but we are not able to hold the masses when starvation brings them out of their holes like rats. I have walked along the streets of this city and I have seen the rats come from their holes by the hundreds in the basements, where they pay five and ten cents for lodgings. I have seen the miserable wretches there in the day begging for a piece of bread, and in the night they lie there in an air that was difficult to breathe. I have been in there at ten, twelve, and two o'clock at night, and when those rats are let out of their holes once and get desperate I would not like to be near them. The time will come that you will see them. You rich men don't want the poor educated. You don't want anybody to be educated. You want to keep them down in the mud so you can squeeze the last drop of blood out of their bones.

We asked the capitalists once at a meeting to discuss the question of labor, and Mr. Gary was invited, and each one of them was invited, and nobody appeared. They didn't want to discuss the question; they didn't care for it. What is the next question? No discussion, more Gatling guns, more militia, and 300 more police. For what? To catch the thieves? I read the daily papers and see that burglaries are taking place all over the city, but I don't see that they catch any. There are some twelve hundred and odd policemen in the city of Chicago, and every day so many burglaries. Maybe they need them to make a case sometimes, and they don't arrest them; but when it comes to arresting a poor workingman they are all there. On May 9, when I came home, my wife, who is delicate, told me that the patrol wagon, with twenty-five police, came to search my house. I must be a very dangerous man to require so many police. They searched the whole house and they found a revolver. That is a deadly weapon and a dangerous weapon. I don't think anybody has revolvers but Anarchists and Socialists and labor agitators. They found a red flag, too—a flag of that size (about a foot square) that my little boy played with, and my wife used at a masquerade ball. My wife told me that when the police—these honorable men who protect law and order—got on the wagon they waved that flag and hollered and hurrahed just like a lot of wild Indians—and they were wild Indians in those days. They searched hundreds of houses, and money was stolen by searching houses, and watches were stolen, and nobody knew whether they were stolen by the police or not. Captain Nobody but Schaack; he knows it. His gang was one of the worst in this city. You need not laugh about it, Captain Schaack. You are one of them. You are an Anarchist, as you understand it. You are all Anarchists, in this sense of the word, I must say.

Well, these are all the crimes I have committed. They found a revolver in my house, and a red flag there. I organized trades unions. I was for reduction of the hours of labor, and the education of laboring men, and the re-establishment of the *Arbeiter-Zeitung*—the workingmen's newspaper. There is no evidence to show that I was connected with the bomb-throwing, or that I was near it, or anything of that kind. So I will ask you to hang me, too; for I think it is more honorable to die suddenly than to be killed by inches. I have a family and children; and if they know their father is dead, they will bury him. They can go to the grave, and kneel down by the side of it; but they can't go to the penitentiary and see their father, who was convicted for a crime that he hadn't had anything to do with. That is all I have got to say. Your honor, I am sorry I am not to be hung with the rest of the men.*

* Oscar Neebe was the only one of the eight defendants who was not condemned to death. He was sentenced to imprisonment for fifteen years.

ADDRESS OF ADOLPH FISCHER

YOUR HONOR: You ask me why sentence of death should not be passed upon me. I will not talk much. I will only say that I protest against my being sentenced to death, because I have committed no crime. I was tried here in this room for murder, and I was convicted of Anarchy. I protest against being sentenced to death, because I have not been found guilty of murder. However, if I am to die on account of being an Anarchist, on account of my love for liberty, fraternity and equality, I will not remonstrate. If death is the penalty for our love of the freedom of the human race, then I say openly I have forfeited my life; but a murderer I am not. Although being one of the parties who arranged the Haymarket meeting, I had no more to do with the throwing of that bomb, I had no more connection with it than State's Attorney Grinnell had. I do not deny that I was present at the Haymarket meeting but that meeting—

(At this point Mr. Salomon stepped up and spoke to Mr. Fischer in a low tone, but the latter waved him off and said:)

Mr. Salomon, be so kind. I know what I am talking about. Now, that Haymarket meeting was not called for the purpose of committing violence and crime. No; but the meeting was called for the purpose of protesting against the outrages and crimes committed by the police on the previous day, out at McCormick's. The State's witness, Waller, and others have testified here, and I only need to repeat it, that we had a meeting on Monday night, and at this meeting—the affair at McCormick's taking place just a few hours previous—took action and called a mass meeting for the purpose of protesting against the brutal outrages of the police. Waller was chairman of this meeting, and he himself made the motion to hold the meeting at the Haymarket. It was also he who appointed me as a committee to have handbills printed and to provide for speakers; that I did, and nothing else. The next day I went to Wehrer & Klein, and had 25,000 handbills printed, and I invited Spies to speak at the Haymarket meeting. In the original of the "copy" I had the line "Workingmen, appear armed!" and my reason for putting those words in was because I didn't want the workingmen to be shot down in that meeting as on other occasions. But as those circulars were printed, or as a few of them were printed and brought over to me at the *Arbeiter-Zeitung* office, my comrade Spies saw one of them. I had invited him to speak before that. He showed me the circular, and said: "Well, Fischer, if those circulars are distributed, I won't speak." I admitted it would be better to take the objectionable words out, and Mr. Spies spoke. And that is all I had to do with that meeting. Well, I went to the Haymarket about 8:15 o'clock, and stayed there until Parsons interrupted Fielden's speech. Parsons stepped up to the stand, and said that it looked like it was going to rain, and that the assembly had better adjourn to Zepf's Hall. At that moment a friend of mine who testified on the witness stand, went with me to Zepf's Hall, and we sat down at a table and had a glass of beer. At the moment I was going to sit down, my friend Parsons came in with some other persons, and after I was sitting there about five minutes the explosion occurred. I had no idea that anything of the kind would happen, because, as the State's witnesses testified, themselves, there was no agreement to defend ourselves that night. It was only a meeting called to protest.

Now, as I said before, this verdict, which was rendered by the jury in this room, is not directed against murder, but against Anarchy. I feel that I am sentenced, or that I will be sentenced, to death because of being an Anarchist, and not because I am a murderer. I have never been a murderer. I have never yet committed a crime in my life; but I know a certain man who is on the way to becoming a murderer, an assassin, and that man is Grinnell—the State's Attorney Grinnell—because he brought men on the witness stand who he knew would swear falsely; and I publicly denounce Mr. Grinnell as being a murderer and an assassin if I should be executed. But if the ruling class thinks that by executing us, hanging a few Anarchists, they can crush out Anarchy, they will be badly mistaken, because the Anarchist loves his principles better than his life. An Anarchist is always ready to die for his principles; but in this case I have been charged with murder, and I am not a murderer. You will find it impossible to kill a principle, although you may take the life of men who confess these principles. The more the believers in just causes are persecuted, the quicker will their ideas be realized. For instance, in rendering such an unjust and barbarous verdict, the twelve "honorable" men in the jury box have done more for the furtherance of Anarchism than the convicted could have accomplished in a generation. This verdict is a death-blow against free speech, free press, and free thought in this country, and the people will be conscious of it, too. This is all I care to say.

ADDRESS OF LOUIS LINGG

COURT OF JUSTICE: With the same irony with which you have regarded my efforts to win, in this "free land of America," a livelihood such as human kind is worthy to enjoy, do you now, after condemning me to death, concede me the liberty of making a final speech.

I accept your concession; but it is only for the purpose of exposing the injustice, the calumnies, and the outrages which have been heaped upon me.

You have accused me of murder, and convicted me; what proof have you brought that I am guilty?

In the first place, you have brought this fellow Seliger to testify against me. Him I have helped to make bombs, and you have further proven that with the assistance of another, I took those bombs to No. 58 Clybourn avenue, but what you have not proved—even with the assistance of your bought "squealer," Seliger, who would appear to have acted such a prominent part in the affair—is that any of those bombs were taken to the Haymarket.

A couple of chemists also have been brought here as specialists, yet they could only state that the metal of which the Haymarket bomb was made bore a certain resemblance to those bombs of mine, and your Mr. Ingham has vainly endeavored to deny that the bombs were quite different. He had to admit that there was a difference of a full half inch in their diameters, although he suppressed the fact that there was also a difference of a quarter of an inch in the thickness of the shell. This is the kind of evidence upon which you have convicted me.

It is not murder, however, of which you have convicted me. The Judge has stated that much only this morning in his *resume* of the case, and Grinnell has repeatedly asserted that we were being tried, not for murder, but for Anarchy, so that the condemnation is—that I am an Anarchist!

What is Anarchy?

This is a subject which my comrades have explained with sufficient clearness, and it is unnecessary for me to go over it again. They have told you plainly enough what our aims are. The State's attorney, however, has not given you that information. He has merely criticized and condemned not the doctrines of Anarchy, but our methods of giving them practical effect, and even here he has maintained a discreet silence as to the fact that those methods were forced upon us by the brutality of the police. Grinnell's own proffered remedy for our grievances is the ballot and combination of Trades Unions, and Ingham has even avowed the desirability of a six hour movement! But the fact is, that at every attempt to wield the ballot, at every endeavor to combine the efforts of workingmen, you have displayed the brutal violence of the police club, and this is why I have recommended rude force to combat the ruder force of the police.

You have charged me with despising "law and order." What does your "law and order" amount to? Its representatives are the police, and they have thieves in their ranks. Here sits Captain Schaack. He has himself admitted to me that my hat and books have been stolen from him in his office—stolen by policemen. These are your defenders of property rights!

The detectives again, who arrested me, forced their way into my room like house breakers, under false pretenses, giving the name of a carpenter, Lorenz, of Burlington street. They have sworn that I was alone in my room, therein perjuring themselves. You have not subpoenaed this lady, Mrs. Klein, who was present, and could have sworn that the aforesaid detectives broke into my room under false pretenses, and that their testimonies are perjured.

But let us go further. In Schaack we have a captain of the police, and he also has perjured himself. He has sworn that I admitted to him being present at the Monday night's meeting, whereas I distinctly informed him that I was at a carpenters' meeting at Zepf's Hall. He has sworn again that I told him that I had learned how to make bombs from Herr Most's book. That, also, is a perjury.

Let us go still a step higher among these representatives of "law and order." Grinnell and his associates have permitted perjury, and I say that they have done it knowingly. The proof has been adduced by my counsel, and with my own eyes I have seen Grinnell point out to Gilmer, eight days before he came upon the stand, the persons of the men whom he was to swear against.

While I, as I have stated above, believe in force for the sake of winning for myself and fellow workmen a livelihood such as men ought to have, Grinnell, on the other hand, through his police and other rogues, has suborned perjury in order to murder seven men, of whom I am one.

Grinnell had the pitiful courage, here in this courtroom, where I could not defend myself, to call me a coward! The scoundrel! A fellow who has leagued himself with a parcel of base, hireling knaves, to bring me to the gallows. Why? For no earthly reason save a contemptible selfishness—a desire to "rise in the world"—to "make money," forsooth!

This wretch—who, by means of the perjuries of other wretches is going to murder seven men—is the fellow who calls me "coward!" And yet you blame me for despising such "defenders of the law"—such unspeakable hypocrites!

Anarchy means no domination or authority of one man over another, yet you call that "disorder." A system which advocates no such "order" as shall require the services of rogues and thieves to defend it you call "disorder."

The Judge himself was forced to admit that the State's attorney had not been able to connect me with the bomb throwing. The latter knows how to get around it, however. He charges me with being a "conspirator." How does he prove it? Simply by declaring the International Workingmen's Association to be a "conspiracy." I was a member of that body, so he has the charge securely fastened on me. Excellent! Nothing is too difficult for the genius of a State's attorney!

It is hardly incumbent upon me to review the relations which I occupy to my companions in misfortune. My friend Spies has already explained how we became acquainted with each other. I can say truly and openly that I am not as intimate with my fellow prisoners as I am with Captain Schaack.

The universal misery, the ravages of the capitalistic hyena have brought us together in our agitation, not as persons, but as workers in the same cause. Such is the "conspiracy" of which you have convicted me.

I protest against the conviction, against the decision of the court. I do not recognize your law, jumbled together as it is by the nobodies of by-gone centuries, and I do not recognize the decision of the court. My own counsel have conclusively proven from the decisions of equally high courts that a new trial must be granted us. The State's attorney quotes three times as many decisions from perhaps still higher courts to prove the opposite, and I am convinced that if, in another trial, these decisions should be supported by twenty-five volumes, they will adduce one hundred in support of the contrary, if it is Anarchists who are to be tried. And not even under such a law, a law that a schoolboy must despise, not even by such methods have they been able to "legally" convict us. They have suborned perjury to boot.

I tell you frankly and openly, I am for force. I have already told Captain Schaack, "If they use cannons against us, we shall use dynamite against them."

I repeat that I am the enemy of the "order" of today, and I repeat that, with all my powers, so long as breath remains in me, I shall combat it. I declare again, frankly and openly, that I am in favor of using force. I have told Captain Schaack, and I stand by it, "If you cannonade us we shall dynamite you." You laugh! Perhaps you think, "You'll throw no more bombs"; but let me assure you that I die happy on the gallows, so confident am I that the hundreds and thousands to whom I have spoken will remember my words; and when you shall have hanged us, then, mark my words, they will do the bomb throwing! In this hope I say to you: I despise you. I despise your order, your laws, your force-propped authority. Hang me for it!

ADDRESS OF GEORGE ENGEL

When, in the year 1872, I left Germany because it had become impossible for me to gain there, by the labor of my hands, a livelihood such as man is worthy to enjoy—the introduction of machinery having ruined the smaller craftsmen and made the outlook for the future appear very dark to them—I concluded to go with my family to the land of America, the land that had been praised to me by so many as the land of liberty.

On the occasion of my arrival at Philadelphia, on the 8th of January, 1873, my heart swelled with joy in the hope and in the belief that in the future I would live among free men, and in a free country. I made up my mind to become a good citizen of this country, and congratulated myself on having left Germany, and landed in this glorious republic. And I believe my past history will bear witness that I have ever striven to be a good citizen of this country. This is the first occasion of my standing before an American court, and on this occasion it is murder of which I am accused. And for what reasons do I stand here? For what reasons am I accused of murder? The same that caused me to leave Germany—the poverty, the misery of the working classes.

And here, too, in this "free republic," in the richest country of the world, there are numerous proletarians for whom no table is set; who, as outcasts of society, stray joylessly through life. I have seen human beings gather their daily food from the garbage heaps of the streets, to quiet therewith their gnawing hunger.

I have read of occurrences in the daily papers which proves to me that here, too, in this great "free land," people are doomed to die of starvation. This brought me to reflection, and to the question: What are the peculiar causes that could bring about such a condition of society? I then began to give our political institutions more attention than formerly. My discoveries brought to me the knowledge that the same societary evils exist here that exist in Germany. This is the explanation of what induced me to study the social question, to become a Socialist. And I proceeded with all the means at my command, to make myself familiar with the new doctrine.

When, in 1878, I came here from Philadelphia, I strove to better my condition, believing it would be less difficult to establish a means of livelihood here than in Philadelphia, where I had tried in vain to make a living. But here, too, I found myself disappointed. I began to understand that it made no difference to the proletarian, whether he lived in New York, Philadelphia, or Chicago. In the factory in which I worked, I became acquainted with a man who pointed out to me the causes that brought about the difficult and fruitless battles of the workingmen for the means of existence. He explained to me, by the logic of scientific Socialism, how mistaken I was in believing that I could make an independent living by the toil of my hands, so long as machinery, raw material, etc., were guaranteed to the capitalists as private property by the State. That I might further enlighten my mind in regard to these facts, I purchased with money earned by myself and family, sociological works, among them those of LaSalle, Marx, and Henry George. After the study of these books, it became clear to me why a workingman could not decently exist in this rich country. I now began to think of ways and means to remedy this. I hit upon the ballot box; for it had been told me so often that this was the means by which workingmen could better their condition.

I took part in politics with the earnestness of a good citizen; but I was soon to find that the teachings of a "free ballot box" are a myth, and that I had again been duped. I came to the opinion that as long as workingmen are economically enslaved they cannot be politically free. It became clear to me that the working classes would never bring about a form of society guaranteeing work, bread, and a happy life by means of the ballot.

Before I had lost my faith in the ballot box the following occurrences transpired which proved to me that the politicians of this country were throughly corrupt. When, in the fourteenth ward, in which I lived and had the right to vote, the Social Democratic party had grown to such dimensions as to make it dangerous for the Republican and Democratic parties, the latter forthwith united and took stand against the Social Democrats. This, of course, was natural; for are not their interests identical? And as the Social Democrats nevertheless elected their candidates, they were beaten out of the fruits of their victory by the corrupt schemes of the old political parties. The ballot-box was stolen and the votes so "corrected" that it became impossible for the opposition to proclaim their candidates elected. The workingmen sought to obtain justice through the courts, but it was all in vain. The trial cost them fifteen hundred dollars, but their rights they never obtained.

Soon enough I found that political corruption had burrowed through the ranks of the Social Democrats. I left this party and joined the International Working People's Association that was just being organized. The members of that body have the firm conviction that the workingman can free himself from the tyranny of capitalism only through force, just as all advances of which history speaks have been brought about through force alone. We see from the history of this country that the first colonists won their liberty only through force; that through force slavery was abolished, and just as the man who agitated against slavery in this country had to ascend the gallows, so also must we. He who speaks for the workingman today must hang. And why? Because this Republic is not governed by people who have obtained their offices honestly.

Who are the leaders at Washington that are to guard the interests of this nation? Have they been elected by the people, or by the aid of money? They have no right to make laws for us, because they were not elected by the people. These are the reasons why I have lost all respect for American laws.

The fact that through the improvement of machinery so many men are thrown out of employment, or at best, working but half the time, brings them to reflection. They have leisure, and they consider how their conditions can be changed. Reading matter that has been written in their interest gets into their hands, and, faulty though their education may be, they can nevertheless cull the truths contained in those writings. This, of course, is not pleasant for the capitalistic class, but they cannot prevent it. And it is my firm conviction that in a comparatively short time the great mass of proletarians will understand that they can be freed from their bonds only through Socialism. One must consider what Carl Schurz said scarcely eight years ago: That, "in this country there is no room for Socialism"; and yet today Socialism stands before the bar of the court. For this reason it is my firm conviction that if these few years sufficed to make Socialism one of the burning questions of the day, it will require but a short time more to put it in practical operation.

All that I have to say in regard to my conviction is, that I was not at all surprised; for it has ever been that the men who have endeavored to enlighten their fellow man have been thrown into prison or put to death, as was the case with John Brown. I have found, long ago, that the workingman has no more rights here than anywhere else in the world. The State's attorney has stated that we were not citizens. I have been a citizen this long time; but it does not occur to me to appeal for my rights as a citizen, knowing as well as I do that this does not make a particle of difference. Citizen or not—as a workingman I am without rights, and therefore I respect neither your rights nor your laws, which are made and directed by one class against the other—the working class.

Of what does my crime consist?

That I have labored to bring about a system of society by which it is impossible for one to hoard millions, through the improvements in machinery, while the great masses sink to degradation and misery.

As water and air are free to all, so should inventions of scientific men be applied for the benefit of all. The statute laws we have are in opposition to the laws of nature, in that they rob the great masses of their rights "to life, liberty, and the pursuit of happiness."

I am too much a man of feeling not to battle against the societary conditions of today. Every considerate person must combat a system which makes it possible for the individual to rake and hoard millions in a few years, while, on the other side, thousands become tramps and beggars.

Is it to be wondered at that under such circumstances men arise who strive and struggle to create other conditions, where humanity shall take precedence of all other considerations? This is the aim of Socialism, and to this I joyfully subscribe.

The State's attorney said here that Anarchy was on trial.

Anarchism and Socialism are as much alike, in my opinion, as one egg is like another. They differ only in their tactics. The Anarchists have abandoned the way of liberating humanity which Socialists would take to accomplish this. I say: Believe no more in the ballot, and use all other means at your command. Because we have done so we stand arraigned here today—because we have pointed out to the people the proper way. The Anarchists are being hunted and persecuted for this in every clime, but in the face of it all Anarchism is gaining more and more adherents, and if you cut off our opportunities of open agitation, then will the work be done secretly. If the State's attorney thinks he can root out Socialism by hanging seven of our men and condemning the other to fifteen years' servitude, he is laboring under a very wrong impression. The tactics simply will be changed—that is all. No power on earth can rob the workingman of his knowledge of how to make bombs—and that knowledge he possesses. I do not wish for State's Attorney Grinnell and his assistant, Furthman, the fate of the chief of police Rumpff.

If Anarchism could be rooted out, it would have been accomplished long ago in other countries. On the night on which the first bomb in this country was thrown, I was in my apartments at home. I knew nothing of the conspiracy which the State's attorney pretends to have discovered.

It is true I am acquainted with several of my fellow-defendants: with most of them, however, but slightly, through seeing them at meetings, and hearing them speak. Nor do I deny, that I, too, have spoken at meetings, saying that, if every working man had a bomb in his pocket, capitalistic rule would soon come to an end.

That is my opinion, and my wish; it became my conviction, when I discovered the wickedness of the capitalistic conditions of the day.

When hundreds of workingmen have been destroyed in mines in consequence of faulty preparations, for the repairing of which the owners were too stingy, the capitalistic papers have scarcely noticed it. See with what satisfaction and cruelty they make their report, when here and there workingmen have been fired upon, while striking for a few cents, increase in their wages, that they might earn only a scanty subsistence.

Can any one feel respect for a government that accords rights only to the privileged classes, and none to the workers? We have seen but recently how the coal barons combined to form a conspiracy to raise the price of coal, while at the same time reducing the already low wages of their men. Are they accused of conspiracy on that account? But when workingmen dare ask an increase in their wages, the militia and the police are sent out to shoot them down.

For such a government as this I can feel no respect, and will combat it, despite its power, despite its police, despite its spies.

I hate and combat, not the individual capitalist, but the system that gives him those privileges. My greatest wish is that workingmen may recognize who are their friends and who are their enemies.

As to my conviction, brought about as it was, through capitalistic influence, I have not one word to say.

ADDRESS OF SAMUEL FIELDEN

And tho' ye caught your noble prey within your hangman's sordid thrall;
And tho' your captive was led forth beneath your city's rampart wall;
And tho' the grass lies o'er her green, where at the morning's early red
The peasant girl brings funeral wreaths—I tell you still—she is not dead!

And tho' from off the lofty brow ye cut the ringlets flowing long,
And tho' ye've mated her amid the thieves' and murderers' hideous throng,
And tho' ye gave her felon fare—bade felon garb her livery be,
And tho' ye set the oakum task—I tell you all—she still is free!

And tho' compelled to banishment, ye hunt her down thro' endless lands;
And tho' she seeks a foreign hearth, and silent 'mid its ashes stands;

And tho' she bathes her wounded feet where foreign streams seek foreign seas;
Yet—yet—she never more will hang her harp on Babel's willow trees!

Ah, no! she strikes it very strong, and bids their loud defiance swell,
And as she marked your scaffold erst, she mocks your banishment as well.
She sings a song that starts you up astounded from your slumbrous seats.
Until your heart—your craven heart—your traitor heart—with terror beats!

No song of plaint, no song of sighs for those who perished unsubdued.
Nor yet a song of irony at wrongs fantastic interlude—
The beggar's opera that ye try to drag out thro' its lingering scenes.
Tho' moth-eaten the purple bee that decks your tinsel kings and queens.

Oh, no! the song those waters hear is not of sorrow, nor dismay—
'Tis triumph song—victorious song—the paeans of the future's day—
The future—distant now no more—her prophet voice is sounding free.
As well as once your Godhead spake: I was, I am, and I will be!

Will be—and lead the nation on the last of all your hosts to meet,
And on your necks, your heads, your crowns, I'll plant my strong, resistless feet!
Avenger, Liberator, Judge—red battles on my pathway hurled,
I stretch forth my almighty arm, till it revivifies the world.

Ye see me only in your cells; ye see me only in the grave;
Ye see me only wandering lone, beside the exile's sullen wave—
Ye fools! Do I not live where ye have tried to pierce in vain?
Rests not a nook for me to dwell in every heart and every brain?

In every brow that boldly thinks, erect with manhood's honest pride—

Does not each bosom shelter me that beats with honor's generous
tide?
Not every workshop, brooding woe? not every hut that harbors grief?
Ha! Am I not the Breath of Life, that pants and struggles for relief?

'Tis therefore I will be—and lead the people yet your hosts to meet,
And on your necks, your heads, your crowns, will plant my strong,
resistless feet!
It is no boast—it is no threat—thus history's iron law decrees—
The day grows hot, oh, Babylon! 'Tis cool beneath thy willow trees!

That is a piece of poetry written by Freiligrath, called "Revolution." Freiligrath is a German writer, and every intelligent German in the civilized world has that piece of poetry upon his book-shelves.

Revolution—it is a crime in what is sometimes called the foremost civilized country in the world, to be a Revolutionist, and yet all those who can read the works of Freiligrath have read that poem with rapture. It makes a great deal of difference, perhaps, what kind of a Revolutionist a man is. The men who have been on trial here for Anarchy have been asked the question on the witness stand if they were Revolutionists. It is not generally considered a crime among intellectual people to be a Revolutionist, but it may be made a crime if the Revolutionist happens to be poor.

Your Honor, I was brought into this court by the police officers and the civil authorities of the city of Chicago to answer to the charge of murder. I was arrested on May 5, held by the coroner's jury on the same evening as accessory to the crime of murder. I was furnished after some time with an indictment which the Grand Jury had passed, or approved, charging me with that crime. I answered that charge in this court. My attorneys in my behalf met that charge; we brought evidence which we thought was competent to rebut and meet the charge of murder. After all our evidence was put in, after all the speeches had been made on both sides, with the exception of one, we were suddenly confronted with the fact—and there is in that statement of the State's attorney, in his closing argument, an acknowledgment that the charge of murder had not been proven—when all the witnesses had been heard, I am suddenly told that I am being tried for Anarchy. If I had known that I was being tried for anarchy I could have answered that charge. I could have justified it under the constitutional right of every citizen of this country, and more than the right which any constitution can give, the natural right of the human mind to draw its conclusion from whatever information it can gain, but I had no opportunity to show why I was an Anarchist. I was told that I was to be hung for being an Anarchist, after I got through defending myself on the charge of murder. Now, your honor, my reputation, my associations, my history, as far as the lynx-eyed detectives of Chicago could get it, has been raked up, as Mr. Foster has said, from the cradle to the grave. I have been charged here with being a disturber of the peace, an enemy of public order, and generally a dangerous man. I choose now, it being the last time that I shall have an opportunity to speak, to go back a few years into my past history, and perhaps in doing so I shall show your honor the reasons that led me to be what I have been, and for which today I am not ashamed and have no apology to make.

I was born, as I have told you, in Lancashire, and if there is a place—I know that the so-called patriots of this country have from mercenary motives of their own, tried to create a quarrel between England and America from time to time in order to get a certain vote, and I know that there is some justification behind it—but if there is a place on this footstool that Americans ought to look to with gratitude, it is Lancashire. I was born there. I learned there to hate slavery. I learned to hate kings and queens, and unlike the State's attorney in this case, I was a Republican, though I was born in a monarchy.

There are some men who never grow out of their environments. They never progress. They never advance one step. If they are born in Russia, Russia is the grandest country in the world, and has the grandest institutions. If they are born in China it is the same. If they were born in Patagonia it would have been the same. But I, as a child, inquired, and I began there to hate Kings, and I tell you that when your cotton ports on the Southern sea-board were blockaded—and this fact has gone into the literature of both countries—the patience of the starving operatives of Lancashire was remarkable, and the noble Lincoln, acknowledging that, sent two ship-loads of provisions to keep them from starving. The propertied class of England, in sympathy with the slaveholders of the South, I know, would have interfered in order to prevent the cementing together of the Union and the success of the North. But the operatives, the intelligent operatives of Lancashire, one of whom I was when a child, were the friends of the North, and they cheerfully and patiently bore with all the starvation which they suffered through that terrible struggle.

I say there are some people who never get out of their environments. I was a Republican when I was a child. I recognized the fact that I might be wrong, and, recognizing that fact, I grew from one point to another. The first speech I ever delivered in my life was in the streets of my native town, and I was but a mere child; it was in support of the Union as against the views of those who denounced the North in their struggle for supremacy in the late war. That was the first speech I delivered, and it shows that then I had some sympathy in my heart for those who could do me no good; that I could feel for others. Mr. Ingham has said that while other people were making their fortunes these men were advocating sedition or drinking beer. It is as noble a thing for a man to drink beer as it is for a man to make his fortune off of other people's labor; and I tell you that a man is of no use to this world, of no use to society or the neighborhood in which he lives, who has no other object in view than making a fortune for himself and his family, little caring what becomes of those around him. And it is because we have recognized this fact—and it is a philosophical fact, a logical fact that no man can get away from, and Mr. Ingham has not got the intelligence to perceive it—that the greatest security to human happiness depends upon the widespread happiness of those around you. You have no security for your fortunes. You can have no security for your comforts as long as there is around you a dissatisfied, a despoiled, and suffering community. I assert here as a fact, that Vanderbilt and Jay Gould would be happier men today if they had but $20,000 to their names and every employee who is now in their employment were above want and above the danger of want. There would be less irritation, less of that trouble and bother of clashing and conflicting of interests than there is, which must necessarily bother these men considerably, and keep them awake nights possibly.

I have never hesitated when I have seen my way clearly according to my lights, to follow it. I have always endeavored to hew to the line, let the chips fall where they would. Some people do not do that. That is what is the trouble with the world. A great many people ask, when they find what their duty is, does it pay? If it pays they will follow it, and they care not where the payment comes from.

About the second speech, perhaps, that I ever made in my life was after I had become a member of the Methodist church, and to show that I was a perambulating talking machine then, I will say here that I visited different towns in Lancashire and spoke in the open air to audiences because my thoroughness of character compelled me to do it. I felt that that religion which I thought I possessed, and which I thought was calculated to better the world, was something that was worth while for me to use my energies in propagating, and I did it. I could not help it. There are sloths that are sometimes called men who are never influenced by anything of that kind, but I was not of that character and that is the reason that I am here today. So intense and earnest was I at that time that I was at one and the same time the Sunday school superintendent of a little Sunday school, a class teacher, a local preacher, and what was called an exhorter; held four different positions.

I came to the United States in 1868. I have preached in Ohio, and I came to Chicago in 1869. There are monuments of beauty, of stability, and evidences of progress in the city of Chicago, and you can hardly go through a street in this city that I have not dropped my sweat upon, that had been produced by the labor of my hands. And just here let me tell you that when the indictment had been procured against me and my comrades here, it was accompanied by the statement that these men had been deluding their dupes in order to make money out of them. When the trial was in progress the only man who could have answered the question as to whether we had made money out of our agitation was Zeller, the Secretary of the Central Labor Union, and when he was asked the question whether we ever received any money for speaking and organizing unions in that organization, the gentlemen who had been instrumental in attaching that to the indictment in order to prejudice the people against us before the trial should come on against us—for there is nothing in the world that can prejudice a man so much as to be charged with having imposed upon some one for mercenary motives, and this is creditable to society—when the trial came on and this man who could have testified to that, who could have substantiated it if it had been true, was asked the question, each one of the gentlemen who were interested in its being proven true for their side of the case at once sprang to their feet and objected to the question being asked. We have been tried by a jury that has found us guilty. You will be tried by a jury now that will find you guilty.

Being of an inquiring disposition or turn of mind, and having observed that there was something wrong in our social system, I attended some meetings of workingmen and compared what they said with my own observation. I knew there was something wrong.

My ideas did not become settled as to what was the remedy, but when they did, I carried the same energy and the same determination to bring about that remedy that I had applied to ideas which I had possessed years before. There is always a period in every individual's life when some sympathetic chord is touched by some other person. That is the open sesame that carries conviction. The ground may have all been prepared. The evidence may all have been accumulated, but it has not formed any shape; in fact, the child has not been born. The new idea has not impressed itself thoroughly when that sympathetic chord is touched, and the person is thoroughly convinced of the truth of the idea. It was so in my investigation of political economy. I knew there was something wrong, but I did not know what the remedy was, but discussing the condition of things and the different remedies one day, a person said to me that Socialism meant equal opportunities—and that was the touch. From that time I became a Socialist; I learned more and more what it was. I knew that I had found the right thing; and I had found the medicine that was calculated to cure the ills of society. Having found it I had a right to advocate it, and I did. The constitution of the United States, when it says: "The right of free speech shall not be abridged," gives every man the right to speak his thoughts.

I have advocated the principles of socialism and social equality, and for that and no other reason am I here, and is sentence of death to be pronounced upon me. What is Socialism? Taking somebody else's property? That is what Socialism is in the common acceptation of the term. No; but if I were to answer it as shortly and as curtly as it is answered by its enemies, I would say it is preventing somebody else from taking your property.

But socialism is equality. Socialism recognizes the fact that no man in society is responsible for what he is; that all the ills that are in society are the production of poverty; and scientific Socialism says that you must go to the root of the evil. There is no criminal statistician in the world but will acknowledge that all crime, when traced to its origin, is the product of poverty. It has been said that it was inflammatory for me to say that the present social system degraded men until they became mere animals. Go through this city into the low lodging houses where men are huddled together into the smallest possible space, living in an infernal atmosphere of death and disease, and I will ask you to draw your silks and broadcloths close to you when these men pass you. Do you think that these men deliberately, with a full knowledge of what they are doing, choose to become that class of animals? Not one of them. They are the products of conditions, of certain environments in which they were born, and which have impelled them resistlessly into what they are. And we have this loadstone. You who wish it could be taken from the shoulders of society, what is it? When those men were children, put them into an environment where they have had the best results of civilization around them, and they would never have willfully chosen a condition like that. Some cynic might say that this would be a very nice thing for these men. Society, with its rapidity of production of the means of existence, is capable of doing that without doing an injury to a single individual; and the great masses of wealth owned by individuals in this and the old world have been produced in exactly the same proportion as these men have been degraded—and they never could have been accumulated in any other way. I do not charge that every capitalist willfully and maliciously conspires to bring about these results, but I do charge that it has been done, and I do charge that it is a very undesirable condition of things, and I claim that Socialism would cure the world of that ulcer.

These are my ideas in short on Socialism. The ultra patriotic sentiment of the American people—and I suppose the same comparative sentiment is felt in England, France and Germany—is that no man in this country need be poor. The class who are not poor think so. The class who are poor are beginning to think differently; that under existing conditions it is impossible that some should not be poor.

Fortunes are made, and I will tell you how it is done. The Chicago *Tribune*, in its New Year's issue of 1885, I believe, drew attention to the production of the means of human use and necessity in the city of Chicago during the previous year. It carefully estimated the cost of the raw material, the cost of machinery, the rent of buildings, the interest on money, and the wages to employees. It went into different lines of production, and, summing up, the result was this: That in a year's time each man working as a wage-laborer in the city of Chicago had added to the wealth of this city—by whomsoever it was possessed makes no difference—$2,764 in a year. The average wages paid for that average product of each worker was $457—a little more than one-sixth. And yet the political economists of the free trade and the protective schools were asking; "Why is it that we have overproduction?" You compel a man to work and produce $2,764 worth of goods, and you give him $457 to buy them with, and you ask: "Why is it that we have overproduction, and why is it that our warehouses are full of goods, and our workshops have to shut up, and our workmen are turned out on the highway because there is nothing to do." What is this tending to? Let me show the change of conditions as shown in Boston in forty years. Charles Dickens, a man of acute perceptions, visited this country forty years ago, and he said in his American notes that the sight of a beggar in the streets of Boston at that time would have created as much consternation as the sight of an angel with a drawn sword. A Boston paper in the winter of 1884-85 stated that there were some quarters in Boston where to own a stove was to be a comparative aristocrat. The poor people who lived in the neighborhood paid a certain sum of money to rent the holes on the top of the stove that belonged to the aristocrats. You see the change, and there is this comparative change in the working classes of that city, and in every large city in the Union. It is a noted fact that within the last twenty or thirty years the farms of this country have been gradually going out of the possession of the actual cultivators until today there is a little more than a quarter of the actual cultivators of farms in this country who are renters; and within twenty years in the States of Iowa and Illinois the mortgages on farms have increased thirty-three per cent of the actual value of the farms. Is it not enough to make any thinking man ask if there is not something wrong somewhere? Possibly it would be answered, "Yes, a man has a right to inquire whether there is something wrong or not, but for God's sake, don't think that Socialism will do it any good, or if you do we will hang you! It is all right to think, but we will punish you for your conclusions."

Parsons, in his testimony, repeated what he had said at the Haymarket on the night of May 4, when he stated that this was an American question, because the patriotic tricksters who have been telling the people to worship the American flag, while they quietly put their hands in their pockets and robbed them—they have said that this is merely a European question. It is an American question, and the close contact of nations cemented by the facilities of civilization, is bringing all the questions that affect one people to affect all people equally all over the world. What affects the European laborer and his employer affects the American laborer and his American employer, and the relationship is the same between the two classes.

In the winter of 1884–85 one hundred and twenty American girls of fourteen and sixteen years of age were driven from their homes by the shutting down of the Merrimac mills in Connecticut, and they were compelled to walk through the bleak New England hills and find refuge in outhouses and haystacks, and numbers of them undoubtedly found their way to lives of shame. And I say here and now that the man who can look upon such conditions as these and not know that society is bringing itself to the verge of a crisis which is terrible to think of, is blind; and the man who can look upon suffering like this and not feel stirred to do something to change such conditions, has not got any thing in his heart but the feelings of the tiger, hungry for prey. In this city of Chicago children are working at very tender ages. Going home one very cold night in the winter of 1884, two little girls ran up to me and begged of me to go home with them. I asked them why. They said: "A man down there has been offering us money." It was 7 o'clock at night and snowing; I asked them where they had been so late. They said: "We have been working in such a store." Children, babies turned out from their mother's hearth to make a living, their fathers perhaps dead—in this case they were. The civilization that will not and cannot support a widow so that she will not have to turn her children out to such temptations as that is not worth respecting, and the man who will not try to change it is no man. Talking with those children as I went home with them—for they lived not far from me—I could notice the comparative boldness in the two children, they being of the same age. One of them told me she had been working three years and the other a year. There was that shyness, at least something remained of it, the coyness, which is about a child of tender age to a stranger, about the one that had only been away from the hearth-side one year; but in the other one, that had been away three years, there was not a particle of it, and she was a head shorter than the child that had the advantage of living at home two years more of her existence.

Carter Harrison noticed the degraded condition of a class of persons in this community, and he called the justices of the peace of this city to consult with him, a year ago last winter. They wanted to get rid of the street-walkers, who were so numerous that it was a disgrace to the city. It was very laudable in Harrison and the justices of the peace to get rid of them if they could. The remedy proposed was to arrest them, and the first time fine them lightly, and the next time fine them more, and they would keep on fining them more and more until they got rid of them. It is a known fact that there is no possibility of a young, unmarried woman, who has not a brother or father to assist her, getting a living in the city of Chicago, with a few exceptions. A friend of mine, a labor agitator, was asked by a young lady to procure her a position. He went to one of your large establishments, and they said: "Yes, we can give her a position, but she has got to dress tastily and nicely and neatly, and look well, and we will give her from three to five dollars a week." And you propose to get rid of these things by fining those who are compelled to resort to such extremes to live. I tell you these things to show you that the question is an American question. It is a question of the nineteenth century.

I am charged with having made some inflammatory harangues within the last few years. It has been testified to here that I made a speech at the Twelfth street Turner Hall in 1885. The language I used on that occasion has been referred to. To show the character of that meeting, and that of the organization to which I belong, I have only to say that that meeting was called in pursuance of a desire on the part of the Socialists to find out whether they were right or wrong, and to compare their views with the views of gentlemen who continually asserted that they were wrong. Those gentlemen were invited there to discuss the question, and would have been given an opportunity and as much time as any Socialistic speaker in that meeting to reply to the creed of Socialism. I do not think it was claimed that I said anything very inflammatory at that meeting. The city was placarded with bills inviting the professional and business men to come there and discuss those questions with us. They did not come in any great force. I was charged with having, at Mueller's Hall, as chairman of the meeting, called upon the audience to dispute with the Socialists and controvert anything that might have been said in behalf of private capitalism, as this would be the last opportunity before we began to take their property. The man who testified to that knows under what circumstances it was said. It was said because the critics on Socialism had charged us with a desire to take the property of others, instead of examining into our position; and the audience understood it was a joke as a sort of a take-off on the criticisms on Socialism.

It is well known that the reporters of the papers are a most intelligent (?) class of men. I do not know any class of people among whom I have found so many stupid people, and I have a very extensive acquaintance with them. With regard to what was stated about me at one time, when I was charged with making inflammatory statements here, I wish to say that at that time I was in Cincinnati, and I can prove it by a thousand persons of Cincinnati. Mr. Spies went with me to the depot the night before and bought me a ticket. I will speak a little further about my friends, the reporters, because the reporters have been depended upon to produce the conviction in this case. It is well known in this and every reading community that reports in the newspapers cannot be depended upon. There is not a public speaker in this country but what has had cause to complain of the reports of his speeches in the newspapers. So intolerable has this become that the chief magistrate of this country, less than a year ago, stated—and it was published all through the country—that there never was an age in the world in which newspaper lying existed to the extent that it does now, and there never was a country in which it existed to the extent that it does in this. Since my incarceration in jail, Mr. Harrison has been so utterly disgusted with the promises of the reporters to correctly report news, that he has given orders to his subordinates at the headquarters of the city department to refuse to give them any more news. "It is no use; you will lie about it. I have tried you and tried you, and you have lied about it, and I will give you no more news," he has said. And yet we have been convicted on this kind of testimony. Reporters have been brought here to prove that I was a conspirator and was intending to sack Michigan avenue, intending to create a riot and revolt in this city, by quotations from my speeches. I have shown you, my friends—I am speaking to you as well as to the court, and I am speaking to the country—that reports of newspapers can not be depended upon, and a man whose life is placed in jeopardy on the bare report of a newspaper reporter, is as liable to be murdered as not. At Twelfth street Turner Hall I made a speech concerning the riot in London. On that occasion I stated that the same causes in Chicago would produce the same results that we had seen in London, and that the privileged classes of this city who had read of the homeless and down-trodden and desperately poor of London creating the havoc and consternation that they had in the east end of London by throwing bricks through the Carleton Club windows, need not be surprised if the same causes here would bring out a mob which would march down Michigan avenue and throw a brick through the window of the Calumet Club. I said that the same causes existing here would produce the same results. A reporter of one of the morning papers came into the hall after I had got through, and was sitting down in the hall, and the next morning he stated that Samuel Fielden had said he would lead a mob down Michigan avenue and he himself would throw a brick through the window of the Calumet Club. And it is on such testimony as this that I have been convicted of murder.

The Board of Trade meeting has been referred to, and it has been claimed by that intellectual class of people, the detectives, that that night I advised the people to go in there, and partake of their twenty dollar supper. Johnson, himself, though not the most truthful of persons, says he did not hear anything of that kind.* I will say here for the edification of the gentlemen who have produced this conviction, I defy them to find a single report of that meeting in any of the morning papers that bears such a statement, and they all contained reports of it. They come in here and give evidence worse than their remarkable reports. Not one reporter in the next morning's papers reported me as having said anything of the kind. What I did say on that occasion, was that the Board of Trade of this city had received considerable eulogy from the press of this country for the grand structure they had erected in which to trade on the means of existence of the people of the country. It was claimed I said that that monument of architectural beauty had cost nearly $2,000,000. I repeat this now, because any of you who read the papers that morning will remember that you have seen this report. I said before it had been in existence many years as a Board of Trade, it would have cost the people of Chicago and the Northwest two billion dollars. I said nothing about going in there. I said that the eulogy that had been given to these men should not go unrebuked; that the working classes, on whose substance the Board of Trade had been built, had been called to that meeting to discuss this question, and to get up a demonstration which would march around the Board of Trade and show them that not all the community was eulogizing them and their business; that there was an element in it which disapproved of Boards of Trade. That was all there was of that speech.

Much has been said of the American Group meetings. In the spring of 1880 a gentleman came here from Washington, and attended our meetings. He had studied the labor question. He listened to what we had to say, and disapproved our position. I challenged him to a public discussion. He came and stayed at the Palmer House, and the next Sunday we had a debate on the principles of Socialism, he claiming that these were not the means by which the condition

* A Pinkerton detective, witness for the State.

of society would be renovated, and I claiming that they were. Since this trial has been in progress that gentleman has written a letter to us informing us that he was willing to come upon the stand here and testify that our meetings were not for the purpose of inciting people to riot, but merely for the discussion of economic questions. And that was all the meetings were for. I was not indicted for inciting to riot. If I had been, I could have brought a good deal of this evidence in. Twenty men were in the witness room ready to testify to the Board of Trade meeting and the language used there on that and on other occasions where we had spoken: but we thought we were being tried for murder. We found out afterwards we were being tried for Anarchy, and that was the reason we did not think it necessary to bring those men upon the stand. There was a separate indictment for inciting to riot, as well as the indictment for murder, and that evidence would have been proper to combat the charge of inciting to riot.

After the Board of Trade demonstration we came back to No. 107 Fifth avenue, and Mr. Parsons and Spies and I spoke from the window. I told the people on that occasion that they had shown that they disapproved of Boards of Trade; that they had possibly put a bee in the bonnet of the Board of Trade men. I advised them to go home and study political economy and learn what was their position in society, but not one word advising them to go to Marshall Field's. But it is very clear why there should have been so much testimony brought in here regarding Marshall Field. The foreman of the jury was one of Marshall Field's salesmen. He depended upon him for his daily wages; he depended on him for preferment. A witness was brought in here who testified before the coroner's jury to hearing a conversation in Crane's alley previous to the Haymarket meeting, between Spies and Schwab, and got them held to the grand jury, and Marshall Field has given that man a job. This is brought in before the man on the jury, who is dependent on Marshal Field for his living. He has given a job to the man who gave such damaging testimony before the coroner's jury in order to get our conviction. Why, was it not plain to anybody why there should have been so much Marshall Field lugged in here? When it was shown to the employee of Marshall Field, who is on the jury, that his employer has given a job to the principle witness against the prisoners, since giving his evidence against them at the coroner's inquest, was it not a hint to the juror as to what kind of a verdict his employer wanted? On no occasion, except as illustrating a point, has anybody, at any Socialistic meeting that I ever attended, advised anybody to go to Marshal Field's and take anything. We have pointed, perhaps, to Marshal Field. I, on the lake front, have pointed to Pullman's building there to illustrate a point; and the English language might as well be changed to the Patagonian language if illustrations are not to be used. At the large demonstration on the Market Square, when there were 10,000 people there before they marched to Ogden's Grove, Parsons and I spoke there, and I distinctly told them that the Socialists did not propose the destruction of property or the robbing of houses. I pointed at the buildings, but did not propose anything of that kind. I have told them so many a time.

All the meetings of the American Group were for the purpose of discussing things. Of course, in the discussion the persons on the different sides always advocate their own views; therefore they were for the advocacy of anything, and the discussion of anything, and many men of different shades of opinion have been at these meetings, and know that there were no meetings of the American Group held for the purpose of treason or inciting to riot. You may have satisfied these twelve jurymen that there was, but these men outside know it was not so.

I went to a special meeting on the night of the 4th of May, at 107 Fifth avenue, and it was necessary that I should go there, for I was Treasurer of the organization, otherwise I should not have been at the Haymarket meeting. On the Sunday previous I met a man at No. 54 West Lake street, who told me he had been at a meeting of the Trade and Labor Assembly, and at that time the organizer of the Central Labor Union came to me and asked me to speak Tuesday night at Workingmen's Hall, No. 376 West Twelfth street. I think I agreed to go there. Monday night I was at No. 54 Lake street, and spoke to the wagon makers, and went home; Tuesday I was out of town all day. I went ten miles in the country as a teamster, in which business I have been engaged in deluding the workingmen and making money out of them! I was out of town all that day, and could not personally have KNOWN of any arrangements for the meeting at the Haymarket until I got to No. 107 Fifth avenue, about eight o'clock. I should have gone to the other meeting, but what little things change so much the current of a man's life! Just the fact of my seeing an advertisement in the *News* will cause my death, for if I had not seen it I should not have gone. I have committed no more crime, and have no more knowledge or intention of committing crime, than I had when I was on my wagon that day. It has been ingeniously urged that the American Group never met there before, meaning to convey the idea to the jury that they went there in pursuance of a conspiracy. The fact of the matter is that they met there many a time, and there were many reasons why an honest man might have assumed that their meeting there that night was not suspicious, for all the halls in Greif's were occupied long before, for the days on which they were to be used came during the eight-hour excitement. Even if it were true that the American Group had not met there before, this is a plausible reason in itself. I have shown the jury here a handbill calling upon the workingwomen of this city to organize, and it was for that reason that I was called to No. 107 Fifth avenue, on the night of the 4th of May; and after Rau came back from the Haymarket, he said there was nobody there but Spies and a large audience. That is enough to show that Spies should know I was at No. 107.

Your honor has repeated my Haymarket speech very frequently here, and it would seem as though it was a tender morsel to roll under the tongue of those interested in this conviction. On that occasion I said that Mr. Foran had made a speech in the House of Congress. I claim here that there is no man that understands the English language but will say that there was more threat, more violence, more of an incitement to riot in the speech of Foran than anything said on the Haymarket that night. Foran's speech was published in Chicago. In discussing the Arbitration Bill he said that it was useless for the workingmen of this country to expect a remedy for their grievances by legislation. He said further: "Only when the rich men of this country understand that it is dangerous for them to live in a community where there are dissatisfied workingmen, then and not till then will the labor question be solved." There is nothing in the speeches of the Haymarket that is as violent as that. What would have been said throughout the country if the police force of Washington had gone into the Chamber of Congress and cleaned it out on account of what Foran had said? Would it have been justified anywhere?

It was claimed here that it was because of the violence of Fielden's speech that the police were called. I would humbly submit to those who make that claim that they read up the testimony given at the coroner's inquest by the detectives and policemen who testified there. There was hardly one of them that knew a word that Fielden had said; but something must be done to hold Fielden. They knew that his statement before the coroner was true. The prosecution knew it. They undoubtedly, with their detectives, had inquired, and they knew he had done nothing. Therefore, they must present this speech to the jury and claim that it was that which brought out the police. The statements before the coroner's jury did not claim anything of that kind, and it was not brought out at the coroner's jury until I made my statement there, and that was the last statement made there. Coroner Hertz said: "Did you say this?" No man knew I had said it until I acknowledged it. Bonfield did not know that Fielden had said anything of that kind, and he did not testify to it. Captain Ward did not know.

There are many things about that coroner's inquest. It has been stated by several policemen and two detectives that when I got down from the wagon I called out: "Here come the bloodhounds; you do your duty and I'll do mine." And a lieutenant of a very intellectual cast of countenance swore here that when the police came up to the crossing, half a block away, he heard Fielden say: "Here come the bloodhounds; you do your duty and I will do mine." He has sworn here—and I think the fact that a policeman could be made to swear to such an apparent lie as this must, to any intelligent person, be disgusting—that when they got to the wagon, and Captain Ward told the meeting to disperse, I deliberately, on that wagon, pulled the revolver and shot at Bonfield and Ward. Bonfield said he could have touched me with his hands when I stepped from the wagon, and Ward said the same thing, and they didn't see it. Lieutenant Steele, in a very significant manner, when asked if he saw me shoot, or heard me say, "Here come the bloodhounds; you do your duty, and I'll do mine," said: "I will tell nothing but what I know." He was standing at the tail end of the wagon, where he could touch me, and he says: "I heard no such language." Wessler stated that he ran up the sidewalk, and when he came back I was firing at the police. He claims that he shot me, and he brings Foley, whom he claims to have run up the sidewalk with him and come back with him, to substantiate the fact that Fielden was standing at the wagon and shooting at the policemen when they came back, and that he shot me as I stood behind the wheel, on the sidewalk. He says: "Fielden rolled under the wagon after he was shot." Foley says the man that Wessler shot at the wagon was lying under the wagon between the two fore wheels, one on each side. If it had been a fair jury would it have convicted any man on that testimony?

Krueger, who claims to have had a duel with me there, claims that as soon as I jumped from the wagon I ran there and began firing at him, and that he shot me as I ran into the alley. And yet I was shooting there as these men came back from up the street, and was shot by Wessler, as they say, after their return. This other man claims he shot me as I was running up the alley. Then comes truthful James Bonfield, who claims to have sneaked around the corridor of the Central Station jail on the night of the fifth of May. He sneaked up against the wall where Fielden could not see him, and he listened to a conversation between Fielden and Knox and Graham, reporters. He is brought on to corroborate the statement of Krueger that Fielden ran into the alley. He claims he overheard Fielden admit to these reporters that he ran through the alley. The State brings the reporter Knox upon the stand. They did not bring Graham after they got through with Knox. Knox was asked: "Did Fielden say to you that he went through the alley?" "No; he said he went around the corner." Now, no man would state that if he had gone into the alley, because the wagon was close to the alley, and the corner meant the corner of Randolph street. I did state that I went around the corner after I had passed the alley. That proves somebody was lying. They did not bring Graham on to substantiate James Bonfield. I ask any reasonable man to consider all this testimony; to consider whether there could have been a jury that was fair-minded that could have said beyond all question of doubt, that Fielden did fire into that crowd of police. That is all I have to say on that question. But even the worst newspaper in the city of Chicago admitted before the conclusion of this case that it was exceedingly doubtful whether Fielden had fired a shot there or not, or whether he had ever hallowed out, "You do your duty and I will do mine. Here come the bloodhounds." Let us put a hypothetical question now: If I had said something which might have been construed into an incitement to riot, but if, when the policemen came there, I did everything a man could do to have the meeting disperse peaceably, in obedience to the demand of Ward to have it disperse—and there is no other claim than this, which is contradicted by the State's Attorney's claim against me, and that I did nothing but walk away peaceably—could a fair minded jury have convicted me? You will remember that the reporter, Freeman—and Freeman is a State witness—who knelt down on the sidewalk within three feet of the wheel where it is said I was shooting, swears positively that there was nobody at that wheel. It is acknowledged by Foley and Wessler that there were two young men standing up against the wall of Crane's factory nearly opposite the wagon. Those men came here voluntarily and swore there was no shooting done from that place; and the State's Attorney in his closing argument practically admits that it is doubtful whether this testimony is the truth. He said if Fielden did not shoot at the police, then he is not made of as good clay as I thought him to be, which means, if Fielden did not shoot, then he is no man. He ought to have done so, if he was any good. This is not garbled, it is not colored. Is it not as strong as it could be against the possibility of my having done anything of that kind there? Now, if I did not shoot there, if I did not call to the people, "Here come the bloodhounds, you do your duty and I will do mine," and if I, as testified by Bonfield, Steele and Ward, went away peaceably, giving an example to the meeting, if some one else goes and commits murder, am I responsible for his act? Mr. Ward will corroborate me when I say that I had no desire that that meeting should be anything else than peaceable, and that there should be resistance to the officers. If it had not been intended that I should be connected with some act of that kind, and by that means, the papers of this city would call Fielden a coward, who would run at the first sight of the police. But no. They elevate me to the very pinnacle of bravery in order to hang me.

I do not suppose that there ever was a criminal asked to state why death should not be passed upon him that ever succeeded in convincing the Judge that it should not. I do not expect that this will be any exception to the rule. I can only conclude that the reason this is asked of each prisoner is that he may, having failed to convince the jury that has tried him, convince the great jury that will sit upon his case when he is gone, that he is not guilty. I expect to succeed in convincing the latter, though I have failed in the former. I claim here now, on a reasonable interpretation of the language which I have used at the Haymarket, and which I have admitted I have used, and there is not a man in the row by the State's Attorney who will claim that I have shown a desire on this witness stand to deny anything that I have done—everything that I have done has been open and above board. If there is anything that I have hated in this world ever since I knew anything at all, it was trickery. If I had been a trickster I could have possibly been somewhere else today.

I have been charged with having said: "Throttle the law!" Your honor will bear in mind that I had quoted from Foran's speech when I had said that, and it was a deduction, assuming that Foran spoke the truth. If it is true, as Foran says, that nothing can be got by legislation—legislation is supposed to be for the interests of the community—if it is not for their interest, it certainly operates aginst that portion of them whose interests it does not subserve.

Legislation cannot be made that will not affect somebody in some particular way. It must affect them in some way. Then if nothing can be got by legislation, and hundreds of men are paid every year to legislate for the community, it is a foregone fact, and its logic cannot be disputed, that if that portion of the community which can receive no benefit from legislation does not throttle that law which is doing this legislation it will throttle them. The word "throttle" is supposed to be a terrible word. There would not have been anybody in this community who would have claimed that the word is a bad word to use if the bomb had not been thrown on the night of May 4th. It is a word widely used as meaning to abolish; if you take the metaphors from the English language, you have no language at all. It is not necessary, your honor, that because a man says "throttle the law" he means "kill the policemen." There is no such necessary connection. If I were to advise a man to kill Phil Armour, would you conclude by that that I had advised somebody to kill his servant or somebody employed by him? I was speaking of these laws which could do no benefit to the working classes, and which have been referred to by Foran. Now, policemen generally are not men of very intellectual calibre. They are not men who ought in any civilized community to be made the censors of speech or of the press. If I, on that night, had used language which could reasonably have been interpreted as being incendiary, how is it that every witness on both sides of this case has testified that the meeting was getting more peaceful during the delivery of my speech? Surely that shows that the meeting did not understand it as inciting to riot, and that it had no such effect upon that meeting.

When Harrison left Mr. Bonfield, it is claimed by both of them that Harrison said to Bonfield, "I guess there is no danger. There will be no trouble." And Bonfield says, "Well, I will keep the police here and see if there will be any trouble." The testimony as to the character of the meeting shows that it became more quiet during the delivery of Fielden's speech. Where was the danger then that justified the marching of 200 armed police upon it? If I had said something that should not have been said—something that was an incitement to riot, there was still no necessity of these policemen provoking a riot that night, because there was no indication that there was going to be trouble. It has never been claimed by the prosecution that we had anything to do with what they had heard as to the possible blowing up of the freight house. They could have let the meeting disperse peaceably, of its own volition, and they could have come to my house and arrested me for that incendiary language, if it had been such. There was no necessity for provoking a collision that night, because the meeting has been proven overwhelmingly to have been a peaceable meeting up to the close, and I claim that the language reasonably interpreted, was not necessarily incendiary. A newspaper of this city is discussing the coal monopoly as it is called—perhaps that is incendiary language. The constitution of the United States has never clearly defined what incendiary language is, that I know of. If it had I should have informed myself of what it was, and tried to keep myself within the bounds.

A recess was taken until two o'clock.

Upon the reconvening of the court in the afternoon, Mr. Fielden continued his speech.

Your honor: When we adjourned for dinner I was speaking to you about my version of the meeting, of the language used at the Haymarket on May 4. I was speaking to you about the character of that meeting and the unjustifiable interruption of it. I was trying to point out to you and show you by the evidence that it was a peaceable meeting; that there was no indication in the demeanor of the crowd of a desire to commit any act which would make them liable to arrest and punishment. I was giving you my version of the sentence, "throttle the law." I told you that it was a deduction based upon an assumption, and, in my opinion, was a logical deduction, that if laws are enacted for the community, which cannot benefit one class in that community, it is the interest of that class that the laws should be abolished and the law-making machines discontinued. I ought to know, myself, what I meant. Your honor has put an interpretation on the expression, "throttle the law," that it meant to kill the police because they were the servants of the law; and that throttling the law could not mean what I said in its literal sense, it being an intangible thing to do. Now, in the light of the principles that have been sworn to on this stand by witnesses for the State, I say in the definition which Parsons gave of the intentions and objects of the Socialists, in addressing the meeting at the Haymarket, it was not the intention of that organization to take any man's life; that it was merely the system that made such men possible that we are aiming at. When we consider that this has been proven by witnesses on both sides that that was the object of the organization to which Mr. Parsons and I belonged, will not the words, "throttle the law," bear another interpretation, and a more plausible one? The law is an institution; the policemen are a necessary part of it. It is the doing away with the institution, not the policeman—and I defy anyone to prove that, on a fair interpretation of the language used that night, there was anything in that speech that could reasonably be called incendiary.

You will bear in mind that I said "Men in their blind rage attacked McCormick's, and the police shot them down." Now, certainly a man who charges a class of people with doing something "in their blind rage" cannot be said to approve of their acts; cannot be said to be encouraging that blindness, and the fact that I said "in their blind rage," shows that I did not approve of attacking McCormick's; that there was an underlying meaning to it, which, when read between the lines, explains all that it should logically have meant. "When men in their blind rage attacked McCormick's the police shot them down." There was a conflict between these men. As I have claimed here and elsewhere in the city, these men did it in their ignorance. They did not understand it. They looked upon McCormick as a cause of their trouble. We have been represented—or at least they had drawn that inference from disputes which had occurred with McCormick in the last year or two—that it was such men as McCormick that was the cause of their trouble, and in their blindness and their ignorance they attacked McCormick's building. It is not disputed that I said the words just quoted. Now, if these men had understood, as Socialists understand it, this industrial question, they would have known that it was foolish and ridiculous to think that they could better their condition by attacking a person's property. If they had understood this social question as Socialists understand it, they would have understood that it was the system and not the instrument of the system, not the victim of that system. I claim that McCormick, Jay Gould, and William H. Vanderbilt are as much the victims of the system which obtains, and which I claim is an unjust one, as are the beggars who walk the streets and crowd the station houses to keep themselves from being frozen to death in the winter. And it is these particular classes that are arrayed against each other. True, one of the victims gets a better share of the profits of the system than the other. They are no less the victims, and the conflicts and quarrels that exist among them affect them both more or less. Therefore I say that when I said, "Men, in their blind rage, attacked McCormick's and the police shot them down," it was carrying out that idea, which was intended to be conveyed to these people, that it was the system which protected McCormick's interests. But, as I went on, I said: "When McCormick attacked their interests the police did not attack McCormick." I had claimed that the present social system is sustained more in the interest of one class than in the interests of another. I claim that it is necessarily so. Now, McCormick's factory may be said to be his tools, if you please—his means of getting a living. And certainly when the rioters attack his factory they attack his means of livelihood. The police came to McCormick's defense. I believe, your honor—and I am well acquainted with the policemen in the district in which I live—that there is not one of them who believes that I entered into a conspiracy to kill a policeman. I have no better friends than the policemen who have traveled that beat. And I do not say that policemen go to attack rioters because it is their desire to do so. It is because they are the preservers of peace under the present social relations, and they were sent there to keep these men from destroying the means of livelihood of McCormick.

I have frequently said that there was a conflict between two classes of society. They must necessarily come into contact with each other under the present regulations. And there are times when McCormick, in his blind conception of what he thinks is his interest, attacks the means of livelihood of those who have no property and no machines. I said that when this side of the case was presented to the present organization, which maintains the present social relation, there was nobody that came to the assistance of the classes which were attacked by McCormick. I drew the inference that the arrangements were wrong, because of the fact that those who protect McCormick when he is attacked, do not protect the working classes when the are attacked by McCormick. They will necessarily come in conflict under these regulations. How? Sometimes McCormick has reduced wages. Wages are the means of existence to those who have no property, and who are compelled to live by the sale of their labor. It is their machinery, and the police have never come to the assistance of the working classes, when their means of living have been attacked in that way. Sometimes they are attacked by a machine. Do not understand me to say that I blame McCormick for buying a machine, because under the present social and industrial system, men have the right to buy machines, if the system is right. But if the system is wrong, they have not, and it is the system that is responsible, and not they.

I am given to understand, and I believe it to be true, that about a year ago McCormick introduced some moulding machines into his factory. McCormick employed about 125 moulders before the introduction of these machines. Before that time he had had a strike of his men owing to a dispute about wages, or about the regulations of the union to which these moulders belonged. McCormick had acceded to certain terms. He had to do it because of the strength of the union. He could not get any moulders to do his work because the union resolved that it would not work except its terms were acceded to. But there was something else which McCormick found out that was not subject to any union. That was a moulding machine. And when McCormick had got possession of the moulding machine he had got possession of machinery which did with the assistance of twenty-five men what it had required 125 men to do before. Don't you think, your honor, that that was an attack upon the interests of these twenty men out of twenty-five, or 100 out of 125? It would not make any difference whether he had a right to do it. I am not speaking of that phase of the question. These men had families after the introduction of those machines as they had before. The families cried for bread. The children cried for shoes, and the women cried perhaps for a sewing machine. These hundred men were turned out, and then McCormick said to the men: "Now, I am master of the situation. I will take back all the conditions that I have made with my men when I needed 125 of them."

The rate of wages is regulated by the number of men who are out of employment. When four men out of five are turned out of employment, there is nothing in this world for these four men to do but to bid and see how much lower each one can work on that man's job who is retained than the others. It tends to a reduction of wages. And the introduction of machinery in that way is a direct attack upon the interests of those who have no means and cannot have any. Maxwell Brothers introduced some box-making machines about a year ago. There was quite a lively quarrel between him and the box-nailers. I understand that after the introduction of those box-making machines only one man was required to do the work that was formerly done by two and a half—two persons could do the work of five. Now, I claimed in public speeches and discussions that these men who fought about the introduction of the box machines did not understand the real question at issue. Improved machinery,

I claim now what I have claimed all along in the discussion of this industrial problem, is calculated to benefit all classes of humanity and society. But it is the use to which they are put. If they can be bought by one person and used in the interests of that person, so that he can hire labor cheap, or dispense with labor, they are a benefit to no person save the man who has money enough to purchase a machine, and they are a direct injury under such regulations to those who cannot purchase a machine. It is ridiculous to argue that it requires men to make machines and it makes work in that way. If it required as much labor to make them and as much expenditure to make them as it did away with labor, why there would be no object in a man's buying the machine. That answers itself. So that under the present regulations—and this language of mine will bear the interpretation which I have given, when you take everything into consideration, and I think it is the more plausible interpretation—and I will say to you here that, when Mr. English brought this report, he admitted it to be but a garbled report of my speech—my conception of justice is this, that a man ought never to be allowed to testify against a man who is on trial for his life, when he admits, before he gives his testimony, that it is incorrect. I do not think that it is in the interest of justice that such testimony should be given. Mr. English admits that before he left the *Tribune* office that night to go to that meeting, he was advised not to bring a correct report. If he had brought a correct report he might have been discharged. He was instructed not to do it. That was his work for that night, to only take what he considered the inflammatory or incendiary portions of the speeches. You can take no speech delivered by any person and do it justice by extracting what you consider the inflammatory portion. I have heard men make speeches in my time, and I have had to pay very strict attention to know what they were driving at. They would take an hour to prove a position. If you judged them in half an hour you would not get at all the position they were trying to prove. It is often the case when listening to public speakers that I have noticed they will speak along and along, and then in the last few minutes of the speech they will show exactly what they mean. There will be some language used there that modifies your conception of their meaning, and opens it all up, and you see the beauty of the whole argument. May be you would not have seen it if it hadn't been for that unlocking of the secret.

I am charged with having spoken of rebellion. But before I speak of that, I will refer again to some of the words which have been introduced here. I am charged with having said "stab the law." No one claims but that it was in connection with my conception of the meaning of Foran's speech, and the word "stab" is not necessarily a threat of violence upon any person. Here at your primary elections you frequently hear the adherents of different candidates state before the primaries are called that they will "knife" so and so. Do they mean that they are going to kill him, stab him, take his life away from him? They are forcible expressions—very emphatic expressions. They are verbs which are used in different ways to carry conviction and perhaps make the language more startling to the audience in order that they may pay attention. I remember now when the dispute was going on in England as to the extension of the franchise in 1866 and 1867, when such large meetings were called all through England to dispute the assertion of Disraeli, afterward Lord Beaconsfield, that the working classes did not want the franchise, that John Bright replied to the letter of Beaconsfield, saying that there might be some excuse for Beaconsfield if he had said this in the heat of a speech, but having sat down and coolly written it out, there was no excuse for it, showing that such a parliamentarian as John Bright is, with perhaps no superior in his time, thought there was an excuse for men dropping into language in the heat of speeches which afterward they might have thought it would have been better not to have used, as their speech might have looked better without it. I say this language does not necessarily mean an incitement to violence. I have used the word "rebellion." Now, you know that the word "rebellion" is not necessarily an incitement to violence. And if it were, let me call your attention to an incident which occurred in the House of Commons a hundred years ago. When the ill-starred attempt was made under Montgomery to capture Quebec and he lost his life, a member of the House of Commons, generous as he was, brought up the question of the death of Montgomery, whom many there had known. He spoke of him as a gallant, brave, generous, able, and amiable gentleman. Another member said he was a gallant, generous, amiable rebel. Lord North rose in his majesty on the floor of the House of Commons, and said: "I am far from conceding that it is a disreputable term to be called a rebel. The very principles and the privileges which we in constitutional England enjoy on this floor today, were acquired by rebellion." That language could be used on the floor of the House of Commons a hundred years ago, and it was not thought to be an incitement to violence.

I return once more to call your attention to the coal monopoly. I believe I called your attention to it before, but did not finish. It has raised the price of coal by restricting the output. It has deprived men of their labor. The coal monopoly wants money for its coal. The miners want coal to burn. They must pay money for the coal. It turns its miners away from the mines and restricts the output, and then it raises the price of coal. Of course it does not need a very great logician to know that when a man is turned out of employment he can pay more for his coal than he could before. Looked at in this way, this is the logic of the coal monopoly and the injustice it has done to the public. A Chicago—I will not mention the paper—a prominent Chicago paper advises the "throttling of the coal monopoly." Henry George, in his work on protection, advises the throttling of protection. He does not mean to say that he wants to throttle Judge Kelly or James G. Blaine. I also said the law turns large numbers out on the wayside! Does anybody deny it? If it is true that the law does not make laws in the interest of the working classes, but makes laws—and it must necessarily make them in the interests of the other class if it does not for them—then it does turn men out upon the wayside. I have reference to the introduction of machinery—twenty out of twenty-five turned out of employment. Are they not turned out upon the wayside? Any question about it? If they were laws that did not turn men out upon the wayside, and I knew that they did not, I would not tell anybody that they did.

Thomas Cooper, a chartist in England, was once visited in his old age by a friend of his. A little girl came up to him with a book in her hand with pictures in it, opened the front of it and showed him the fly leaf, and she said. "Mr. Cooper, write something for me." And Mr. Cooper wrote:

"Love truth, my child, love truth;
It will gladden thy morn of youth,
And in the noon of life,
Though it cost thee pain and strife
To keep the truth in its brightness,
Still cleave to thy uprightness."

If I am to be convicted—hanged for telling the truth—the little child that kneels by its mother's side on the West Side today, and tells its mother that she wants her papa to come home, and to whom I had intended, as soon as its prattling tongue should commence to talk, to teach that beautiful sentiment—then the child had better never be taught to read; had better never be taught that sentiment—to love truth. If they are to be convicted of murder because they dare tell what they think is the truth, then it would be better that every one of your school houses were reduced to the ground and not one stone left upon another. If you teach your children to read, they will acquire curiosity from what they read. They will think, and they will search for the meaning of this and that. They will arrive at conclusions. And then, if they love the truth, they must tell to each other what is truth or what they think is the truth. That is the sum of my offending. It turns them out upon the wayside when it is used as it is.

Mr. Powderly, in his official address to a large assembly of the representatives of labor at Richmond, Va., said the other day that Anarchy was the legitimate product of monopoly. I have said you must abolish the private property system. Mr. English said that I said "it had no mercy; so ought you." Probably if I said "it had no mercy," I did not say the latter part of the sentence in that way. I probably said, "So you ought not to have any mercy." Is it doubted by anybody that the system has no mercy? Does it not pursue its natural course irrespective of whom it hurts or upon whom it confers benefits? The private property system then, in my opinion, being a system that only subserves the interests of a few, and can only subserve the interests of the few, has no mercy. It cannot stop for the consideration of such a sentiment. Naturally it cannot. So you ought not to have mercy on the private property system, because it is well known that there are many people in the community with prejudices in their minds. They have grown up under certain social regulations, and they believe that these social regulations are right, just as Mr. Grinnell believes that everything in America is right, because he happened to be born here. And they have such a prejudice against any one who attacks those systems. Now, I say they ought not to have any mercy upon a system that does not maintain their interests. They ought not to have that respect for them that would interfere with their abolishing them. And that is all that they can possibly mean by any kind of gymnastics. When I say it does turn them out upon the wayside; when I know—and Captain Schaack knows how many men there were last winter, and the winter before that, who came to him and asked him if he would please allow them to sleep on the station floor, to keep them from the inclemency of the weather—I say it has no mercy. And why should such men have mercy upon it as to keep it in existence? Why should they not destroy it as long as it is destroying them?

Your honor, after the Haymarket meeting, after I had escaped from the showers of bullets with a slight wound, and after I had been around, as I told you on the witness stand, trying to find my comrades who had been in the meeting to find out whether they were alive or not, I went home. The explosion of the bomb was as much a surprise to me as it was to any policeman. You can judge how I felt at that time, not knowing what damage had been done, the suddenness of such a calamity coming down upon one, and knowing, as I must have, that I should be held in some respect, at least responsible. After getting my wound dressed I went home. It was late. My mind was racked with the thoughts of what would occur on the morrow, and I finally resolved, as any innocent man would have done, if they wanted me to explain my connection with this catastrophe, let them come and ask me to do so. Mr. Slayton has testified here that, when he came to my house. I was sitting in my room.

I didn't attempt to run away. I had been out walking around the street that morning, and there was plenty of opportunity for me to have been hundreds of miles away. When he came there I opened the door to him. He said he wanted me. I know him by sight and I knew what was his occupation. I said: "All right, I will go with you." I have said here that I thought, when the representatives of the State had inquired by means of their policemen as to my connection with it, that I should have been released. And I say now, in view of all the authorities that have been read on the law and regarding accessories, that there is nothing in the evidence that has been introduced to connect me with that affair. One of the Chicago papers, at the conclusion of the State attorney's case, said that they might have proved more about these men, about where they were and what they were doing on the 2d and 3d of May. When I was told that Captain Schaack had got confessions out of certain persons connected with this affair, I said. "Let them confess all they like. As long as they will tell only the truth I care nothing for their confessions." I had nothing to do with it, no knowledge of it, and the gentlemen there know it.

I am going to speak about something that has not come out in the testimony. I have a right to tell it now. I do not do it with any vindictive feeling. I do not do it to hurt anybody, but in the hope that, in the last few days that I have to live, I may do some good by telling it, and I hope what I am going to state will have the tendency to do some good. I was arrested and brought to the Central Station. I had always understood that a man who was arrested on suspicion of having committed a crime was to be considered innocent until he was proven guilty. I have received a great deal more consideration since I have been proven guilty in this court than I did before I was so proven—in the opinion of the jurors. I was taken into the corridor of the court house. Lieutenant Shea was sitting on the table with about twenty-five detectives around him. Mr. Slayton said, "This is Fielden." Lieutenant Shea said, "You——Dutchman, before you came to this country people were getting good wages." I said, "Mr. Shea, I am not a Dutchman." He said, "You are——worse, you——." That is the language of the officers of the law. It makes no difference whether they are Democratic or Republican officers, I speak of them as a whole. And this is a prominent official in the police department of the city of Chicago. I replied to him somewhat sharply, using no epithets. It certainly occurred to me when I looked around at those policemen, that perhaps this man, who will treat a helpless prisoner in this way, is trying to provoke me. Perhaps he will shoot me. I think it was a logical conclusion to draw. A man who is mean enough and contemptible enough to use that language to a helpless prisoner, would go further. And I said to myself, "If he does, who is there here to testify that he murdered me? Are there not twenty-five professional liars here to testify that I tried to murder him?" These were the thoughts that went through my mind, and I said no more. I said "You have me here now, you can do as you like with me." I will not repeat that again in your Honor's presence and in the presence of ladies. I am sorry that I repeated it now. It came out unthinkingly, and it is a very unpleasant word to use anywhere, and ought not to be used by anybody. I was met by the worthy Chief before I got down into the cellar, Mr. Ebersold. He was informed that I was wounded and told me to take off the bandage and show him. I did so. He said: "—your soul, it ought to have gone in here," (pointing to his head between the eyes). This is the Chief. And when I was about to be brought here, and had begged and begged for some one to dress my wound (because the doctor who dressed it the night before had told me that it must be dressed in the afternoon following), I was told by a detective whose name I don't know, or an official, that they ought to put strychnine in it. Your Honor may not believe this. I know that it is the custom of all classes of criminals who are charged with crime to turn around and charge indiscriminately everything that they can possibly imagine against those who arrest them. I can only make the statement. Your Honor may not believe me. Mr. Shea and Mr. Ebersold may come here and say they did not say it. You may believe them in preference to me. But I will tell you one thing, there is no man who knows Samuel Fielden but will believe him.

Your Honor, we are charged with being opposed to the law. I believe your Honor knows a great deal better than I do what the law is. It would take a man a great number of years to find out what it is. I have seen wagon loads of books brought into this court to find out what the law is. It is generally thought and asserted, and I believe it is a fundamental principle of the law, that no man is to be exempted from punishment for a violation of the law because of his ignorance of it. Now, working at my occupation as teamster fourteen hours a day, I don't think that I could have read all of those authorities that have been quoted here to find out what the law is, in ten lifetimes. But we are required to answer to the charge of being lawless individuals who violated the law, who advised the abolition of the law and all government. Your Honor has put it "The government," as though we were conspirators against this particular government.

The very fact that hundreds of authorities can be quoted on both sides and on a dozen sides of any particular question, is because of the impossibility of any one man prescribing laws to fit any other man or number of men.

I believe there is a law, and I don't know that there is any authority which can be quoted against it, that before a man can go into a house of a citizen, he must have the authority of the law, and show that he is an officer of the law and in pursuit of a lawful purpose. If any man calling himself a policeman may go and search a house and say, "I am an officer of the law. I want to search your house," the law requires, if I understand it, that before anyone can search a house he shall have a search warrant. In every instance that any house has been searched in the prosecution of this case, there has been no search warrant presented. Now, if men can violate the law who are its sworn supporters, and who get their living by the pursuit of the law, do you think it naturally tends to produce respect for the law on the part of those on whom they prey, when they violate the law? If you say that very often justice could not under circumstances and emergencies be carried out if every technicality of the law were obeyed, does it not show the impossibility then of applying the laws justly and rightly to every case? Now, I think that it is the natural tendency to beget disrespect for the law when those who are its representatives show so little respect for it. And I wish to say that I was arrested without a warrant. Another violation of law; I was taken out upon the sidewalk, while three men went through my house, turned it upside down, as the leader has admitted here, although they found nothing that indicated that I was a dangerous character—not even an empty cartridge of a revolver. They not only did this, but my wife tells me that about ten men went back there again, and, without presenting any search warrant, went through the house—her husband and protector in jail. Your honor, I merely state these things to show that men hired by the law to defend it are the very ones who throw discredit upon it. Any one could have gone there at any time, searched that house, and robbed it of everything there was in it, and have just as much justification in going in as any of these men had. I wish to call your attention for a little while—it is going back to the question I spoke of before, but I think it is necessary in my own defense—one of this class of persons who have been in the habit of going into houses without authority of law, testified at the coroner's inquest, and he testified upon this case in court, that he had said in the coroner's jury room that he had heard me say, "Here come the bloodhounds; you do your duty and I will do mine." I would submit to your honor that it would be a very good thing for you to ask one of the counsel on either side of this case to allow you look at the report of the coroner's jury, and see whether that man lied here or not. I have no fear of the result of that investigation.

An interview has been held with Mr. Grinnell, and published in one of the papers of this city since his return from his vacation, in which Mr. Grinnell is reported to have said—but perhaps the reporter lied; I should not wonder if he had, they have done it before, and it would not be surprising—"Why, these men have no principles. They did not defend themselves with their principles." I have said before that we were not here to defend our principles. We were here to respond to the charge of murder. If we were guilty of murder we were guilty whether we had principles or not. After we got all our testimony in we were then told that we were being tried because we had no principles. What are the duties of a prosecuting attorney? The lawyers can give technical definitions, I suppose, but the general idea of the duties of a prosecuting attorney is—and I do not call in question the fact that they are necessary under our present social regulations—to see to it that no guilty man shall escape, if he can possibly prevent it. It is also the duty of the prosecuting attorney, as much as it is of the defendant's attorney, to see to it that no innocent man should suffer for any crime. Lawyers have a peculiar code of morals. Their success in their particular avocation depends upon their gaining suits. And I am afraid there are lawyers to be found who care little as to whether their suit is right or in the interest of justice and truth, so long as they can gain their case and make a reputation for themselves. Now, it is not the duty of the prosecuting attorney to take that view of his position. And when I call upon your honor to go back and review the proceedings of the coroner's inquest, I also ask Mr. Grinnell to review them. I ask him to see whether any man testified at the coroner's inquest, with the events of the 4th of May fresh in his mind, that Fielden said on that night, "Here come the bloodhounds; you do your duty and I will do mine." I will state further that Coroner Hertz came to me shortly after my incarceration in this building, and asked me to sign a synopsis which he had of the testimony given in the coroner's room, in which synopsis there was not one word of the kind attributed to me in this trial.

We claim that the foulest criminal that could have been picked up in the slums of any city in Christendom, or outside of it, would never have been convicted on such testimony as has been brought in here if he had not been a dangerous man in the opinion of the privileged classes. We claim that we are convicted, not because we have committed murder. We are convicted because we were very energetic in advocacy of the rights of labor. I call your attention to a very significant fact—that on this day, at this time when the sentence of death is going to be passed on us, the Stock Yards employers have notified their employees that they will be required to work ten hours next Monday or they will shut down. I think it is a logical conclusion to draw that these men think they have got a dangerous element out of the way now and they can return again to the ten-hour system. I know that I had considerable to do with the eight-hour question, although I only spoke once in that neighborhood, every man there being a stranger to me—but I went down there in March previous and made an eight-hour speech and formed the nucleus of an eight-hour organization there, and the Stock Yards succeeded in starting the eight-hour system, though they have not been able to keep it up in its entirety. We claim that we have done much.

Mr. Neebe has told you of the advantages that have been gained by classes of workingmen in this city through his organization of trades unions for the purpose of getting a reduction of the hours of labor. If we have succeeded to the extent that he has told you, our lives will not have been spent in vain.

And whatever may be our fate—and there seems to be but one conclusion on that question—we feel satisfied that we have not lived in this world for nothing; that we have done some good to our fellowmen, and done what we believe to be in the interests of humanity and for the furtherance of justice. It is a satisfaction to know that. I repeat the language, as near as I can remember it, of Lady Cavendish, after the murder of her husband, in Phoenix

Park. She said: "If the death of my darling has tended in any way to bring about a better understanding and a better condition of things between these two elements, I willingly give him up." If my life is to be taken for advocating the principles of Socialism and Anarchy, as I have understood them and honestly believe them to be in the interests of humanity, I say to you that I gladly give it up; and the price is very small for the result that is gained.

Your Honor, with due respect to your years, I wish to say this: That it is quite possible you can not understand, having lived in a different atmosphere from what we have lived in, how men can hold such ridiculous ideas. I have no doubt you felt that way. Yet it is well known that persons who have lived to a ripe old age seldom change their opinions. I impute no wrong motive in that. It is a natural result. But we do claim that our principles will bear discussion, investigation and criticism. We claim that so far as we have been able to find out in trying to find a cure for the ills of society we have not found out anything that has seemed to fit the particular disease which society, in our opinion, is afflicted with today better than the principles of Socialism, and your honor, Socialism, when it is as thoroughly understood in this community and in the world as it is by us, I believe that the world, which is generally honest, prejudiced though it may be, will not be slow to adopt its principles. And it will be a good time, a grand day for the world; it will be a grand day for humanity; it will never have taken a step so far onward towards perfection, if it can ever reach that goal, as it will when it adopts the principles of Socialism. They are principles that ignore no man. They are the principles that consider the interest of every one. They are the principles which will do away with wrong and injustice and suffering will be reduced at least to a minimum under such an organization of society. As compared to the present struggle for existence, which is degrading society and making men, as I have said in the Haymarket speech, merely things and animals, Socialism will give them opportunities of developing the possibilities of their nature. But under our present existing economic relations, there can be nothing. And, your honor, it is only, in my opinion, a short time before this system will have outlived itself, so as to compel the adoption of the Socialistic system. The existence of the vast army of unemployed men; the existence of crime which is becoming almost an intolerable burden upon the different communities in this country and in Europe to keep in check, is showing us that there is something radically wrong. These conditions will force us to ask what that wrong is, and force us to adopt some antidote for the evil.

I have read somewhere of a historical character who in ancient times is reported to have killed his comrade. Spartacus was a gladiator who lived to pander to the amusement of the Roman nobles of old. He is reported as having on one occasion spoken to his fellow slaves in some such words as these—or, rather, these are his sentiments. In speaking of his home, before he became a captive, he tells them of the pleasures of his youth; he tells them, as they listen to the Numidian lion's roar, that tomorrow it will feast and satisfy its hunger upon them, "Yesterday I met in the arena a gladiator, and I killed him. I thought of the time when I was a child on the hills of Thrace, of a little boy that belonged to a neighbor, and who shared with me my humble meal as we tended our separate flocks on the hillsides, and when I lifted the cowl of the gladiator that I had killed, I found that it was the comrade of my youth. Why should it be that we should struggle? Why should it be that we should fight? Why should it be that we should kill each other for the amusement of the Roman nobles?" And I say now, in an era in which there is an intense struggle for existence among the class that has no money or property, that it is a struggle for the amusement of the property nobles. The children that play together in the streets of Chicago and the villages that dot this continent from the Atlantic to the Pacific, will grow up and engage in a life and death struggle for existence, for the amusement and for the benefit of nobody but their masters, the American nobles. I say, my friends, as you draw the line tighter and tighter, the conflicts that are going on and will go on between these men, will array them against their masters. If I can say anything in the interests of humanity, in the interests of liberty, equality, and fraternity, I would say it now. Take heed, take heed! The time, my friends, is not far off. The swift process of reduction of the masses into a condition of depravity and degradation, as is evinced by the number of men out of employment, shows us clearly where we are going. We cannot deny it. No thinking man, no reasoning man, no friend of his kind, can ignore the fact that we are going rapidly on to a precipice. If I call a halt, I consider that in the interest of humanity. I make no threats. I have never made any threats. I have merely spoken and told the people what was the natural result of present existing conditions.

I tell them now that I do not advise any man to commit any act which would render himself liable to the law or to punishment; but I say to those who have the means of existence in their possession, that there may come a time when the people will no longer be crowded together, when the rats, as Mr. Grinnell has said, will come out of their holes. I would ask you to read Victor Hugo, read in that grand work, the "Hunchback of Notre Dame," the description of the vermin that crawled out of the Latin quarter. Unpleasant as these are, they are human beings. Look at the result of the degradation that the masses had been brought to, and at the time of the French Revolution of 1789, they knew nothing. They only knew the blind rage of an enraged tiger to kill something—to destroy something, when their condition had become so desperate that life was no longer desirable and death had no terrors. It is a lesson of history. No man ever willfully throws his life away.

It is not probable that there will be any revolt in America; that there will be any rebellion in any country under the sun, until the time has come when the people can no longer live. They will never do it until then. It is for society to think; it is for them to compare. It will not do for a man to look around at his little home, his own hearthstone, and imagine how comfortable he is, and think because of that, that everything is lovely and everything is safe. It is not. Outside are the men who are suffering; men with appetites; men with passions; men with desires; men with sentiments as fine, perhaps, some of them, as those of some of the most intelligent portions of the community; men being driven to the wall. They will continue to be unless this system is changed. When I have told you, or indicated, rather, how the people's means of existence have gradually been concentrated into the hands of the smaller quantity and number of the community, it is an indication that points unerringly to a danger. I wish society would avert this. I have said upon the witness stand that it was not pleasant for me to contemplate anything of the kind. It is not a pleasant thing, but it is in the interest of peace, as I told these people.

Your Honor, there is one thing I wish to say about my own peculiar case, and then I have done. Dynamite has been spoken of here, and it has been charged by Mr. Ingham that all of us knew that violence was to be used at the Haymarket. If he didn't say as much, it was indicated as much in that assertion that we were all equally guilty. That may be so. I don't know the extent to which any of the others are guilty. Fischer, Lingg, and Engel are men that I have not associated with for a year. I knew Fischer; I didn't know Lingg. Mr. Engel I have seen, but quite a while before the Haymarket affair, and I know at one time he did not belong to our organization—had left it, and so had Fischer, and I didn't know they belonged to it. I could not have been then conspiring with them to do anything in the Haymarket square on the 4th of May. I hadn't seen these other gentlemen since the Sunday previous. I believe I didn't see Mr. Parsons on that Sunday at all and had not seen him for a week before that. I don't know what the ingredients of dynamite are. I had never seen, before I came into this court room, a dynamite bomb. I have never seen any experiments or taken part in any experiments with dynamite in any shape or form. And I never knew—and I only know now, if I may believe the testimony of the detectives in this case—that there was dynamite kept in the *Arbeiter-Zeitung* building. I say these things, not because I believe that I shall be believed—because I know, as I have stated before, that every defendant, almost, asserts his innocence, and it is about all that he can do—and it undoubtedly has been the case that many a man, as guilty as he could possibly be, has said with as much apparent sincerity as I say it today, that he was innocent, and yet was guilty—but I wish to say this, that if the State's Attorney or the authorities of this city should arrest your honor tomorrow for any crime they choose to charge you with, they could prove you guilty if they wanted to. That is an advantage that they have. Whether it is intentional—and I am not going to charge anything of the kind against any man—I know that intentional falsehoods have been stated here, I will charge that where I know it—I will not injure any man's feelings; I will not charge for the sake of saving my life, any man with being a murderer, until I know him to be that; I do not and cannot know, having been confined the length of time I have, what influences may have been brought to bear upon the State's attorney, that there should have been the evidence brought in here against me which has been, and which I know to be false—therefore, I will not charge that it was intentional to convict me on his part, but I have suggested here that he can find out many things if he will look up certain records that I have referred to which will controvert much that has been asserted here in my particular case.

Your honor, I have worked at hard labor since I was eight years of age. I went into a cotton factory when I was eight years old, and I have worked continually since, and there has never been a time in my history that I could have been bought or paid into a single thing by any man or for any purpose which I did not believe to be true. To contradict the lie that was published in connection with the bill by the grand jury charging us with murder, I wish to say that I have never received one cent for agitating. When I have gone out of the city I have had my expenses paid. But often when I have gone into communities, when I would have to depend upon those communities for paying my way, I have often come back to this city money out of my pocket, which I had earned by hard labor, and I had to pay for the privilege of my agitation out of the little money I might have in my possession.

Today as the beautiful autumn sun kisses with balmy breeze the cheek of every free man, I stand here never to bathe my head in its rays again. I have loved my fellowmen as I have loved myself. I have hated trickery, dishonesty, and injustice. The nineteenth century commits the crime of killing its best friend. It will live to repent of it. But, as I have said before, if it will do any good, I freely give myself up. I trust the time will come when there will be a better understanding, more intelligence, and, above the mountains of iniquity, wrong and corruption. I hope the sun of righteousness and truth and justice will come to bathe in its balmy light an emancipated world. I thank your honor for your attention.

ADDRESS OF ALBERT R. PARSONS

FREEDOM.

Toil and pray! The world cries cold;
Speed thy prayer, for time is gold.
At thy door Need's subtle tread;
Pray in haste! for time is bread.

And thou plough'st and thou hew'st,
And thou rivet'st and sewest,
And thou harvestest in vain;
Speak! O, man; what is thy gain?

Fly'st the shuttle day and night,
Heav'st the ores of earth to light,
Fill'st with treasures plenty's horn;
Brim'st it o'er with wine and corn.

But who hath thy meal prepared,
Festive garments with thee shared;
And where is thy cheerful hearth,
Thy good shield in battle dearth?

Thy creations round thee see
All thy work, but naught for thee!
Yea, of all the chains alone thy hand forged,
These are thine own:

Chains that round the body cling,
Chains that lame the spirits wing,
Chains that infants' feet, indeed
Clog! O, workman! Lo! Thy meed.

What you rear and bring to light,
Profits by the idle wight,
What ye weave of diverse hue,
'Tis a curse—your only due.

What ye build, no room insures,
Not a sheltering roof to yours,
And by haughty ones are trod—
Ye, whose toil their feet hath shod.

Human bees! Has nature's thrift
Given thee naught but honey's gift?
See! the drones are on the wing.
Have you lost the will to sting?

Man of labor, up, arise!
Know the might that in thee lies,
Wheel and shaft are set at rest
At thy powerful arm's behest.

Thine oppressor's hand recoils
When thou, weary of thy toil,

Shun'st thy plough thy task begun,
When thou speak'st: Enough is done!

Break this two-fold yoke in twain;
Break thy want's enslaving chain;
Break thy slavery's want and dread;
Bread is freedom, freedom bread.

That poem epitomizes the aspirations, the hope, the need of the working classes, not alone of America, but of the civilized world.

Your honor: If there is one distinguishing characteristic which has made itself prominent in the conduct of this trial, it has been the passion, the heat, and the anger, the violence both to sentiment and to person, of everything connected with this case. You ask me why sentence of death should not be pronounced upon me, or, what is tantamount to the same thing, you ask me why you should give me a new trial in order that I might establish my innocence and the ends of justice be subserved. I answer you and say that this verdict is the verdict of passion, born in passion, nurtured in passion, and is the sum totality of the organized passion of the city of Chicago. For this reason I ask your suspension of the sentence and the granting of a new trial. This is one among the many reasons which I hope to present before I conclude. Now, what is passion? Passion is the suspension of reason; in a mob upon the streets, in the broils of the saloon, in the quarrels on the sidewalk, where men throw aside their reason and resort to feelings of exasperation, we have passion. There is a suspension of the elements of judgment, of calmness, of discrimination requisite to arrive at the truth and the establishment of justice. I hold that you cannot dispute the charge which I make, that this trial has been submerged, immersed in passion from its inception to its close, and even to this hour, standing here upon the scaffold as I do, with the hangman awaiting me with his halter, there are those who claim to represent public sentiment in this city, and I now speak of the capitalistic press—that vile and infamous organ of monopoly of hired liars, the people's oppressor—even to this day these papers are clamoring for our blood in the heat and violence of passion. Who can deny this? Certainly not this Court. The Court is fully aware of these facts.

In order that I may place myself properly before you, it is necessary, in vindication of whatever I may have said or done in the history of my past life, that I should enter somewhat into details, and I claim, even at the expense of being lengthy, the ends of justice require that this shall be done.

For the past twenty years my life has been closely identified with, and I have actively participated in, what is known as the labor movement in America. I have some knowledge of that movement in consequence of this experience and of the careful study which opportunity has afforded me from time to time to give to the matter, and what I have to say upon this subject relating to the labor movement or to myself as connected with it in this trial and before this bar—I will speak the truth, the whole truth, be the consequences what they may.

The United States census for 1880 report that there are in the United States 16,200,000 wage workers. These are the persons who, by their industry, create all the wealth of this country. And now before I say anything further it may be necessary in order to clearly understand what I am going to state further on, for me to define what I mean and what is meant in the labor movement by these words, wage worker. Wage workers are those who work for wages and who have no other means of subsistence than by the selling of their daily toil from hour to hour, day to day, week to week, month to month, and year to year, as the case may be. Their whole property consists entirely of their labor—strength and skill or, rather, they possess nothing but their empty hands. They live only when afforded an opportunity to work, and this opportunity must be procured from the possessors of the means of subsistence—capital—before their right to live at all or the opportunity to do so is possessed. Now, there are 16,200,000 of these people in the United States, according to the census of 1880. Among this number are 9,000,000 men, and reckoning five persons to each family, they represent 45,000,000 of our population. It is claimed that there are between eleven and twelve million voters in the United States. Now, out of these 12,000,000 voters, 9,000,000 are wage workers. The remainder of the 16,200,000 is composed of the women and children employed in the factories, the mines and the various avocations of this country. This class of people—the working class—who alone do all the useful and productive labor of this country are the hirelings and dependents of the propertied class.

Your Honor, I have, as a workingman, espoused what I conceive to be the just claims of the working class; I have defended their right to liberty and insisted upon their right to control their own labor and the fruits thereof, and in the statement that I am to make here before this court upon the question why I should not be sentenced, or why I should be permitted to have a new trial you will also be made to understand why there is a class of men in this country who come to your honor and appeal to you not to grant us a new trial. I believe, sir, that the representatives of that millionaire organization of Chicago, known as the Chicago Citizens' Association stand to a man demanding of your honor our immediate extinction and suppression by an ignominious death. Now, I stand here as one of the people, a common man, a workingman, one of the masses, and I ask your honor give ear to what I have to say. You stand as a bulwark; you are as a brake between them and us. You are here as the representative of justice, holding the poised scales in your hands. You are expected to look neither to the right nor the left, but to that by which justice, and justice alone, shall be subserved. The conviction of a man, your honor, does not necessarily prove that he is guilty. Your law books are filled with instances where men have been carried to the scaffold and after their death it has been proven that their execution was a judicial murder. Now, what end can be subserved in hurrying this matter through in the manner in which it has been done? Where are the ends of justice subserved, and where is truth found in hurrying seven human beings at the rate of express speed upon a fast train to the scaffold and an ignominious death? Why, if your honor please, the very method of our extermination, the deep damnation of our taking off, appeals to your honor's sense of justice, of rectitude, and of honor. A judge may also be an unjust man. Such things have been known. We have, in our histories, heard of Lord Jeffreys. It need not follow that because a man is a judge he is also just. As everyone knows, it has long since become the practice in American politics for the candidates for judgeships, throughout the United States, to be named by corporations and monopoly influences, and it is a well known secret that more than one of our chief justices have been appointed to their seats upon the bench of the United States Supreme Court at the instance of the leading railway magnates of America—the Huntingtons and Jay Goulds. Therefore the people are beginning to lose confidence in some of our courts of law.

Now, I have not been able to gather together and put in a consecutive shape these thoughts which I wish to present here for your consideration. They have been put together hurriedly in the last few days, since we began to come in here, first, because I did not know what you would do, nor what the position of your honor would be in the case, and secondly, because I did not know upon what ground the conclusion of the prosecution would be made denying us the right of a rehearing, and, therefore, if the method of the presentation of this matter be somewhat disconnected and disjointed, it may be ascribed to that fact, over which I had no control.

I maintain that our execution, as the matter stands just now, would be a judicial murder, rank and foul, and judicial murder is far more infamous than lynch law—far worse. Bear in mind, please, this trial was conducted by a mob, prosecuted by a mob, by the shrieks and the howls of a mob, an organized, powerful mob. But that trial is now over. You sit here judicially, calmly, quietly, and it is now for you to look at this thing from the standpoint of reason and common sense. There is one peculiarity about the case that I want to call your attention to. It was the manner and the method of its prosecution! On the one side, the attorneys for the prosecution conducted this case from the standpoint of capitalists as against laborers. On the other side, the attorneys for the defense conducted this case as a defense against murder, not for laborers and not against capitalists. The prosecution in this case throughout has been a capitalistic prosecution, inspired by the instinct of capitalism, and I mean by that, by class feelings, by a dictatorial right to rule, and a denial to common people of the right to say anything or have anything to say to these men, by that class of persons who think that working people have but one right and one duty to perform, viz., obedience. They conducted this trial from that standpoint throughout, and, as was very truthfully stated by my comrade, Fielden, we were prosecuted ostensibly for murder, until, near the end of the trial, when all at once the jury is commanded, yea, commanded to render a verdict against us as Anarchists. Your honor, you are aware of this; you know this to be the truth; you sat and heard it all. I will not make a statement but what will be in accord with the facts, and what I do say is said for the purpose of refreshing your memory and asking you to look at both sides of this matter and view it from the standpoint of reason and common sense.

Now, the money makers, the business men, those people who deal in stocks and bonds, the speculators and employers, all that class of men known as the money making class, have no conception of this labor question; they don't understand what it means. To use the street parlance, with many of them it is a difficult matter to "catch onto" it, and they are perverse also; they will have no knowledge of it. They don't want to know anything about it, and they won't hear anything about it, and they propose to club, lock up, and, if necessary, strangle those who insist on their hearing this question. Can it be any longer denied that there is such a thing as the labor question?

I am an Anarchist. Now strike! But hear me before you strike. What is Socialism, or Anarchism? Briefly stated, it is the right of the toiler to the free and equal use of the tools of production, and the right of the producers to their product. That is Socialism. The history of mankind is one of growth. It has been evolutionary and revolutionary. The dividing line between evolution and revolution, or that imperceptible boundary line where one begins and the other ends can never be designated. Who believed at the time that our fathers tossed the tea into the Boston harbor that it meant the first revolt of the revolution separating this continent from the dominion of George III. and founding this Republic here in which we, their descendants, live today. Evolution and revolution are synonymous. Evolution is the incubatory state of revolution. The birth is the revolution—its process the evolution.

What is the history of man with regard to the laboring classes? Originally the earth and its contents were held in common by all men. Then came a change brought about by violence, robbery and wholesale murder, called war. Later, but still way back in history, we find that there were but two classes in the world—slaves and masters. Time rolled on and we find a labor system of serfdom. This serf labor system existed in the sixteenth and seventeenth centuries, and throughout the world the serf had a right to the soil on which he lived. The lord of the land could not exclude him from its use. But with the discovery of America and the developments which followed that discovery and its settlement, a century or two afterwards, the gold found in Peru and Mexico by the invading hosts of Pizarro and Cortez, who carried back to Europe this precious metal, infused new vitality into the commercial stagnant blood of Europe and set in motion those wheels which have rolled on and on, until today commerce covers the face of the earth time is annihilated and distance is known no more. Following the abolition of the serfdom system was the establishment of the wage labor system. This found its fruition, or birth, rather, in the French revolution of 1789 and 1793. It was then for the first time that civil and political liberty was established in Europe. We see, by a mere glance back into history, that the sixteenth century was engaged in a struggle for religious freedom and the right of conscience—mental liberty. Following that in the seventeenth and eighteenth centuries was the struggle throughout France which resulted in the establishment of the Republic and the founding of the right of political liberty. The struggle today, which follows on in the line of progress and in the logic of events, is the industrial problem, of which we were the representatives, as the State's attorney has said we were, selected by the grand jury because we were the leaders, and are to be punished and consigned to an ignominious death for that reason, that the wage-slaves of Chicago and of America may be horrified, terror-stricken, and driven like rats back to their holes, to hunger, slavery, misery and death. The industrial question, following on in the natural order of events, the wage system of industry is now up for consideration; it presses for a hearing; it demands a solution; it cannot be throttled by this district attorney, nor all the district attorneys upon the soil of America. Now, what is this labor question which these gentlemen treat with such profound contempt for advocating, which these distinguished "honorable" gentlemen would throttle and put us to ignominious death and hurry us like rats to our holes? What is it? You will pardon me if I exhibit some feeling. I have sat here for two months, and these men have poured their vituperations out upon my head and I have not been permitted to utter a single word in my own defense. For two months they have poured their poison upon me and upon my colleagues. For two months they have sat here and spit like adders the vile poison of their tongues, and if men could have been placed in a mental inquisition and tortured to death, these men would have succeeded here now, for we have been vilified, misrepresented, held in loathsome contempt, without a chance to speak or contradict a word. Therefore, if I show emotion, it is because of this, and if my comrades and colleagues with me here have spoken in such strains as these, it is because of this. Pardon us. Look at it from the right standpoint. What is this labor question? It is not a question of emotion; the labor question is not a question of sentiment; it is not a religious matter; it is not a political problem; no, sir, it is a stern economic fact, a stubborn and immovable fact. It has, it is true, its emotional phase; it has its sentimental, religious, political aspects; but the sum total of this question is the bread and butter question, the how and the why we shall live and earn our daily bread. This is the labor movement. It has a scientific basis. It is founded upon fact, and I have been to considerable pains in my researches of well known and distinguished authors on this question to collect and present to you briefly what this question is and what it springs from. I will first explain to you briefly what capital is:

Capital is the stored-up and accumulated surplus of past labor; capital is the product of labor. The function of capital is to appropriate or confiscate for its own use and benefit the "surplus" labor product of the wage laborer. The capitalistic system originated in the forcible seizure of natural opportunities and rights by a few, and then converting those things into special privileges which have since become vested rights, formally entrenched behind the bulwarks of statute law and government. Capital could not exist unless there also existed a majority class who were propertyless, that is, without capital, a class whose only mode of existence is the selling of their labor to capitalists. Capitalism is maintained, fostered, and perpetuated by law; in fact, capital is law—statute law—and law is capital. Now, briefly stated, for I will not take your time but a moment, what is labor? Labor is a commodity and wages is the price paid for it. The owner of this commodity sells it, that is, himself, to the owner of capital in order to live. Labor is the expression of energy, the power of the laborer's life. This energy or power he must sell to another person in order to live. It is his only means of existence. He works to live, but his work is not simply a part of his life; it is the sacrifice of it. His labor is a commodity which under the guise of free labor he is forced by necessity to hand over to another party. The whole of the wage laborer's activity is not the product of his labor—far from it. The silk he weaves, the palace he builds, the ores he digs from out the mines, are not for him. The only thing he produces for himself is his wages, and the silk, the ores, and the palace which he built, are simply transformed for him into a certain kind of means of existence, namely, a cotton shirt, a few pennies, and the mere tenancy of a lodging-house. In other words, his wages represent the bare necessities of his existence, and the unpaid-for or "surplus" portion of his labor product constitutes the vast superabundant wealth of the non-producing or capitalist class.

That is the capitalist system defined in a few words. It is this system that creates these classes, and it is these classes that produce this conflict. This conflict intensifies as the power of the privileged classes over the non-possessing or propertyless classes increases and intensifies, and this power increases as the idle few become richer and the producing many become poorer, and this produces what is called the labor movement. This is the labor question. Wealth is power; poverty is weakness.

If I had time I might stop here to answer some suggestions that probably arise in the minds of some persons, or perhaps of your honor, not being familiar with this question. I imagine I hear your honor say, "Why, labor is free. This is a free country." Now, we had in the Southern States for nearly a century a form of labor known as chattel slave labor. That has been abolished, and I hear you say that labor is free; that the war has resulted in establishing free labor all over America. Is this true? Look at it. The chattel slave of the past—the wage slave of today; what is the difference? The master selected under chattel slavery his own slaves. Under the wage slavery system the wage slave selects his master, and he has got to find one or else he is carried down here to my friend, the goaler, and occupy a cell along side of myself. He is compelled to find one. So the change of the industrial system, in the language of Jefferson Davis, ex-President of the Southern Confederacy, in an interview with the *New York Herald* upon the question of the chattel slave system of the South and that of the so-called "free laborer," and their wages—Jefferson Davis stated positively that the change was a decided benefit to the former chattel slave owners who would not exchange the new system of wage labor at all for chattel labor, because now the dead had to bury themselves and the sick take care of themselves, and now they don't have to employ overseers to look after them. They give them a task to do—a certain amount to do. They say: "Now, here, perform this piece of work in a certain length of time," and if you don't (under the wage system, says Mr. Davis), why, when you come around for your pay next Saturday, you simply find in the envelope which gives you your money, a note which informs you of the fact that you have been discharged. Now, Jefferson Davis admitted in his statement that the leather thong dipped in salt brine, for the chattel slave, had been exchanged under the wage slave system for the lash of hunger, an empty stomach and the ragged back of the wage-slave of free born American sovereign citizens, who, according to the census of the United States for 1880, constitute more than nine-tenths of our entire population.

But you say the wage slave had advantages over the chattel slave. The chattel slave couldn't get away from it. Well, if we had the statistics, I believe it could be shown that as many chattel slaves escaped from bondage with the bloodhounds of their masters after them as they tracked their way over the snow-beaten rocks of Canada, and via the underground grape vine road—I believe the statistics would show today that as many chattel slaves escaped from their bondage under that system as can, and do escape today from wage bondage into capitalistic liberty.

I am a Socialist, I am one of those, although myself a wage slave, who holds that it is wrong, wrong to myself, wrong to my neighbor, and unjust to my fellowmen for me, wage slave that I am, to undertake to make my escape from wage slavery by becoming a master and an owner of slaves myself. I refuse to do it, I refuse equally to be a slave or the owner of slaves. Had I chosen another path in life, I might be upon the avenue of the city of Chicago today, surrounded in my beautiful home with luxury and ease and slaves to do my bidding. But I chose the other road, and instead I stand here today upon the scaffold. This is my crime. Before high heaven this and this alone is my crime. I have been false and a traitor to the infamies that exist today in capitalistic society. If this is a crime in your opinion I plead guilty to it.

Now, be patient with me; I have been with you, or rather, I have been patient with this trial. Follow me, if you please, and look at the oppressions of this capitalistic system of industry. As was depicted by my comrade Fielden, this morning, every new machine that comes into existence comes as a competitor with the man of labor, as a drag and menace and a prey to the very existence of those who have to sell their labor in order to earn their bread. The man is turned out to starve and whole occupations and pursuits are revolutionized and completely destroyed by the introduction of machinery, in a day, in an hour as it were. I have known it to be the case in the history of my own life—and I am yet a young man—that whole pursuits and occupations have been wiped out by the invention of machinery.

What becomes of these people? Where are they? They become competitors of other laborers and are made to reduce wages and increase the work hours. Many of them are candidates for the gibbet, they are candidates for your prison cells. Build more penitentiaries; erect new scaffolds, for these men are upon the highway of crime, of misery, of death. Your Honor, there never was an effect without a cause. The tree is known by its fruit. Socialists are not those who blindly close their eyes and refuse to look, and who refuse to hear, but having eyes to see, they see, and having ears to hear, they hear. Look at this capitalistic system; look at its operation upon the small business men; the small dealers, the middle class. *Bradstreet's* tells us in last year's report that there were 11,000 small business men financially destroyed during the past twelve months. What became of those people? Where are they, and why have they been wiped out? Has there been any less wealth? No; that which they possessed has simply been transferred itself into the hands of some other person. Who is that other? It is he who has greater capitalistic facilities. It is the monopolist, the man who can run corners, who can create rings and squeeze these men to death and wipe them out like dead flies from the table into his monopolistic basket. The middle classes destroyed in this manner join the ranks of the proletariat. They become what? They seek out the factory gate, they seek in the various occupations of wage labor for employment. What is the result? Then there are more men upon the market. This increases the number of those who are applying for employment. What then? This intensifies the competition, which in turn creates greater monopolists, and with it wages go down until the starvation point is reached, and then what? Your honor, Socialism comes to the people and asks them to look into this thing, to discuss it, to reason, to examine it, to investigate it, to know the facts, because it is by this, and this alone, that violence will be prevented and bloodshed will be avoided; because, as my friend here has said, men in their blind rage, in their ignorance, not knowing what ails them, knowing that they are hungry, that they are miserable and destitute, strike blindly, and do as they did with Maxwell here, and fight the labor saving machinery. Imagine such an absurd thing, and yet the capitalistic press has taken great pains to say that Socialists do these things; that we fight machinery; that we fight property. Why, sir, it is an absurdity; it is ridiculous; it is preposterous. No man ever heard an utterance from the mouth of a Socialist to advise anything of the kind. They know to the contrary. We don't fight machinery; we don't oppose the thing. It is only the manner and methods of employing them that we object to. We desire that all the forces of nature, all the forces of society, of the gigantic strength which has resulted from the combined intellect and labor of the ages of the past shall be turned over to man, and made his servant, his obedient slave forever. This is the object of Socialism. It asks no one to give up anything. It seeks no harm to anybody. But, when we witness this condition of things, when we see little children huddling around the factory gates, the poor little things whose bones are not yet hard; when we see them clutched from the hearthstone, taken from the family altar and carried to the bastilles of labor and their little bones ground up into gold dust to bedeck the form of some aristocratic Jezebel, then it stirs us and we speak out. We plead for the little ones; we plead for the helpless; we plead for the oppressed, we seek redress for those who are wronged; we seek knowledge and intelligence for the ignorant; we seek liberty for the slave; Socialism secures the welfare of every human being.

Your honor, if you will permit it, I would like to stop now and resume tomorrow morning.

The court here adjourned until 10 o'clock the following day, when Mr. Parsons resumed his address.

Your honor, I concluded last evening at that portion of my statement before you which had for its purpose a showing of the operations and effects of our existing social system, the evils which naturally flow from the established social relations, which are founded upon the economic subjection and dependence of the man of labor to the monopolizer of the means of labor and the resources of life. I sought in this connection to show that all the ills that afflict society—social miseries, mental degradations, political dependence—all resulted from the economic subjection and dependence of the man of labor upon the monopolizer of the means of existence; and as long as the cause remains the effect must certainly follow. I pointed out what *Bradstreet's* had to say in regard to the destruction of the middle class last year. As it affects the small dealers, the middle class men of our shop streets, the same influences are likewise at work among the farming classes.

According to statistics ninety per cent of the farms of America are today under mortgage. The man who a few years ago owned the soil that he worked, is today a tenant, and a mortgage is placed upon his soil, and when he, the farmer whose hand tickles the earth and causes it to blossom as the rose and bring forth its rich fruits for human sustenance—even while this man is asleep the interest upon the mortgage continues. It grows and it increases, rendering it more and more difficult for him to get along or make his living. In the meantime the railway corporations place upon the traffic all that the market will bear. The Board of Trade sharks run their corners until—what? Until it occurs as stated in the Chicago *Tribune* about three months ago, that a freight train of corn from Iowa consigned to a commission merchant in Chicago, had to be sold for less than the cost of freight, and there was a balance of $3 due the commission man on the freight of after he had sold the corn. The freightage upon that corn was three dollars more than the corn brought in the market. So it is with the tenant farmers of America. Your honor, we do not have to go to Ireland to find the evils of landlordism. We do not have to cross the Atlantic ocean to find Lord Lietrim's rackrenters, or landlords who evict their tenants. We have them all around us. There is Ireland right here in Chicago and everywhere else in this country. Look at Bridgeport where the Irish live! Look! Tenants at will, huddled together as State's Attorney Grinnell calls them, like rats; living as they do in Dublin, living precisely as they do in Limerick—taxed to death, unable to meet the extortions of the landlord.

We were told by the prosecution that law is on trial; that government is on trial. That is what the gentlemen on the other side stated to the jury. The law is on trial, and government is on trial. Well, up to near the conclusion of this trial we, the defendants, supposed that we were indicted and being tried for murder. Now, if the law is on trial and if the government is on trial, who placed it upon trial? And I leave it to the people of America whether the prosecution in this case have made out a case; and I charge it here now frankly that in order to bring about this conviction the prosecution, the representatives of the state, the sworn officers of the law, those whose obligation it is to the people to obey the law and preserve order—I charge upon them a willful, a malicious, a purposed violation of every law which guarantees right to American citizens. They have violated free speech. In the prosecution of this case they have violated a free press. They have violated the right of public assembly. Yea, they have even violated and denounced the right of self-defense. I charge the crime home to them. These great blood bought rights, for which our forefathers spent centuries of struggle, it is attempted to run them like rats into a hole by the prosecution in this case. Why, gentlemen, law is upon trial; government is upon trial, indeed. Yea, they are themselves guilty of the precise thing of which they accuse me. They say that I am an Anarchist and refuse to respect the law. "By their works ye shall know them," and out of their own mouths they stand condemned. They are the real Anarchists in this case, while we stand upon the constitution of the United States.

I have violated no law of this country. Neither I nor my colleagues here have violated any legal right of American citizens. We stand upon the right of free speech, of free press, of public assemblage, unmolested and undisturbed. We stand upon the constitutional right of self-defense, and we defy the prosecution to rob the people of America of these dearly bought rights. But the prosecution imagines that they have triumphed because they propose to put to death seven men. Seven men to be exterminated in violation of law, because they insist upon the inalienable rights granted them by the constitution. Seven men are to be exterminated, because they demand the right of free speech and exercise it. Seven men by this court of law are to be put to death, because they claim their right of self-defense. Do you think, gentlemen of the prosecution, that you will have settled the case when you are carrying my lifeless bones to the potter's field? Do you think that this trial will be settled by my strangulation and that of my colleagues? I tell you that there is a greater verdict yet to be heard from. The American people will have something to say about this attempt to destroy their rights, which they hold sacred. The American people will have something to say as to whether or not the Constitution of this country can be trampled under foot at the dictation of monopoly and corporations and their hired tools.

Your honor read yesterday your reasons for refusing us a new trial, and I want to call your attention to it, if you please, on some points on which I think you are laboring under misapprehension. Your honor says that there can be no question in the mind of any one who has read these articles (referring to the *Alarm* and *Arbeiter-Zeitung*), or heard these speeches, which were written and spoken long before the eight hour movement was talked of, that this movement which we advocated was but a means in their estimation toward the ends which we sought, and the movement itself was not primarily of any consideration at all. Now, your honor, I submit that you are sitting in judgment not alone upon my acts, but also upon my motives. That is a dangerous thing for any man to do; any man is so liable to make a mistake in a matter of that kind. I claim that it would not be fair for you to assume to state what my motives were in the eight hour movement; that I was simply using it for another purpose. How do you know that? Can you read my heart and order my actions? If you go by the record, it will disprove your honor's conjecture, because it is a conjecture!

The State's attorney has throughout this trial done precisely what Mr. English, the reporter of the *Tribune*, said he was instructed to do by the proprietor of the *Tribune*, when he attended labor meetings. It was the custom of the chief editors of the large dailies to instruct those who went to these labor meetings to report only the inflammatory passages of the speaker's remarks. That is precisely the scheme laid out by the prosecution. They have presented you here copies of the *Alarm* running back for three years, and my speeches covering three years back. They have selected such portions of those articles, and such articles, mark you, as subserve their purpose, such as they supposed would be calculated to inflame your mind and prejudice you and the jury against us. You ought to be careful of this thing. It is not fair and is not right for you to conclude that from the showing made by these gentlemen we were not what we pretended to be in this labor movement. Take the record. Why, I am well known throughout the United States for years and years past and I have come in personal contact with hundreds of thousands of workingmen from Nebraska in the West to New York in the East, and from Maryland to Wisconsin and Minnesota. I have traversed the States for the past ten years, and I am known by hundreds and thousands who have seen and heard me.

Possibly I had better stop a moment, and explain how this was. These labor organizations sent for me. Sometimes it was the Knights of Labor; sometimes it was the Trades Unions; sometimes the Socialistic organizations; but always as an organizer of workingmen, always as a labor speaker at labor meetings. Now, if there is anything for which I am well known it is my advocacy of the eight hour system of labor; so it is with my colleagues here. But because I have said in this connection that I did not believe it would be possible to bring about a reform of this present wage system, because of the fact that the power of the employing class is so great that they can refuse to make any concessions, you say that I had no interest in the eight hour movement. Is it not a fact that the present social system places all power in the hands of the capitalist class? They can and do refuse to make any concessions, and where they grant anything they retract it when they choose to do so. They can do it. The wage system gives them the power. The tyranny and the despotism of the wage system of labor consists in the fact that the wage laborer is compelled under penalty of hunger and death by starvation to obey and accept terms laid down to him by his employer. Hence I have pointed out that it might be difficult for this reason to establish an eight-hour rule. What have I said in this connection? I have said to the employers, to the manufacturers and the corporations—the monopolists of America: "Gentlemen, the eight-hour system of labor is the olive branch of peace held out to you. Take it. Concede this moderate demand of the working people. Give them better opportunities. Let them possess the leisure which eight hours will bring. Let it operate on the wants and the daily habits of the people." I have talked this way to the rich of this country in every place I have gone, and I have told them, not in the language of a threat; not in the language of intimidation; I have said: "If you do not concede this demand, if, on the other hand, you increase the hours of labor, and employ more and more machinery, you thereby increase the number of enforced idle; you thereby swell the army of the compulsory idle and unemployed; you create new elements of discontent; you increase the army of idleness and misery." I said to them: "This is a dangerous condition of things to have in a country. It is liable to lead to violence. It will drive the workers into revolution. The eight hour demand is a measure which is in the interest of humanity, in the interest of peace, in the interest of prosperity and public order."

Now, your honor, can you take your comments there and say that we had other motives and ulterior motives? Your impression is derived from the inflammatory sections and articles selected by the prosecution for your honor to read. I think that I know what my motives were, and I am stating them deliberately and fairly and honestly, leaving you to judge whether or not I am telling the truth. You say that "the different papers and the speeches furnish direct contradiction to the arguments of the counsel for the defense that we proposed to resort to arms only in case of unlawful attacks of the police." Why, the very article that you quote in the *Alarm*—a copy of which I have not, but which I would like to see, calling the American Group to assemble for the purpose of considering military matters and military organization, states specifically that the purpose and object is to take into consideration measures of defense against unlawful and unconstitutional attacks of the police. That identical article shows it. You forget surely that fact when you made this observation; and I defy any one to show, in a speech that is susceptible of proof, by proof, that I have ever said aught by word of mouth or by written article except in self-defense. Does not the constitution of the country, under whose flag myself and my forefathers were born for the last 260 years, provide that protection, and give me, their descendant, that right? Does not the constitution say that I, as an American, have a right to keep and to bear arms? I stand upon that right. Let me see if this court will deprive me of it.

Let me call your attention to another point here. For some of these articles that appear in the *Alarm*, I am no more responsible than is the editor of any other paper. And I did not write everything in the *Alarm*, and it might be possible that there were some things in that paper which I am not ready to endorse. I am frank to admit that such is the case. I suppose you could scarcely find an editor of a paper in the world, but what could conscientiously say the same thing. Now, am I to be dragged up here and executed for the utterances and the writings of other men, even though they were published in the columns of a paper of which I was the editor? Your honor, you must remember that the *Alarm* was a labor paper, published by the International Working People's Association, belonging to that body. I was elected its editor by the organization, and, as labor editors generally are, I was handsomely paid. I had saw-dust pudding as a general thing for dinner. My salary was eight dollars a week, and I have received that salary as editor of the *Alarm* for over two years and a half—$8 a week! I was paid by the association. It stands upon the books. Go down to the office and consult the business manager. Look over the record in the book and it will show you that A. R. Parsons received $8 a week as editor of the *Alarm* for over two years and a half. This paper belonged to the organization. It was theirs. They sent in their articles—Tom, Dick and Harry; everybody wanted to have something to say, and I had no right to shut off anybody's complaint. The *Alarm* was a labor paper, and it was specifically published for the purpose of allowing every human being who had a wrong to ventilate it; to give every human being who wore the chains of monopoly an opportunity to clank those chains in the columns of the *Alarm*. It was a free press organ. It was a free speech newspaper.

But your honor says: "Oh, well, Parsons, your own language, your own words, your own statements at these meetings—what you said." Well, possibly I have said some foolish things. Who has not? As a public speaker, probably I have uttered some wild and possibly incoherent assertions. Who, as a public speaker, has not done so? Now, consider for a moment. Suppose, as is now the case with me, here I see little children suffering, men and women starving. There I see others rolling in luxury and wealth and opulence, out of the unpaid-for labor of the laborers.

I am conscious of this fact. I see the streets of Chicago, as was the case last winter, filled with 30,000 men in compulsory idleness; destitution, misery and want upon every hand. I see this thing. Then on the other hand I see the First Regiment out in a street-riot drill, and reading the papers the next morning describing the affair, I am told by the editor of this capitalistic newspaper that the First Regiment is out practicing a street-riot drill for the purpose of mowing down these wretches when they come out of their holes that the prosecution talks about here in this case; that the working people are to be slaughtered in cold blood, and that men are drilling upon the streets of the cities of America to butcher their fellowmen when they demand the right to work and partake of the fruits of their labor. Seeing these things, overwhelmed as it were with indignation and pity, my heart speaks. May I not say some things then that I would not in cooler moments? Are not such outrageous things calculated to arouse the bitterest denunciations?

Your honor, I want to call your attention to some of the reasons which I propose here today to offer in justification of the words and utterances, and the acts, whatever they may have been, of myself, or my colleagues, on the question of force, on the question of arms, and on the question of dynamite. Now, going back to 1877, what do we find? The railroad strikes occurred. During the conflict of that year the following utterances were made by heavy employers and manufacturers and monopolists in this country. I will give you a few samples. This, mark you, is published in the *Alarm* of November 8, 1884, but the same extracts have been kept standing in the labor papers, published by the Knights of Labor, the trades unions, and the Socialists of the United States, there being somewhere over three hundred of these papers. Now listen: "Give them (the strikers) a rifle diet for a few days, and see how they like that kind of bread," said Tom Scott, president of the Pennsylvania Central Railway, addressing Gov. Hartranft of Pennsylvania, and calling upon him to send his army of militiamen to Pittsburg, to put down his railroad strikers, who were asking for a little more pay, and some of them asking for pay enough to get their hungry children bread. His answer is "give them a rifle diet for a few days and see how they like that kind of bread." Mark you, this was in 1877. "If the workingmen had no vote they might be more amenable to the teachings of the times," says the Indianapolis *News*. "There is too much freedom in this country rather than too little," says the Indianapolis *Journal*. In 1878, the New York *Tribune*, in an editorial upon strikes, used these words: "These brutal strikers or creatures can understand no other meaning than that of force, and ought to have enough of it to be remembered among them for many generations." "Hand grenades should be thrown among these union sailors who are striving to obtain higher wages and less hours. By such treatment they would be taught a valuable lesson, and other strikers could take warning from their fate," said the Chicago *Times*. "It is very well to relieve real distress wherever it exists, whether in the city or in the country, but the best meal that can be given a ragged tramp is a leaden one, and it should be supplied in sufficient quantities to satisfy the most voracious appetite." New York *Herald*, 1878: "The American laborer must make up his mind to be not so much better than the European laborer. He must be contented to work for less wages and must be satisfied with that station in life to which it has pleased God to call him." The New York *World* uttered these sentiments in 1878. I could go through the whole gamut of the monopolistic press of America and show similar expressions of sentiment. These sentiments were used against strikers, against men who were simply seeking to improve their condition. They only asked for less hours of labor and for increased pay. These are the bloody, bitter words of these papers. Now, what follows? It is the experience nowadays and has been since that time, when workingmen strike, to call out the militia. That has been the practice since these utterances and declarations in 1878, growing out of the great railroad strike. It has become the custom in America to call out the militia if there is a strike, or even if there is one contemplated. Why, look at the packing houses in the city of Chicago. Only yesterday the packing house bosses, who employ 25,000 men, called for an army of Pinkerton men to go down there, and advertised for them to come. That was before there was a strike—in mere contemplation of it, your honor. This in America—the United States! Why, is it surprising that the working people should feel indignant about these things and say to Mr. Gould or to Tom Scott: "If you are going to give us a rifle diet instead of a bread diet, as was asked of Christ, when we ask you for bread you give us a stone, and not only give us a stone, but at the point of the bayonet compel us to swallow it, where is the constitutional right of resistance to these outrages?" If I am to be deprived of my rights of defense against the administration of a rifle diet, and strychnine put upon my bread and food, which was advocated by the Chicago *Tribune* when it said that, when tramps come around in the neighborhood, give them a slice of bread with strychnine upon it, and other tramps will take warning and keep out the of the neighborhood; if I am to be deprived of my right, what shall I do? Are not such expressions as this calculated to exasperate men? Is there no justification for these, what you denominate violent speeches? Did not these monopolists bring about the inception of this language? Did they not originate it? Were they not the first to say: "Throw dynamite bombs among the strikers, and thereby make a warning to others?" Was it not Tom Scott who first said, "Give them a rifle diet"? Was it the *Tribune* which first said "Give them strychnine"? And they have done it. Since that time they have administered a rifle diet; they have administered strychnine. They have thrown hand grenades, and the hand grenade upon the Haymarket on the night of the 4th of May was thrown by the hand of a monopolist conspirator sent from the city of New York for that specific purpose, to break up the eight hour movement and bring these men to the gallows in this court. Your honor, we are the victims of the foulest and blackest conspiracy that ever disgraced the annals of time. If these men will preach these things; if the *Tribune* thinks that strychnine is good enough for us; if the *Times* thinks that hand grenades are good enough for us, why have we not got a right to say they will use it? They say they believe in it. They say they think it. What right have we to say that they will not hire some mercenary to carry out what they think, and put into practice that which they believe?

In this connection I want to call your attention to the way armed men, militiamen and Pinkerton's private army are used against workingmen, strikers; the way they are used to shoot them, to arrest them, to put up jobs on them and carry them out. In the *Alarm* of Oct. 17, 1885, there is printed the following: "Pinkerton's Army. They Issue a Secret Circular Offering their Services to Capitalists for the Suppression of Strikers. The secretary of the Minneapolis, Minn., Trades and Labor Assembly, sends us the following note: Minneapolis, Minn., Oct. 6, 1885. Editor of the *Alarm*. Dear Sir: Please pay your respects to the Pinkerton pups for their extreme kindness to labor. Try to have the government of your city do away with its metropolitan police and employ the Pinkerton protectors." (Of course this is sarcastic.) "The enclosed circular fell into the hands of the Minneapolis Trades Assembly, which thought it not out of place to pass it around. Please insert it in your paper. Yours fraternally, T. W. Brosnan.'" That letter is under the seal of the Trade and Labor Assembly of the city of Minneapolis, Minn. Then follows the circular. Then, after referring to the services rendered the capitalists, corporations, and monopolists during the strikes in all parts of the country during the past year, the circular closes with the following paragraphs, which we give in full as illustrative of the designs of these secret enemies upon organized labor. Let every workingman ponder over the avowed purposes of these armies of thugs. It says: "The Pinkerton Protective Patrol is connected with Pinkerton's National Detective Agency, and is under the same management. Corporations or individuals desirous of ascertaining the feelings of their employees, whether they are likely to engage in strikes or are joining any secret labor organizations, such as the Knights of Labor, with a view of compelling terms from corporations or employers, can obtain upon application to the superintendent of either of the offices a detective suitable to associate with their employees and obtain this information." This circular continues: "At this time, when there is so much dissatisfaction among the labor classes, and secret labor societies are organizing throughout the United States, we suggest whether it would not be well for railroad companies and other corporations, as well as individuals who are extensive employers, to keep a close watch for designing men among their own employees, who, in the interest of secret labor societies, are influencing their employees to join these organizations and eventually cause a strike. It is frequently the case that, by taking a matter of this kind in time, and discovering the ring-leaders, and dealing promptly with them"—"discovering the ring-leaders," mark you, "and dealing promptly with them, serious trouble may be avoided in the future. Yours respectfully, William A. Pinkerton, General Superintendent Western Agency, Chicago; Robert A. Pinkerton, General Superintendent Eastern Division, New York.'"

Now here is a concern, an institution which organizes a private army. This private army is at the command and control of those who grind the faces of the poor, who keep wages down to the starvation point. This private army can be shipped to the place where they are wanted. Now it goes to the Hocking Valley to subjugate the starving miners; then it is carried across the plains to Nebraska to shoot the striking miners in that region. Then it is carried to the East to stop the strike of the factory operatives and put them down. The army moves about to and fro all over the country, sneaks into the labor organizations, worms itself into the these labor societies, finds out, as it says, who the ring-leaders are and deals promptly with them. "Promptly," your honor, "with them." Now, what does that mean? It means this: that some workingman who has got the spirit of a man in his organization, who gets up and speaks out his sentiments, protests, you know, objects, won't have it, don't like these indignities and says so; is set down as a ring-leader, and these spies go to work and put up a job on him. If they can not aggravate him and make him, as the New York *Tribune* says, violate the law so they can get hold of him, they go to work and put up a scheme on him, and concoct a conspiracy that will bring him into court. When he is brought into court he is a wage-slave; he has no friends, he has got no money—who is he? Why, he stands here at the bar like a culprit. He has neither position, wealth, honor, nor friends to defend him. What is the result? Why, sixty days at the Bridewell or a year in the county jail. The matter is dismissed with a wave of the hand. The bailiff carries the ring leader out. The strike is suppressed. Monopoly triumphs and the Pinkertons have performed the work for which they receive their pay. Now, it was these things that caused the American group to take an exceeding interest in this manner of treatment on the part of the corporations and monopolies of the country, and we became indignant about it. We expostulated, we denounced it. Could we do otherwise? We are a part and parcel of the miseries brought about by this condition of things. Could we do otherwise than expostulate and object to it and resent it? Now, to illustrate what we did, I read to you from the *Alarm*, December 12, 1885, the proceedings of the American Group, of which I was a member, as a sample. I being present at that meeting, and that meeting being reported in this paper, I hold that this report of the meeting, being put into the *Alarm* at that time, is worthy of your credence and respect, as showing what our attitude was upon the question of force and of arms and of dynamite. The article is headed "street riot drill. Mass Meeting of Working People held at 106 East Randolph Street." This was the regular hall and place of meeting. The article reads: "A large mass meeting of workingmen and women was held by the American Group of the International last Wednesday evening at their hall, 106 East Randolph street. The subject under discussion was the street-riot drill of the First Regiment on Thanksgiving day. William Holmes presided. The principal speaker of the evening was Mrs. Lucy E. Parsons. She began by saying that the founders of this republic, whose motto was that every human being was by nature entitled to life, liberty, and the pursuit of happiness, would turn in their graves if they could read and know that a great street-riot drill was now being practiced in times of peace. 'Let us,' said she, examine into this matter and ascertain, if we can, what this street-riot drill of the military is for. Certainly not for the purpose of fighting enemies from without; not for a foreign foe, for if this was the case we would be massing our armies on the sea-coast. Then it must be for our enemies within. Now, then, do a contented, prosperous, and happy people leave their avocations and go out upon the streets to riot? Do young men and maidens who are marrying and given in marriage forsake the peaceful paths of life to become a riotous mob? Then who is this street-riot drill for? For whom is it intended? Who is to be shot? When the tramp of the military is heard, and grape and canister are sweeping four streets at a time, as is contemplated by this new-fangled drill which was so graphically described in the capitalistic press which gave an account of it, it is certainly not for the purpose of shooting down the *bourgeoisie*, the wealthy, because this same press makes a stirring appeal to them to contribute liberally to a military fund to put them on a good footing and make the militia twice as strong as it is at present, because their services would soon be needed to shoot down the mob.' The speaker then read an extract from a capitalistic account of the street-riot drill on Thanksgiving Day."

Your honor, this meeting was held the week following Thanksgiving day, and the drill took place on Thanksgiving day. This article, which is a description of the drill copied from a capitalistic paper, reads as follows: "As a conclusion the divisions were drawn up in line of battle and there was more firing by companies, by file and by battalion. The drill was creditable to the regiment, and the First will do excellent service in the streets in case of necessity. Opportunities, however, are needed for rifle practice, and Colonel Knox is anxious to have a range established as soon as possible. Instead of 400 members, the regiment should have 800 members on its rolls. Business men should take more interest in the organization and help put it in the best possible condition to cope with a mob, for there may be need for its service at no distant day." That article appeared either in the *Times* or *Tribune* of the next day. I don't know which. The speaker says: "What must be the thought of the oppressed in foreign lands when they hear the tramp of the militia beneath the folds of the stars and stripes? They who first hung this flag to the breeze, proclaimed that beneath its folds the oppressed of all lands would find a refuge and a haven and protection against the despotism of all lands. Is this the case today when the counter-tramp of two millions of homeless wanderers is heard throughout the land of America; men strong and able and anxious and willing to work, that they may purchase for themselves and their families food; when the cry of discontent is heard from the working classes everywhere, and they refuse longer to starve, and peaceably accept a rifle diet and die in misery according to law, and order is enforced by this military drill? Is this military drill for the purpose of sweeping them down as a mob with grape and canister upon the street?" This is the language of the speaker at the meeting: "We working people hear these ominous rumblings, which create inquiry as to their origin. A few years ago we heard nothing of this kind; but great changes have taken place during the past generation. Charles Dickens, who visited America forty years ago, said that what surprised him most was the general prosperity and equality of all people, and that a beggar upon the streets of Boston would create as much consternation as an angel with a flaming sword. What of Boston today? Last winter, said a correspondent of the Chicago *Tribune*, writing from that city, 30,000 persons were destitute, and there were whole streets of tenant houses where the possession of a cooking stove was regarded as a badge of aristocracy, the holes of which were rented to other less wealthy neighbors for a few pennies per hour.

"So, too, with New York, Chicago and every other industrial center in this broad land. Why is this? Have we had a famine? Has nature refused to yield her harvest? These are grave and serious questions for us, the producers and sufferers, to consider, at least. Take a glance at the wealth of this country. In the past twenty years it has increased over twenty billions of dollars. Into whose hands has this wealth found its way? Certainly not the hands of the producers, for if it had there would be no need for street-riot drills. This country has a population of 55,000,000, and a statistical compilation shows that there are in the cities of New York, Philadelphia and Boston twenty men who own as their private property over $750,000,000, or about one-twenty-sixth of the entire increase which was produced by the labor of the working class, these twenty individuals being as one in three millions. In twenty years these profit-mongers have fleeced the people of the enormous sum of $750,000,000, and only three cities and twenty robbers heard from. A government that protects this plundering of the people, a government which permits the people to be degraded and brought to misery in this manner is a fraud upon the face of it, no matter under what name it is called, or what flag floats over it; whether it be a republic, a monarchy, or an empire," said the speaker. "The American flag protects as much economic despotism as any other flag on the face of the earth today to the ratio of population. This being the case, of what does the boasted freedom of the American workingman consist? Our fathers used to sing,

> 'Come along, come along; make no delay;
> Come from every nation, come from every way;
> Come along, come along; don't be alarmed—
> Uncle Sam is rich enough to give us all a farm.'

The stars and stripes in those days floated upon every water as the emblem of the free, but today it obeys only the command, and has become the ensign of monopoly and of corporations, of those who grind the face of the poor and rob and enslave the laborer. Could Russia do more than drill in its streets to kill the people? But alas! Americans creep and crawl at the foot of wealth and adore the golden calf. Can a man amass millions without despoiling the labor of others? We all know he cannot. American workingmen seem to be degenerating. They do not seem to understand what liberty and freedom really consist of. They shout themselves hoarse on election day—for what? For the miserable privilege of choosing their master; which men shall be their boss and rule over them; for the privilege of choosing just who are the bosses and who shall govern them. Great privilege! These Americans—sovereigns—millions of them do not know where they could get a bed or a supper. Your ballot—what is it good for? Can a man vote himself bread, or clothes, or shelter, or work? In what does American wage slaves' freedom consist? The poor are the slaves of the rich everywhere. The ballot is neither a protection against hunger nor against the bullets of the military. Bread is freedom; freedom bread. The ballot is no protection against the bullets of those who are practicing the street-riot drills in Chicago. The ballot is worthless to the industrial slave under these conditions. The palaces of the rich overshadow the homes or huts of the poor, and we say with Victor Hugo, that the paradise of the rich is made out of the hells of the poor. The whole force of the organized power of the government is thrown against the workers, whom the so-called better class denominate a mob. Now, when the workers of America refuse to starve according to law and order, and when they begin to think and act, why, the street drill begins. The enslavers of labor see the coming storm. They are determined, cost what it may, to drill these people and make them their slaves by holding in their possession the means of life as their property, and thus enslave the producers. Workingmen—we mean the women, too—arise! Prepare to make and determine successfully to establish the right to live and partake of the bounties to which all are equally entitled. Agitate, organize, prepare to defend your life, your liberty, your happiness against the murderers who are practicing the street riot drill on Thanksgiving Day.

> "'Tis the shame of the land that the earnings of toil,
> Should gorge the god Mammon, the tyrant, the spoiler.
> Every foot has a logical right to the soil,
> And the product of toil is the meed of the toiler.
> The hands that disdain
> Honest industry's stain
> Have no share in its honor, no right to its gain,
> And the falsehood of Wealth over Worth shall not be
> In 'the home of the brave and the land of the free.'"

"Short addresses were made by comrades Fielden, Dr. Taylor, William Snyder, William Holmes, and others. This concluded the meeting, after criticisms."

Now, I challenge your Honor, to find a sentence or an utterance in that meeting—and that is one of the fullest reported of the many meetings held by the American Group for public discussion of such matters as the Thanksgiving drill of the First Regiment—I challenge you to find a single word or utterance there that is unlawful, that is contrary to the constitution, or that is in violation of free speech, or that is in violation of free press, or that is in violation of public assembly or of the right of self-defense. And that is our position, and has been all the while. Imagine for a moment, the First Regiment practicing the street-riot drill as it was described—learning how to sweep four streets from the four corners at once. Who? The *Tribune* and *Times* say "the mob." Who are the mob? Why, dissatisfied people, dissatisfied workingmen and women; people who are working for starvation wages, people who are on a strike for better pay—these are the mob. They are always the mob. That is what the riot drill is for. Suppose a case like that occurs. The First Regiment is out with a thousand men armed with the latest improved Winchester rifles. Here are the mobs; here are the Knights of Labor and the Trades Unions, and all of the organizations without arms. They have no treasury, and a Winchester rifle costs $18. They cannot purchase those things. We can not organize an army. It takes capital to organize an army. It takes as much money to organize an army as to organize industry, or as to build railroads; therefore, it is impossible for the working classes to organize and buy Winchester rifles. What can they do? What must they do? Your honor, the dynamite bomb, I am told, costs six cents. It can be made by anybody. The Winchester rifle costs $18. That is the difference. Am I to be blamed for that? Am I to be hanged for saying this? Am I to be destroyed for this? What have I done? Go, dig up the ashes of the man who invented this thing. Find his ashes and scatter them to the winds, because he gave this power to the world. It was not I. General Sheridan—he is the commander in chief of the United States army, and in his report to the president and congress two years ago he had occasion to speak of the possible labor trouble that may occur in the country, and what did he say? In this report he says that dynamite was a lately discovered article of tremendous power, and such was its nature that people could carry it around in the pockets of their clothing with perfect safety to themselves, and by means of it they could destroy whole cities and whole armies. This was General Sheridan. That is what he said. We quoted that language and referred to it. I want to say another word about dynamite before I pass on to something else. I am called a dynamiter by the prosecution here. Why? Did I ever use dynamite? No. Did I ever have any? No. Do I know anything about dynamite bombs? No.

Why, then, am I called a dynamiter? Listen, and I will tell you. Gunpowder in the fifteenth century marked an era in the world's history. It was the downfall of the mail armor of he knight, the freebooter, and the robber of that period. It enabled the victims of these highway robbers to stand off at a distance in a safe place and defend themselves by the use of gunpowder, and make a ball enter and pierce into the flesh of their robbers and destroyers. Gunpowder came as a democratic instrument. It came as a republican institution, and the effect was that it immediately began to equalize and bring about an equilibrium of power. There was less power in the hands of the nobility after that; less power in the hands of the king; less power in the hands of those who would plunder and degrade and destroy the people after that.

So today dynamite comes as the emancipator of man from the domination and enslavement of his fellowman. [The Judge showed symptoms of impatience.] Bear with me now. Dynamite is the diffusion of power. It is democratic; it makes everybody equal. General Sheridan says "arms are worthless." They are worthless in the presence of this instrument. Nothing can meet it. The Pinkertons, the police, the militia, are absolutely worthless in the presence of dynamite. They can do nothing with the people at all. It is the equilibrium. It is the annihilator. It is the disseminator of power. It is the downfall of oppression. It is the abolition of authority; it is the dawn of peace; it is the end of war, because war cannot exist unless there is somebody to make war upon, and dynamite makes that unsafe, undesirable, and absolutely impossible. It is a peace-maker; it is man's best and last friend; it emancipates the world from the domineering of the few over the many, because all government, in the last resort, is violence; all law, in the last resort, is force. Everything is based upon force. Force is the law of the universe; force is the law of nature, and this newly discovered force makes all men equal and therefore free. It is idle to talk of rights when one does not possess the power to enforce them. Science has now given every human being that power. It is proposed by the prosecution here to take me by force and strangle me on the gallows for these things I have said, for these expressions. Now, force is the last resort of tyrants; it is the last resort of despots and of oppressors, and he who would strangle another because that other does not believe as he would have him, he who will destroy another because that other will not do as he says, that man is a despot and a tyrant and unworthy to live.

Now, I speak plainly. Does it follow, because I hold these views, that I committed this act at the Haymarket? Does that follow? Why, you might just as consistently charge General Phil. Sheridan with the act, and for the same reason, for while he did not go into the matter perhaps as extensively in his encomium upon dynamite as I have done, yet he furnished me the text from which I have drawn my knowledge of this thing.

But, you say, my speeches were sometimes extravagant, unlawful. During the discussion of the question of the extension of chattel slavery into the new Territories, into Kansas and the west, while Charles Sumner was yet a member of the United States senate, and that gallant man stood as the champion of freedom upon that floor, he was expostulated with on one occasion and reprimanded by a friend, who said to him: "Sumner, you are not expedient; you must have more policy about what you say, you should not express yourself in this manner; you should not be so denunciatory and fanciful against this slavery, this enslavement. I know it is wrong; I know it should be denounced, but keep inside of the law; keep inside of the constitution."

Your Honor, I quote from the speech of Charles Sumner, that great American, in answer and in reply to that remark. Said he: "Anything for human rights is constitutional. No learning in books, no skill acquired in courts, no sharpness in forensic dealings, no cunning in splitting hairs can impair the vigor thereof. This is the supreme law of the land, anything in the constitution or laws of any state to the contrary notwithstanding." I never said anything that could equal that in lawlessness. Go, gentlemen of the prosecution, dig up the ashes of Sumner and scatter them in disgrace to the wind, tear down the monument that the American people have erected to his honor, and erect thereon some emblem of your contempt!

I will read you now an extract from the *Alarm*, a little editorial: "Any pretense called freedom, however loudly heralded, which does not bring peace, plenty and comfort to all the members of the human race, is a lie and a fraud on the face of it." Another expression from the *Alarm*—a little editorial: "A man gets rich by meanness and poor because he is generous. How long can we tolerate the vile system which rewards meanness and starves generosity?"

Your Honor, one of the most startling facts in connection with this trial, the labor movement, and the general situation of affairs is to be found in the fact that during the last two or three years at least one-half of the large industrial establishments of the United States, the larger corporations, monopolies, and industries, have been conducted under military supervision. A startling fact this is. Armed men, armed guards, either the Pinkertons or the police, the police of the municipalities in the cities, or the militia, or the United States army, as has been done in some cases, are supervising one-half of the industries of America, that is, the larger industries. It is a positive fact. Think of this! Who is doing this! Now, as an offset to this state of affairs, we find 1,200 delegates assembled in Richmond, Va., representing our American workingmen in the convention of the Knights of Labor. That congress, that organization is the reply which is being made by peaceable laborers to the rifle diet advice, the strychnine business, and the hand grenade business, and club business advice by the Chicago, New York, Philadelphia, and other large papers in this country. These men are assembled in self-defense. The conflict is the struggle between liberty and authority—authority in any and every form. Those who are in authority tell the workingmen that if they want to enjoy the law and the protection of the law, they must render a cheerful obedience to the law. Why a man, when he flogs his slave for disobedience tells him the same thing. Your honor, according to your construction of sentence, or the reason which you propose as a portion of the ground work upon which you expect to render your proposed sentence, you deny the right of Americans to defend themselves against the rifle diet, and to protest against these outrageous things, to object to the strychnine business. These are the things that have made us what we are. If there be any wrong in me I am the product of these conditions. I am the creature of circumstance; I am the effect of a cause. Now, where is that cause? What is that cause? But, if it comes to that, the right of free speech, the right of free press, the right of peaceable assemblage, and the right of self-defense is denied to the workingmen; if that is going to be denied us by the courts of law, what is going to be the result? Why, the workingmen will immediately say as a matter of necessity, "Why, of what use to us is the law? What is the constitution for? Of what value is it to us? It certainly must belong to somebody. Yes, it is used for somebody else's benefit and protection, not surely for ours." This will be the natural conclusion, inevitably.

There was no evidence produced to implicate me with the Haymarket bomb. Why, the evidence that was produced only touched two of us, only implicated two of us, and that evidence, as your honor must know, was paid for. Everybody knows it. Your honor knows it. Your honor does not credit that testimony of Gilmer. You cannot do it. It was overwhelmingly and irresistibly impeached. This man is the slender thread that connects two of us with that Haymarket affair. Now, what are the facts about this Haymarket affair? On Tuesday evening, May 4, several thousand persons, working people, assembled at the Haymarket to discuss their grievances, namely the eight hour strike, and the attack and killing of several workingmen by the police the day before. Those citizens, thus assembled in the peaceable exercise of free speech, free press, and public assembly under their constitutional rights, were upon the eve of adjourning, it being after 10 o'clock, when they were charged upon by 200 armed police, and under pain and penalty of instant death and wholesale slaughter, commanded to disperse, ordered like slaves to sneak and cringe and crawl away from the presence of their masters. Now, was not that an affront? Was not that a most grievous outrage? Was not that a violation of all of those principles for which our forefathers struggled in this country? At this juncture some unknown and unproven person throws a bomb among the police, killing several men. You say that I did it, or you say that I knew of it. Where is your proof, gentlemen of the prosecution? You have none. You didn't have any. Oh, but you have a theory, and that theory is that no one else could have had any motive to hurl that missile of death except myself, and, as is the common remark of the great papers of the city, the police are never short of a theory. There is always a theory on hand for everything. A theory they have got, and especially the detectives; they hatch out a theory at once and begin to follow that up. There was a theory carried out during this trial. Let us examine that theory. I say that a Pinkerton man, or a member of the Chicago police force itself, had as much inducement to throw that bomb as I had, and why? Because it would demonstrate the necessity for their existence and result in an increase of their pay and their wages. Are these people any too good to do such a thing? Are they any better than I am? Are their motives any better than my own? Let us look at this thing from every standpoint. Perhaps, on the other hand, the dread missile was hurled in revenge by some poor man or woman, or child even, whose parents or protector or friend was killed by the police in some one of their numerous massacres of the people before. Who knows? And if it was, are we seven to suffer death for that? Are we responsible for that act? Or, might it not be that some person with the fear of death in his eyes threw that bomb in self-defense? And if they did, am I responsible for it? Am I to be executed for that? Is it law to put me to death for that? And who knows? My own deliberate opinion concerning this Haymarket affair is that the death-dealing missile was the work, the deliberate work, of monopoly, the act of those who themselves charge us with the deed. I am not alone in this view of the matter.

Let me first of all call your attention to the pre-existing conspiracy of monopoly against the American people, which I believe culminated in the Haymarket there. I will give you a brief outline or history of this great crime; of the principles of the long antecedent conspiracy on the part of the Chicago *Times* and *Tribune* to use hand grenades, recommending the rifle diet for strikers, and arsenic and strychnine for the unemployed, as the outcome of Gould's admonition in the New York *Tribune* that it is soon that American workingmen must prepare to submit to the same wages as their European brethren, that of the coercive policy of the hand grenade and rifle diet. This all resulted from the deliberate attempt of corporations to pay interest and dividends on bonds and stock which were clear water without a speck of dye in it, and, to keep up these double, treble and sometimes quadruple payments above the actual cash valuation of all the existing capital and innumerable corporations which girdle and reticulate the land, not only was production, transportation and telegraphic industry taxed four-fold, that it should bear in excess of ten per cent, upon actual cash cost, and this conducted on a contracted volume of money in order to enhance its purchasing power and usurious value, and enable them to dictate the price of labor and its products; but the greatest crime of all: congress framed a bill by which when bankrupted, the middle classes are brought to the verge of want by foreclosure of mortgage upon their farms. The managers of these corporations then turn their whole attention to the reduction of expenses, which follows as a direct blow at the wages of those by whose skill and labor the railroad, telegraph, and telephone, and other corporations do their work, knowing that the overcrowded labor market would compel their employees to accept their wages to supply their wants or starve. An industrial war follows, because the wage system enables monopoly to do these things. Now, upon this the wage question has its basis. The crisis was reached when organized labor struck against long hours on the 1st of May, 1886, following the protest in April of the 15,000 employees of Gould's Missouri railway system of the southwest against the wages of fifty-five and seventy cents a day to which Gould's corporation and Manager Hoxie had reduced the army of skilled railroad operatives; but these events were precipitated on the first by the massed labor unions, and the latter by the district assemblies of the Knights of Labor of the southwest. What was the issue? On railroad stocks alone on all the roads within the United States, at a cost of two billion dollars, there was a capitalization of six billions. Now, imagine the effect of this false and fictitious value of labor, for skill and labor alone gives any value to the stocks and bonds and enables these monopoly inflationists to build up vast incomes on that which has merely cost the paper on which these false calculations were issued. The employees of these public institutions and their patrons cannot understand why these holders, and issuers of fictitious stocks and bonds regard it as a crime to strike. That was an issue in 1877, and it is an issue now in 1886 between the monopoly inflationists who hold that a strike for higher wages, which also aims to prevent other labor vocations from accepting the meager wage doled out to labor, is a blow struck at the liberty of contract, which is the only means left them to realize dividends and interest on their fictitious wealth. Noble and sacrificing! These monopolists care nothing for liberty, but everything for the power to contract with competing starving laborers.

Now, your Honor, the victims of these wrongs are numbered by the millions in the United States, one million of whom it is officially reported by the Labor Bureau are out of employment.

The Chicago *Tribune*, about this time, published the following sentiment: "The simplest plan probably when one is not a member of the Humane Society is to put arsenic in the supplies of food furnished the unemployed or the tramp. This produces death in a short time, and is a warning to other tramps to keep out of the neighborhood." The unemployed are kept for better uses now—to take the place of strikers. They don't want to kill them off with strychnine now. The Chicago *Times* used the same advice with reference to the same matter while the great railroad strike of 1877 was pending, and the President of the Pennsylvania Company—Tom Scott—says: "Give them the rifle diet and see how they like that kind of bread." I have spoken here of monopoly conspiracy. Now, to show my words are not extravagant I want to call your attention to the expressions of three Senators on the floor of the United States Senate in the last session of the American Congress. They had a long discussion of the Bland silver bill and the currency question, and during the debate on that question Senator Teller used these words—he said: "There was a conspiracy all over the world on the part of capital against labor, a conspiracy which did not exist in the United States alone, but in which this government was an active agent—a conspiracy for the purpose of increasing the value of the dollar and of decreasing the value of man's production everywhere in the world." It was a conspiracy, as Mr. Teller said for those who had power to take advantage of, and perpetuate the outrage and the wrong upon those who were helpless and powerless. Mr. Vest, in the discussion upon the floor of the Senate used these words. He said he also preferred the House resolutions. He said that the question was one between gold and silver, between gold and greenbacks; between the man who wanted to make money dear and the man who borrowed the money; and unless this trouble was terminated on equitable and fair grounds it would result in a sectional struggle between the east and the west. That was the plain meaning of the whole thing. It was a conspiracy! Senator Jones, of Nevada, discussing the same thing, said that his belief was "that the shrinking volumes of money had inflicted more evil, more suffering, more penalties upon the American people than they had ever suffered from war, pestilence, or famine. What the people want is money; not gold nor silver, but dollars and what liquidates the debt and keeps the red flag of the sheriff away from the window." Your honor will observe he did not refer to the red flag of the commune in that particular. Now, to the mind of this United States senator, the only red flag that is dangerous in the United States is the sheriff's—the flag of the auctioneer, denoting the death of what? Denoting the financial demise of some business man who has been destroyed by these conspiracies spoken of by Senator Vest, Senator Teller, and Senator Jones, of the United States senate. These organized, legalized conspiracies that are bringing about wholesale bankruptcies; conspiracies that inflate the railway stock of the country from two billion dollars to six billion dollars; which compel the people of this country to pay interest upon four billion dollars of watered stock upon railroads alone, compelling the workingmen of America to pay in wages for this inflation, for labor in the end must foot the bill. Now, these men urge this is a conspiracy. So do I, and so do the workingmen of this country. We agree with them. Now, this is a part of the programme culminating here in this Haymarket affair on the 4th of May last. This deplorable conspiracy to which I referred incidentally before, and which I now wish to give to the court in detail, to break down the eight hour movement and avenge itself upon the leaders of the labor movement, furnishes indisputable proof that we, the eight hour men, here at this bar, are the victims of that foul conspiracy to rob and enslave the American people.

What are the real facts of that Haymarket tragedy? Mayor Harrison, of Chicago, has caused to be published his opinion, because, mark you, your honor, this is all a matter of conjecture. It is only presumed that I threw the bomb. They have only assumed that some one of these men threw that bomb. It is only an inference that any of us had anything to do with it. It is not a fact, and it is not proven. It is merely an opinion. Your honor admits that we did not perpetrate the deed, or know who did it, but that we, by our speeches, instigated some one else to do so. Now, let us see the other side of this case. Mayor Harrison of Chicago, has caused to be published in the New York *World*, and which was copied in the *Tribune* of this city, this statement: "I do not believe that there was any intention on the part of Spies and those men to have bombs thrown at the Haymarket. If so, why was there but one thrown?

It was just as easy for them to throw a dozen or fifty, and to throw them in all parts of the city, as it was to have thrown one. And again, if it was intended to throw bombs that night the leaders would not have been there at all, in my opinion. Like commanders in chief, they would have been in a safe place. No, it cannot be shown that there was any intention on the part of these individuals to kill that particular man who was killed at that Haymarket meeting." Now, your honor, this is the Mayor of Chicago. He is a sensible man. He is in a position to know what he is talking about. He has first-rate opportunities to form an intelligent opinion, and his opinion is worthy of respect. He knows more about this thing than the jury that sat in this room, for he knows—I suspect that the Mayor knows—of some of the methods by which most of this so-called evidence and testimony was manufactured. I don't charge it, but possibly he has had some intimation of it, and if he has he knows more about this case and the merits of this case than did the jury who sat here. There is too much at stake to take anything for granted. Your Honor can't afford to do that.

Is it nothing to destroy the lives of seven men? Are the rights of the poor of no consequence? Is it nothing, that we should regard it so lightly, as a mere pastime? That is why I stand here at such length to present this case to you, that you may understand it; that you may have our side of this question as well as that of the prosecution. Now, this opinion of Mayor Harrison was based upon personal observation on the ground at the Haymarket meeting. Mark you, he was there, and this is his opinion, both as to the character of the speeches and the deportment both of the speakers and of the audience, on the night of the 4th of May, in which opinion Inspector Bonfield himself concurred with the mayor: that it was a peaceable meeting, calling for no interference to within ten minutes of the unlawful order to disperse the same by the guardians of the peace and the preservers of order. Now, the two witnesses for the prosecution, who are they? Waller and Schroeder. Those were the state's informers, called "squealers," upon whom the State attempted to base the proof and charged the conspiracy against us. Have they made out a case on the testimony of these men? Let us take the evidence for a moment. These men were the first witnesses called, and they absolutely and completely negative the idea, and not alone the idea, but the fact itself, that the collision of the Haymarket was ever contemplated at that meeting, much less provided for by any perpetrator whatever. Now, that stands as a fact in the testimony here. It was not brought about by any person or by any individual, or by any member of the so-called armed group, and your honor won't claim that we have not a right to have an armed group. Your honor will not say it is unlawful to have an armed group if we want it. As I understand the law and the constitution, if we want an organized group we have the right to it. The constitution defines that treason against the government consists in the fact, only in the fact, of an overt act proven, indisputably proven, by at least two persons. This is what I, as an American, understood the constitution to mean. You say in your remarks upon the sentence that there can be no doubt but what this was an unlawful combination. Well, suppose it was. If I am a member of an unlawful combination, am I to be hung for that? Are seven men to be exterminated for that? Are there not surely some degrees in punishment? Because I belong to an unlawful combination am I to be put to death? Why, that would be cruel. That would be a verdict of hate. That would be a penalty of vengeance, not of justice, and it is not proven; it has not been alleged, even, nor has it been shown, that I was a member of an unlawful combination. That question has not been put in consideration in this court; it has not been here to be established by this jury whether or not I am now or ever was a member of an unlawful combination. Now, for proof of the charge to which I wish to call your honor's attention, that there was no conspiracy, and given out of the mouths of these witnesses of the State, I will cite the very words of the witness Waller himself. In reply to interrogatories by the State's attorney as to what was said at the meeting after he had called it to order, Waller said, "It was said that these men had been killed at McCormick's," referring to the strikers killed by the police the day before.

Engel brought forward a resolution at the April meeting, and what did Engel say? He said that if through the fall of the strikers the other men should come into conflict with the police, we should aid them. He then told us that the northwestern group had resolved to bring aid to these men; that if, on account of this work, something should happen to the police; we must assemble at the corners. What else did Engel say? He said that if tumults occurred in the city, then we should meet in Wicker Park. If the word should appear in the paper, that the northwestern group and the Lehr-und Wehr-Verein should assemble in the park with arms. After Engel said this, a committee was appointed to watch the movements in the city and report to us if a riot should occur.

Now then, take into consideration this language. Just consider the situation. Look at the attitude of these capitalist papers for years toward the workingmen; and not only that, but the actual use of these armed hirelings at East St. Louis, at Saginaw, at Pittsburg, all over the country, and at McCormick's the day before. Look at the condition of affairs, and I ask you if these men were not justified in making some preparation by which they could defend themselves, because there is no proposition here to assault anybody. There is no proposition here to make war upon anybody, either their persons or their property:

Q. "Now, was anything said about having a meeting of workingmen the next day?"

A. "Yes, sir; I proposed that a meeting should be held the next afternoon, but that was rejected. It was decided to have a meeting in the evening, as more could come then."

Q. "Who proposed calling a meeting in the evening?"

A. "Fischer. He proposed having one at the Haymarket and it was finally resolved to call the meeting at 8 o'clock."

Q. "Was anything said as to what should be done at that meeting?"

A. "It was intended to cheer up the workmen so that if anything should happen they should be prepared for a conflict. It was decided to call this meeting by means of hand-bills. The getting up of this was entrusted to Fischer, but he did not say where they should be printed. It was decided that as a body we should not participate in the Haymarket meeting, but should meet at halls. While only a committee should be at the Haymarket, if the committee reported that something happened, we should attack the police where it was arranged for each group to do so; if necessary, in addition to the police, we would attack the militia and fire department."

Now, then, in the first part of this it says that in the case of the police coming upon the strikers, shooting the strikers down, destroying them, interfering with the people, interfering unlawfully, interfering with the right of the people to assemble, interfering with the right of the people to express their views, mark you, it was said in such a contingency they would defend themselves. Now, these men here upon the stand, Schroeder and Waller who were giving the testimony, used the word "attack." When it was translated "attack," you must not take that as the literal meaning of these men. It was defense. They meant by this word defense. If it had been literally translated as these men meant it, and as the spirit of the testimony shows, the word would not have been "attack," but would have been defense. In every instance the whole preparation and proof about it shows that it was for defense. What could they attack? What can a handful of men attack? There was only a handful of men there at best. What can they attack? Who can they attack? What could they capture? What could they take? Wouldn't it be ridiculous for them to undertake to attack the city of Chicago, to attack the authorities, to undertake to seize the city? Why, that would be nonsense. It would be ridiculous. Upon the very face of it, it is an absurdity. It was for defense. They said that it was for defense, and for no other purpose, in the event that the police invaded the meetings of workingmen and unlawfully—as Judge McAllister had told the workingmen of the city, that the police of Chicago could not lawfully invade their meetings, and break them up—Judge McAllister had told us this in his decision. We believed that that was what the law was. We believed that we had the constitutional right to assemble. Now, why shouldn't we protect ourselves in such a contingency?

In this connection right here [Judge Gary indicated his impatience]—please bear with me for a few minutes. In 1877—to show you what the police will do, and what they will do unlawfully—they broke down the doors; they entered the hall at West Twelfth street Turner Hall, where the Furniture Workers' Union was in session considering the eight hour movement just as we were at the Haymarket that night, and the question of wages. They broke into that hall. They drove the people out of that hall with club and pistol, and fired among them, and they killed one of the people in that hall, and

Judge McAllister, upon the trial afterward declared that that was an outrageous assault, that it was cruel, bloody murder, and that if every single policeman—and there were about twenty-five or thirty who went into that establishment—Judge McAllister said that if every policeman, if every single one of them had been killed on the spot, no one could have been harmed for doing it. This was the decision of the Judge; that has stood as the law. These things had been done in Chicago. The police swept down through the lumber yards at McCormick's the day before. Those things were done all over the country and through the city to put down strikes everywhere. Now, where is the crime in our having said that we would, if no other remedy or redress was left us, that we would follow the law laid down by Judge McAllister and use our right, our constitutional right, our legal right to defend ourselves?

Well, now, mark you, this Schroeder and this Waller were witnesses for the State; they were what is called "squealers," and they were men—now, don't forget this point—these men were telling their story under a great bribe. What was that bribe? Liberty and life, two of the greatest and sweetest things known to man. Life and liberty were offered to Schroeder and Waller. Was it from the fact that they were given money, as was testified to by both of them, and uncontradicted by the prosecution? Aside from that fact, life and liberty were given to these men if they would tell a story that would fit a theory and carry out a certain line of the prosecution to bring about a certain verdict. They gave that kind of testimony. You will remember that Seliger's wife upon the stand testified that these men were kept by Captain Schaack in the station, under durance vile, and herself also, until both Seliger and Waller were compelled, under intimidation to sign four different statements in writing; that is an uncontradictable statement. Consider the condition under which these men gave this testimony, and even with all that, they only testify that the meeting was for the purpose of defense, and not for any action at the Haymarket meeting, and had nothing to do with the Haymarket meeting, had no connection with the Haymarket meeting. This is the statement of the witnesses for the State on the part of the conspirators, so-called. On cross-examination the question was asked: "Well, didn't Engel say in reference to the plan of action agreed upon by the armed group on Monday night and on Sunday that it was to be carried out in case the police should interfere with your right of free speech and free assemblage?" "If the police should attack us, yes."

That this plan was to be followed only when the police would—I believe Captain Black asked this question—"would by brutal force interfere with your right of free assemblage and free speech?"

A. "It was said that we would use or resort to this plan or the execution of it whenever the police should attack us."

Now, listen to that, your honor. Up here, you understand, in one part of this testimony it is said we got ready to attack the police, and down here on the cross-examination it shows that the witness himself meant that we should defend ourselves—not attack the police. It was an absurdity—perfectly absurd—to talk about a handful of men attacking the authorities of this city. What if they got the city of Chicago, wouldn't it be a white elephant? What, in the name of common sense, could they do with it? It reminds me of some people who are afraid that if the world should be made free and the workingmen should come into their liberty that they would steal the world and run off with it. What would they do with it if they did? It is an absurd proposition. Now, the statement of these men under cross-examination shows what their intention was, and they used the word "defense," whereas, in the direct examination, and by the translation of the district attorney, they are made in English to use the word "attack":

Q. "You say that nothing was said at the Monday night meeting with reference to an action to be taken by you at the Haymarket?"

A. "We said we would do nothing there; we were not to do anything at the Haymarket."

Q. "Was it not the plan that you should not be there at all?"

A. "Yes, sir."

These are the state's witnesses upon which they propose to show and prove a conspiracy against us, your Honor.

Q. "And you also say that you did not anticipate that the policemen would come to the Haymarket?"

A. "No, we did not think the police would come to the Haymarket."

Q. "For this reason no preparations were made for meeting any police attack on the Haymarket square?"

A. "Not by them."

Q. "Was it not the sole purpose of the meeting at the Haymarket to protest against the action of the police in the shooting of the workingmen at McCormick's factory?"

A. "Yes, sir."

This was the testimony of the state's witness, Waller.

Mr. Schroeder, another witness upon whom the state rested to prove there was a concerted plot to entrap and destroy the police swore: "Lingg was not present. We talked about the condition of the workingmen, and the remark was made that the members of the northwestern group should go to Wicker Park in case the police should make an attack on them"—you understand, your Honor, police can make attacks. Judge McAllister says that they can make unlawful and unconstitutional attacks. Now, shall it be held by you that the police, like the kings of old, can do no wrong, because forsooth, there happens to be here upon this trial eight poor men, eight workingmen, eight men without money or friends? Are we to be offered up and immolated as a sacrifice upon the altar of Mammon to satisfy the vindictive hatred and greed of the monopolists of this city? For that is the sum total of what it amounts to, your honor.

Q. "How should they defend themselves? Was anything said about dynamite?"

A. "No; as well as anyone could, if anyone had anything with him."

Q. "How long were you at Greif's Hall on that Monday night previous to the Haymarket meeting?" (This is Schroeder.)

A. "Three quarters of an hour."

Q. "What was discussed there?"

A. "If the police made an attack upon the workmen"—now, your honor, keep this in mind;the prosecution has tried to make out that there was a meeting held; that there was a conspiracy entered into, and that it was resolved upon to attack the police. Their own witnesses here, their own testimony, shows that there was nothing of the kind intended—"if the police made an attack upon the workmen they would help the workmen to help themselves."

Q. "Was anything said about bombs?"

A. "No."

Q. "At any of the meetings?"

A. "No; not while I was present."

Q. "Well, while you were present at the Monday night meeting they talked about how they would help the workmen defend themselves?"

A. "Yes, sir."

Q. "And nothing was said about throwing bombs on Monday night, or at any other time?"

A. "No."

Q. "Was it not talked about throwing bombs at the Haymarket meeting?"

A. "No; not while I was there."

Q. "Then it was talked about throwing dynamite to destroy the police at the next meeting at the Haymarket?"

A. "There was nothing said about it while I was there."

Q. "You went to the Haymarket meeting?"

A. "Yes, sir: I was in a saloon when the bomb exploded."

Q. "Did you go there with any dynamite in your pocket?"

A. "I don't what dynamite is; don't know dynamite."

Q. "Did you know there would be trouble at that meeting?"

A. "Well, I know that much, that when the police should attack the workingmen that each one should help themselves as best they could."

Q. "At the time you left the meeting, the meeting was quiet and peaceable?"

A. "Yes."

And this is the testimony, your honor, which was relied upon to prove a conspiracy on my part. Now, I did not belong to this meeting; I did not know that there was such a meeting. In fact, I was not in Chicago. I was in Ohio and the meeting was conducted in German; I cannot speak German; I do not understand it. I never saw Schroeder or Waller in my life until I saw them on the witness stand here. Lingg, the first time I ever saw him in my life was when I came into this court room and surrendered for trial, and saw him sitting in the prisoner's box. Why, your honor, it is ridiculous. It is an absurdity; it is a misconception of the whole situation and conjunction of circumstances in connection with this whole affair when I was away from the city, and this is a sentence passed upon me for being connected with a conspiracy which, the prosecution claims, was organized for the purpose and resulted in the death of Mathias Degan at the Haymarket Square on the 4th of May.

Referring again to the informer Waller's testimony; the State's attorney is reported by the *Herald* of July 17 as saying after the adjournment: "This man's testimony is going to convict the prisoners"; that is, Waller. How preposterous! The two informers disclosed no fact that bore the semblance of a conspiracy, which in law is an agreement to do a criminal act. Now, I was not there. I did not know anything about it. I do not speak German. I do not know these men. I never saw them before. I don't know who the men were at the meeting. The only man that I know that is connected with this matter, I believe, is Engel; him I have met before, I don't know whether he was at the meeting or not. I did not know anything about it. I did not know there was such a meeting. I never requested it to be called. Now, the State's attorney says that this man's testimony is the thread upon which he proposed to connect me with this conspiracy to do an unlawful thing, which resulted in the death of Mathias Degan at the Haymarket on the 4th of May. How preposterous! These informers disclose no fact that bears the semblance of a conspiracy, but on the contrary, their testimony simply revealed a noble and a fraternal and a patriotic purpose; that—quoting the language of Schroeder himself—"if the police made an attack upon the workingmen unlawfully again, they would help the workingmen to resist it, or to defend themselves." Waller testified in chief, and reiterated it in cross-examination, that Engel and Fischer, these noble and brave Germans, offered a resolution at Greif's Hall, on the announcement that six men had been wantonly and brutally murdered by the police at McCormick's that if other men should come into encounter with the police we should aid them, and further swore that this plan was to be followed only when the police, by brutal force, should interfere with the workman's right of free assemblage and free speech.

Now, then, where is the foul and dastardly criminal conspiracy here? Where is it? So preposterous was it on its face to call such a noble compact to do a lawful thing a conspiracy, that it became necessary, in face of a dozen witnesses, both for the prosecution and the defense, to swear that the bomb came from the pavement on Desplaines street, south of the alley, between the alley and Randolph street, a statement made by Bonfield himself to reporters about half an hour after the tragedy occurred, and published in the *Times* on May 5, the following morning—Louis Haas, Bonfield's special detective on the ground, at the Coroner's inquest, swore the bomb was thrown from the east side of Desplaines street and about fifteen feet, he believed, south of the alley, a statement confirmed by the witness Burnett, for the defense, who located it fifteen feet even further south than Haas or Bonfield did—still, on the impeached testimony of Gilmer, who swore the bomb was thrown from within the alley, we are convicted, because he was also willing to perjure himself by swearing that Spies lit the fuse of the fatal missile. The idea of a man striking a match in an alley to light a bomb in the midst of a crowd, the people and police standing all around him! It seems to me that such a statement as that ought to, among sensible men, on the face of it, carry its own refutation. Perfectly absurd! If this statement bore the semblance of truth with regard to Gilmer, or was the truth, not one of these defendants would shrink from the responsibility of the right of self-defense, your honor, and of free speech, and the right of the people peaceably to assemble. It is because this is not the work of the Anarchists or of the workingmen, that we repel the charge, which proves there was no concerted action, and that it was none of the plans of these groups. It is not unlawful to repel an invasion of our meetings. In the case of the People vs. Miller the learned Judge McAllister expounded the law of Illinois under which the people had the right to assemble at the Haymarket. He said they were entitled to be as free from molestation as in our castle and our homes. We were not obstructing traffic on the highway. As there is no travel thereon at night there was and can be no pretense on that score, because the Mayor of the city of Chicago was present and did not interfere, and, in fact, directed the Inspector of Police, after 10 o'clock, that there was no occasion for police interference. He, therefore, as the sole judge, under the law, recognized that assemblage not only as a lawful assemblage, but more, a peaceful assemblage, within the law and the constitution of both the State and the Federal government, and entitled to the protection of both, which we have here and now claimed in vain, as this court refuses in this instance, or has up to this time, to enforce this right of the people. For these reasons I ask the suspension of your sentence, for the reasons that have been stated here; that there was no conspiracy; that it was an organization for defense; that the meeting was peaceable; that it was a lawful meeting; as the Mayor of the city of Chicago declared it upon the stand to be, and as Bonfield and Haas both said, the morning after the Haymarket tragedy, that the bomb did not come from the alley, but south of it. I ask your honor to suspend your judgment and give us innocent men a chance, in a new trial, to prove these facts beyond any question. The meeting, your honor, was sacred from intrusion or trespass—as sacred as a man's home, which is his castle; even more, for an assemblage of the people is the primary seat of action on their part, of all authority on their part in a republic, and is guarded by the first amendment to the constitution of the United States from any abridgment, as it is also by the constitution of the State of Illinois, now violated by this unconstitutional verdict. You have read the decision of Judge McAllister in this case; I have it here. It would consume time before this court to read it, and I will just submit it. Your honor has read it, of course, and I will not take up your time with the reading of it. I offer it, however, as a part of the statement that I wish to make in connection with our view of our defense, and our appeal to you for a new trial in this case.

Now, then, I want to call your attention to what I regard as the origin of this bomb at the Haymarket. I believe it was instigated by Eastern monopolists to produce public sentiment against popular movements, especially the eight-hour movement then pending, and that some of the Pinkerton's were their tools to execute the plan. To sustain this accusation, I submit to you the following facts: Just exactly four days before the grand strike for eight hours throughout the United States, and only one week before the Haymarket tragedy, the New York *Times*, one of the leading organs of railroad, bank, coal, telegraph and telephone monopoly, published the following notice, under date of April 25, 1886, in an editorial on the condition of the market and the causes of the existing decline and the panicky symptoms which existed. The New York *Times* says: "The strike question is, of course, the dominant one, and is disagreeable in a variety of ways. A short and easy way to settle it is urged in some quarters, which is to indict for conspiracy every man who strikes and summarily lock him up. This method would undoubtedly strike a wholesome terror into the hearts of the working classes. Another way suggested is to pick out the leaders and make such an example of them as would scare others into submission." This was the 25th of April, an editorial in the New York *Times*, written in view of the contemplated strike on the 1st of May for eight hours. The New York *Tribune*, now no longer the oracle of the great American tribune, Horace Greeley, that defender of oppressed humanity, but the servile organ of the most oppressive forms of monopoly, said just about this time in an editorial: "The best policy would be to drive workingmen into open mutiny against the law." The New York *Herald*, at the date suggested by its contemporaries to make examples of the leaders in the short hour movement, said: "Two hours taken from ten hours of labor throughout the United States by the proposed short hour movement would make a difference annually of hundreds of millions in value, both to the capital invested in industries and to existing stock." The issue of the hour, then, with the New York and Chicago Stock Exchanges and Board of Trade and Produce Exchanges was how to preserve the steadiness of the market and maintain the fictitious values then and there rapidly falling under the paralyzing influence of the simultaneous eight-hour demand throughout the United States.

Your honor, so common is this impression among people, so common is this belief among the labor organizations and workingmen of this country, that I wish to impress upon you the view which I present. I am a member of the Knights of Labor, that is an organization of nearly a million American workingmen. I am a member of my union, the Printers' Union, and have been for fourteen years in the city of Chicago. This is a national and international organization with some sixty odd thousand members in the United States. These organizations publish a great many newspapers in America, and every single one of them believe that that bomb at the Haymarket was instigated by the monopolists to break down the eight-hour movement. Hear our side. You have heard the Citizens' Association's side of this question, you have heard the bankers' side, you have heard the railway magnates' side, you have heard the Board of Trade's side; I ask you now to listen also to the side of the workers. I might read you here extract after extract from these papers to show you that what I state is true. I will read you one among the many I have. The *Knights of Labor*, a paper printed in the city of Chicago by the Knights of Labor, says: "It would seem that Pinkerton's detective agency has contracted to carry out this policy, and to at least make the public believe that workingmen are rebels against the law. It may not be long until people will see that those detective gangs, instead of being gangs of peace, are really the agencies of monopolists to trump up charges and produce public sentiment against the popular movements of the people." Now, on this subject, a paper printed at Marinette, Wis., the Marinette *Eagle*, says: "The blowing up of the street cars in St. Louis by dynamite during the strike there last summer was directly traceable to Pinkerton's agents, who put up the job. Gould's officials once tore down and destroyed a telegraph pole, and the satanic press made but a feeble remonstrance while the perpetrators of the dastardly act were never prosecuted, and yet the wage earners are called Anarchists." As I said before, I could quote and take up a great deal of time in quoting and reading the sentiments of anti-monopoly, greenback, labor, Knights of Labor, Trade Union and Socialist newspapers, holding the monopolists responsible for this act in the United States. I will not take up your time, but I will call your attention in this connection to one thing.

In the strike down here at East St. Louis last summer, where the railroad companies called for "men of grit," and advertised to pay men of grit "that meant business" five dollars a day, they got a lot of men, and these men fired upon people that were walking along peaceably on a railroad track in East St. Louis, and killed seven men and one woman. Those men were in the pay of this pool of railways. The grand jury of St. Louis refused to indict those men even, you understand, refused even to indict them; and they were sent home with pay and honor. But here in Chicago a mass-meeting of workingmen occurs, and at that meeting there is a bomb thrown; some men are killed. The deed is fastened upon the men who spoke at that meeting, and they are made responsible for it, and they are brought in here and railroaded through in double-quick time to the scaffold, and, your honor, will you now refuse to give us a chance to have this matter heard fairly, to give us a chance in a new trial? The charge made by the labor papers that the monopolists were at the bottom of the Haymarket tragedy, and that the Pinkertons were employed to carry it out, supplies the key to the solution of the mystery as to who did throw that bomb, for it has not been proven upon one of these defendants, without contradicting the history of that night, as given by Bonfield to the *Times* reporter, and also by Lieutenant Haas, Whiting, Allen, the reporter, and seven witnesses, all told, for the State, and Burnett, Taylor and Simonson, and a number of witnesses, for the defense. That is all the thread that connects it. Now, who will believe his silly story that one of these men or myself had any knowledge of the party who hurled the deadly bomb on its awful mission of death? It rests on Gilmer's testimony alone.

The New York *Times* of April 27 urged as an easy way to settle the eight-hour movement to pick out the leaders and make such an example of them as to scare the others into submission. The wicked cabal of monopolists, with an organ capable of making such an utterance and giving such atrocious advice, is capable of putting it into execution, and force was to be used if blood flowed and the innocent perished. The McCormick difficulty of the day before, where unarmed working people were attacked by the police, transpired within five days of this threat in the east. Stocks went down. The great commercial stock centers were convulsed with apprehensions of a swift decline in values if the eight-hour strike succeeded. The wheels of industry remained paralyzed by the thousands of laborers who were out making the strike in favor of the eight-hour movement. Something must be done to stop this movement, and it was felt that its strongest impulse was at the west, where forty thousand men were on a strike for eight hours in the city of Chicago, and in order to make such an example of them—to quote the language of the *Times*—as to scare the others into submission, I repeat, that the men in New York, capable of making such a suggestion, are capable of carrying it out, of putting it into execution. Now, isn't that a fair presumption? Was it not worth hundreds of millions of dollars to them annually to have it done? Pinkerton's agency, in my opinion, contracted to carry it out; they have done such things on previous occasions. Often before have they done such things; it has been proven on them on numerous parallel cases of conspiracy to bring odium upon popular movements in all parts of the country, and I read to you that official circular of Pinkerton's offering himself to monopolists who wanted just such conspirators and schemes as were laid down by the *Herald* of New York, and the *Times*, *Tribune* and other papers. The Pinkertons, in their circular addressed to these monopolists, said they had the men ready; they were prepared to furnish the information, and they could build up and provide a conspiracy that would break down any contemplated effort on the part of men to receive better pay or an improvement in their condition. That is Pinkerton's own circular. He would carry out that which he proposes to carry out. He offers himself for sale to do that kind of work; he openly declares in the circular that that is his business; that he makes his living and his money by that occupation.

Nor are we wanting in the clear links of circumstantial evidence to point to the culprits who will yet call upon the rocks to hide them from the wrath of an outraged people. There is in the possession of this court in this case on file the sworn testimony of John Philip DeLuce of Indianapolis, a saloon keeper, whose story was printed in the papers at the time he first made it public, in May of this year. He swears that at 7 o'clock one morning in May, this year, an unknown man wearing a mustache, dressed in dark clothes, five feet five or five feet six inches in height, came to his place, and setting a small satchel on the bar, asked for a drink. Taking a drink, the customer said he came from New York, was on his way to Chicago, and the stranger closed with the remark that the saloon keeper would shortly hear of trouble in Chicago. Pointing to his satchel he said: "I have got something in there that will work; you will hear of it." Turning at the door as he departed, he held up his satchel, and, pointing at it, remarked: "You will hear of it soon." Shortly after this episode the news of the Haymarket tragedy reached DeLuce. The deponent appeals to a certain Oscar Smith as a witness to this conversation, and Smith follows with an affidavit to the truth of this statement; that was away back in May. Now, if this is to be a case of conjecture, if this is to be a case of opinion, I submit if that man's testimony is not as worthy of the consideration of this court as is the testimony of Harry Gilmer. Or, if your honor still assumes that we instigated some one else to hurl the bomb, I submit if the threats of the monopolist papers, and the proposals of Pinkerton to carry it out, do not show that some mercenary in their employ performed the deed resulting in the Haymarket tragedy. The Pinkerton force advertises to carry on this kind of work. Pinkerton advertises in his circular that he is ready to do this kind of a job. The New York *Herald* and New York *Times* say the market is going down in consequence of the contemplated strike on the first of May, and say that the leaders must be arrested and thrust into prison, and thus terrify the others into submission by making examples of the leaders. This is what the *Times* says; this is what Pinkerton says. About this time some one, as testified to by two reputable witnesses, stopped at Indianapolis; that was in May; the Haymarket tragedy was the fourth. This man testifies to that fact. A stranger stops there. He says: "I am going to Chicago. I have something that will work. You will hear from it." The man was in his cups, no doubt; probably he drank too much. The Pinkertons are not all temperance men; they sometimes take a little, and sometimes possibly take a little too much; possibly he talked a little more than he ought to have talked; possibly he didn't care, but at any rate it is sworn to that he said it; he came to Chicago, and the bomb was heard from and heard around the world. Your honor, is this an unreasonable assumption? It is far more likely, much more reasonable than your honor's surmise that I instigated some one to do it. Is this not within the possibility of human events? Might this not be the case? Is it proven your honor, incontestibly and uncontrovertibly, that it was not done by this man, that it was not done by a Pinkerton? Is it proven beyond any possibility of a doubt that I and some of these men here threw that bomb, or knew of its being thrown? It is not established. The testimony does not show it.

These squealers for the State, Waller and Schroeder, both state that this meeting was for defense, that it had no reference to the Haymarket, had nothing to do with it; they were not even to go there; there was no difficulty expected there. These are the State's own witnesses and against the testimony of Gilmer, that Spies lit the bomb, which is ridiculous in itself, absurd, the very idea of such thing. Mr. Bonfield and Lieutenant Haas said that the bomb was thrown south of the alley about fifteen feet, and Burnett comes upon the stand—a man who is unimpeached—and swears that he stood by the man who did throw the bomb, and saw him light and throw it. All this against Gilmer, the affidavit of DeLuce, and the statements of the witnesses on the part of the prosecution. I submit that we, for this reason are entitled, and have a right to stand here and claim a new hearing before you. I am told that it is a statement from the prefecture of the Paris police, that the police themselves instigate troubles often to bring about certain results. In police circles such persons are known as procurators or provocatives. I don't know whether this is true or not. You are a judge and a court; you are familiar with these things. Now, this description of the stranger dressed in dark clothes, and not tall in height, exactly corresponds with Burnett's description of the man he saw, both light and hurl the bomb, and Burnett stood there. You remember it; Burnett was standing right about here when he testified; he said that he was standing by the side of the man and saw the man light the bomb, and hurl it in that direction. It tallies with the man sworn to here by John Philip DeLuce, the man called for by the New York *Times*, *Herald* and *Tribune*, by implication at least, that this thing must be stopped. Pinkerton comes out in a circular and offers to do this kind of work. It is the hand of the police. Now, is it anything beyond human reason that these men could not carry out that which they said they were ready to do—to do that which they themselves claimed it would be worth to them millions to do? I am not putting statements in their mouths. They stated here that they were ready to do such work, perhaps they may have overdone the work; perhaps they killed more men than they intended to kill; perhaps that may be true. Perhaps they did not intend that it should be so great a sacrifice as it was; but I will continue with reference to this; Burnett's description of the identical man he saw both light and hurl the bomb thirty-five feet south of the alley, show that the prediction of the stranger from Chicago, "You will hear from it," was verified within twenty-four hours, because it was not a dynamite, but an infernal bomb, of which this stranger boasted in his cups when pointing to the satchel and saying, "I have something in here that will work; you will hear of it; you will shortly hear of trouble in Chicago," speaking of the pending troubles in this city.

Within twenty-four hours after this incident at Indianapolis, as sworn to before this court, the something in that satchel was heard from, and its detonation is still ringing in the ears of a startled world. The day following, the 5th of May, the *Daily News*, of Chicago, published the first description in print of the man who threw the bomb, from one who swore he was neither a Socialist, an Anarchist, nor a Communist, but a mere idle and curious spectator at the meeting. The *News* said on May 5th: "The police have a good description of the man who threw the bomb at the Anarchists' meeting last night. The fellow stood in front of John Burnett, a candy maker in the employ of Mr. Berry, at the corner of Washington and Sangamon streets, and was seen by him to throw the missile of death. The atrocious murderer was a young man, a little above medium height, and well dressed. He was seen to take the bomb from his pocket and light it just as the police drew near. Burnett said he stood within two feet of the man, and would certainly be able to identify him should he meet him again. Hardly a moment elapsed after the bomb was lighted until the man lifted his arm preparatory to casting it from him. Every detail of this performance was witnessed by Burnett, who did not know what to make of the strange action. Presently the fuse attached to the bomb commenced to burn, and then, for the first time, Burnett realized what was about to happen. The man, with a quick jerk of his arm, sent the bomb flying through the air, and the next instant turned to run. Burnett attempted to follow, but a stray bullet struck him in the arm and he fell to the sidewalk. When he got up all was confusion. The foregoing is the substance of the story told the reporter this morning. Detectives were sent out to hunt for Burnett, but they were unable to find him."

Your honor, this was the fifth day of May, the day following the Haymarket affair. Mr. Burnett was found and repeated the above facts to the District Attorney, reaffirming the statement to which he subsequently swore in court for the defense, that the strange man stood thirty-five feet south of the alley; that he saw him light the fuse and then throw the bomb; that he wore dark clothes; and it was proven on trial that Rudolph Schnaubelt, the man Gilmer implicated, wore light clothes that night, and this Pinkerton man had a mustache and no chin or side whiskers, while Schnaubelt, the Anarchist had both; and he was a man of medium size, whereas Schnaubelt is noted for his great height; he is six feet two inches. The district attorney had to stultify his own witnesses by the unsupported, manufactured, perjured evidence of Gilmer, because for forty pieces of silver, he was willing to swear that Spies lit the fuse while another man threw the bomb—a very tall man in height, in light clothes, with a light or sandy beard. Gilmer swore that when Fielden was speaking he was looking for a party he expected to find there, "and I went back in the alley between the Crane building and the building on the south of it. I stopped in the alley and noticed some parties in conversation across the alley on the south side. Some one said: 'Here come the police.' There was a man who jumped from the wagon down to the parties somewhere standing on the south side of the alley, and lit a match and touched off something or other, and the man gave a couple of steps forward and tossed it over into the street." Side by side with this, we give the precise words of Mr. Bonfield, as published in the Chicago *Times* of May 5, to a knot of reporters gathered around him at the station house half an hour after the tragedy occurred. He is reported in the *Times* of May 5 to have said: "The exact scene of the explosion is near the center of the street and exactly opposite the alley on the east side which separates No. 9 South Desplaines street from Crane Brothers' foundry. At intervals between this alley and Randolph street there are large, heavy, box-like frames at the edge of the sidewalk, and it is here that the bomb was thrown." Lieutenant Haas located the spot there also, as some fifteen feet south of the alley, not in the alley, as Gilmer would have it. Yes, the prediction of the Indianapolis stranger was verified. The bomb was heard from, and heard around the world. The purpose avowed in the New York city papers to pick out the labor leaders and make such examples of them as to scare the others into submission, was put into successful execution, and well was the diabolical and nefarious plot executed.

Eight men—"leaders"—three labor editors and five labor organizers and orators—now before you, are here to receive sentence of death in pursuance of that vile plot, of which the Haymarket tragedy, in the hands of a Pinkerton detective, was the entering wedge; and Gilmer's testimony is but a part of a scheme to divert attention from the evidence of twelve witnesses, exclusive of Bonfield's, to the *Times* reporter, that the infernal machine was hurled from fifteen to thirty-five feet south of the alley, just where the short man in dark clothes actually stood when the angel of death was sped on its infernal mission, not only to sacrifice purposely the lives of the policemen on the ground, but that the labor leaders might be arrested and doomed to death under a charge of the commission of the offense, in order, as avowed by the New York *Times*, the agent and representative of the falling stock markets of the East, to scare the other workingmen into submission and frighten them back into the acceptance of the ten hour plan.

Your honor, if you please, I would like to take a short recess. I am much fatigued. I have a few more words to say, and I will finish them this afternoon.

The Court—I had intended not to have but one session of the court today; there has been now two hours and three-quarters this morning and an hour yesterday, three hours and three-quarters of time spent upon that which, as the speaker and the auditors know, has had very little to do with the question that is before me, and it does not seem to me that I ought to have repeated sessions of court in listening to repetitions from newspapers, etc., which never could be used upon any trial, never could have been, and never can be. I would very much prefer to finish up the matter. I shall not restrict you as to time.

Mr. Parsons—I will say, your honor, I am now in the midst of that part of my statement which refers more directly to the Haymarket matter.

The Court—Go on, and say all that you wish to say.

[It was plain to be seen, however, that the speaker was physically unable to "go on."]

Mr. Parsons—The absolute proof that the missile thrown was not dynamite, but what was known in the late civil war as an infernal bomb, is in the evidence of every surgeon who testified that all incisions were clean, and that the flesh was torn as from an explosive in the interior. It was testified by these scientific men, your honor, that dynamite is percussive, and had a shell the size of Lingg's manufacture, on exhibition in evidence, been thrown in the closed ranks of the police, as was this infernal machine, instead of killing but one on the spot, and wounding a few others, it would have blown to unrecognizable fragments the platoons in the vicinity, and the wounds, where there were wounds, would have been as clean as with solid projectiles.

This was an infernal bomb from New York, brought there by the Indianapolis traveler, and not a dynamite bomb, the description in its effects upon its victims, exactly corresponding with the description of those explosives, when once used in battle on the Potomac. The hollow bullets within the shell, after entering the victim, exploded, lacerating the flesh and inflicting ugly internal and really infernal wounds.

But, dynamite is an explosive which annihilates its victims. All experiment and experience demonstrates that fact. The State of Illinois, to convict any man for using a dynamite bomb at the Haymarket, must show that it was dynamite; because the absolutely necessary link to connect these defendants with the explosion (and especially Lingg, whom they charge, and are going to hang, for merely its supposed manufacture by him), is the proof that it was a dynamite bomb, and not an infernal machine, as they were called in war times. The positive proof that it was not such a bomb as Lingg made, lies in the fact that but one man was killed outright, and others being merely wounded, though the bomb fell between two close platoons of heavily massed men.

Mark, sir, dynamite is an explosive which annihilates its victims. A pound displaces the air within a radius of one thousand feet. The adjacent platoon would have been blown, as we have already said, into unrecognizable atoms, had it been a Lingg dynamite bomb. I cite the case of France, and Doran, and Berrige, at Warren, Pennsylvania. In each case the singular characteristic of their death, is the fact of the complete annihilation of matter, especially of the human body. Beside human, the iron frames of wagons, and even ponderous nitroglycerine safes, have been removed from human vision as effectually as if they had never been formed.

This is not merely circumstantial evidence. It is proof positive that it was not a dynamite bomb, such as the alleged conspirators distributed at the Monday night meeting of the armed group, which did not attend the Haymarket, Lingg himself being absent some miles distant. It is confirmation strong as proof of Holy Writ that the agency used to destroy our lives and the eight hour movement was a New York infernal machine.

Six of these condemned men were not even present at the Haymarket meeting when the tragedy occurred. One of them was five miles away at the Deering Harvester Works in Lake View, addressing a mass-meeting of 2,000 workingmen. Another was at home in bed and knew not of the meeting being held at all until the next day. These facts, your honor, stand uncontradicted before this court. Only one witness—Gilmer—and his testimony is overwhelmingly impeached, as I remarked before—connected the other two—two only—of these men with the tragedy at the Haymarket at all.

Now, with these facts, the attempt to make out a case of conspiracy against us is a contemptible farce. What were the facts testified to by the two so-called informers? They said that two of these defendants were present at the so-called conspiracy meeting Monday night. What then have you done with the other six men who were not members-who were not present, and did not know of the meeting being held Monday night? These two so-called informers testified that at the so-called conspiracy meeting of May 3, it was resolved that in the future, when police and militia should attack and club and kill workingmen at their meetings, then, and then only, they were in duty bound to help defend these working people against such unlawful, unrighteous, and outrageous assaults. That was all that was said or done. Was that a conspiracy? If it was, your honor, it was a conspiracy to do right and oppose what is wrong.

But your sentence says that it is criminal for the workingmen to resolve to defend their lives and their liberties and their happiness against brutal, bloody and unlawful assaults of the police and militia.

Look at this jury for a moment, observe the material of which it was composed. There was Juryman Todd; when he was accepted on the jury he described himself as a clothing salesman, and a Baptist. As soon as the verdict had been rendered he was, of course, interviewed. He said:

"This was a picked jury; they were all gentlemen. You see Major Cole, who was the first juror accepted, and myself took the other jurors in hand as soon as they were accepted." Major Cole, you will remember, described himself as a bookkeeper, and an Episcopalian. Todd, in his interview, went on to tell how, notwithstanding their virtuous professions, when they went into the jury room they played cards; they also played the fiddle and guitar and piano, and sang songs. In fact, these gentlemen had a very merry time of it while engaged in the trial of the seven Anarchists for their lives, and they had to bring a verdict as becomes gentlemen, of course. What with songs, music, carriage drives and high life at a fashionable hotel, parlor theatricals in the evening, these twelve gentlemen managed to kill their time, an finally returned a verdict to kill these abominable seven Anarchists, these workingmen, whose lives, of course, were beneath the serious consideration of the elegant gentlemen—these nice gentlemen.

Before the trial began, during its prosecution, and since its close, a satanic press has shrieked and howled itself wild like ravenous hyenas for the blood of these eight workingmen. Now this subsidized press, in the pay of monopoly and of labor enslavers, commanded this court and commanded this jury and this prosecution to convict us.

As a fitting climax to this damnable conspiracy against our lives and liberty, what follows? [The speaker raised his arms and pointing his fingers to the statute of the blind "Goddess of Justice" over the judge's stand.] Oh! hide your eyes now; hide them! hide them! It is well that your eyes are bandaged and your vision obscured, for could you have witnessed, the corruption and infamy practiced in your name during this trial, you would have fled from this temple forever! As a fitting climax to this damnable conspiracy against our lives and liberty, some of Chicago's millionaires proposed to raise a purse of $100,000 and present it to the jury for their verdict of guilty against us. This was done, as everybody knows, in the last days of the trial, and since the verdict, so far as anybody knows to the contrary, this blood money has been paid over to that jury; besides, these jurymen, since the rendition of their verdict, have been feted. They have been wined, and dined, and banqueted, and costly gifts have been bestowed upon them with a lavish hand by the enemies of human rights and human equality. "Oh! shame, where is thy blush! Oh, virtue, hast thou fled to brutish beasts!"

No man was permitted to serve on this jury who was tainted with the slightest sympathy for the working class in their struggles against monopoly. But to every one of the 1,139 men, who were summoned as jurors by the State's attorney, the State's attorney put this question: "Are you a member of a trade and labor union? Are you a member of the Knights of Labor? Have you any sympathy with Communists, Anarchists, and Socialists?" And every one who answered in the affirmative was summarily told that he was excused. Only five such persons out of 1,200 jurymen who were summoned were among the list: I mean there were only five workingmen of the 1,200 called. The deputy sheriff, Mr. Rice—I believe that is his name—it has been sworn to in our plea for a new trial, your honor, that he summoned this jury, and the affidavit is on file before you that Deputy Sheriff Rice, who had charge of the summoning of those jurymen, declared he would summon those who would hang us to death. Such infamy is unparalleled.

The jury was a packed one; the jury was composed of men who arrogate to themselves the right to dictate and rob the wage workers whom they regard as their hired men; they regard workingmen as their inferiors and not "gentlemen." Thus a jury was obtained, whose business it was to convict us of Anarchy whether they found any proof of murder or not. The whole trial was conducted to condemn Anarchy. "Anarchy is on trial," said Mr. Ingham. "Hang these eight men and save our institutions," shouted Grinnell; "these are the leaders; make examples of them," yelled the prosecution in addressing the court and jury. Yes, we are Anarchists, and for this, your honor, we stand condemned. Can it be that men are to suffer death for their opinions? "These eight defendants," said the State's attorney to the jury, "were picked out and indicted by the grand jury. They are no more guilty than are the thousands who follow them. They were picked out because they were leaders." "Convict them and our society is safe," shouted the prosecution. And this in America, the land for which our fathers fought and freely shed their blood that we, their posterity, might enjoy the right of free speech, free press, and unmolested assemblage.

This diabolical conspiracy against man's inalienable rights, finds its best portrayal in the words of State's Attorney Grinnell, himself one of the chief actors in this gigantic crime. At the conclusion of the trial he was interviewed by the agent of the Associated Press, who sent out a full report, from which I quote as follows:

"Do you propose to go ahead at once and bring other leaders of Anarchy to the halter?" Mr. Grinnell replied: "We intend to leave the Anarchists alone for a time, and see whether they have now learned what the right of free speech means in this country, and whether they still hold it to mean that they may incite men to riot, murder, and plunder. But I will say this: We have had in this trial men who were called 'squealers' and 'informers,' three or four of them. From these men we have obtained the names of all the principal Anarchists in Chicago. We have them on the list, and the Anarchists don't know it. I want them to know it now; I want them to know that they are marked men, and if ever a hand is raised to injure a hair of the heads of any juror or person connected with the trial that is now over, every Anarchist might as well consider that his death knell is sounded. We have their names and will bring every one of them to the gallows. Let them understand that."

I suppose your honor has attended the opera bouffe called "The Mikado." You will recollect that the lord high executioner of the Mikado of Japan, like Grinnell, had them all on the list. Grinnell proposes to continue to perpetrate acts which Mayor Harrison says could not be done in any monarchical country with safety, and which, if done in London, would shake Queen Victoria's throne itself. Mr. Grinnell proposes to keep this racket up, to continue it *ad infinitum*. This man, clothed with a little brief authority, spreads himself like a green-bay tree and gasconades with the fulsomeness of an autocrat. He would with the mailed hand of power silence the people's discontent and preserve law and order with silence of the graveyard and the order that reigned in Warsaw. At the behoof of this petty usurper the *Alarm*, the paper of which I was an editor, was seized and suppressed. This man seized it; he destroyed the files and the documents connected with the office. He did the same with the German workingman's daily paper, the *Arbeiter-Zeitung*, and for several weeks, yes, several weeks, this man compelled its publishers and its editors to submit their editorials to him for his press censorship, his running his blue pencil through such articles as his majesty Grinnell saw fit to interdict.

In an interview concerning this matter, published in the Chicago papers, Grinnell said: "Very rigid measures will be adopted toward the *Arbeiter-Zeitung*. Any reference to alleged bribery of the jury or other incendiary utterances will cause its instant suppression. We are going to see this matter clear through."

Thus the men who are selected to enforce the law and who are sworn and paid to obey it and enforce it trample the law and the constitution under their feet at the behest of a few rich men when they find it convenient to punish the poor. Thus the blasphemous conspiracy against free speech, free press and public assemblage was concocted, engineered and consummated.

In the effort of the prosecution to hold up our opinions to public execration they lost sight of the charge of murder. Disloyalty to their class, and their boasted civilization is in their eyes a far greater crime than murder. Anarchy, in the language of Grinnell, is simply a compound of robbery, incendiarism and murder. Now, your honor, this is the official statement of Mr. Grinnell, and against his definition of Anarchy I would put that of Mr. Webster. I think that is pretty near as good authority as that gentleman's.

What is Anarchy? What is the nature of the dreadful thing—this Anarchy, for the holding of which this man says we ought to suffer death? The closing hours of this trial, yes, for five days the representatives of a privileged, usurped power and of despotism sought to belie, misrepresent, and vilify the doctrine in which I believe. Now, your honor, let me speak of that for a moment. What is Anarchy? What are its doctrines—

General Parsons—For which you are called upon to die.

Mr. Parsons—For which I am called upon to die. First and foremost, it is our opinion, or the opinion of an Anarchist, that government is despotism; government is an organization of oppression, and law, statute law is its agent. Anarchy is anti-government, anti-rulers, anti-dictators, anti-bosses and drivers. Anarchy is the negation of force; the elimination of all authority in social affairs; it is the denial of the right of domination of one man over another. It is the diffusion of rights, of power, of duties, equally and freely among all the people. But Anarchy, your honor, like many other words, is defined by Webster's dictionary as having two meanings. In one place it is defined to mean, "without rulers or governors." In another place it is defined to mean, "disorder and confusion." Now, this latter meaning is what we call "capitalistic Anarchy," such as is now witnessed in all portions of the world and especially in this court room; the former, which means without rulers, is what we denominate Communistic Anarchy, which will be ushered in with the social revolution.

Socialism is a term which covers the whole range of human progress and advancement. Socialism is defined by Webster—I think I have a right to speak of this matter, because I am tried here as a Socialist. I am condemned as a Socialist, and it has been of Socialism that my friend Grinnell and these men had so much to say, and I think it right to speak before the country, and be heard in my own behalf, at least. If you are going to put me to death, then let the people know what it is for.

Socialism is defined by Webster as "a theory of society which advocates a more precise, more orderly, and more harmonious arrangement of the social relations of mankind that has hitherto prevailed." Therefore everything in the line of progress, in civilization in fact, is Socialistic. There are two distinct phases of socialism in the labor movement throughout the world today. One is known as Anarchism, without political government or authority, the other is known as State Socialism or paternalism, or governmental control of everything. The State Socialist seeks to ameliorate and emancipate the wage laborers by means of law, by legislative enactments.

The State Socialists demand the right to choose their own rulers. Anarchists would have neither rulers nor lawmakers of any kind. The Anarchists seek the same ends by the abrogation of law, by the abolition of all government, leaving the people free to unite or disunite, as fancy or interest may dictate, coercing no one, driving no party.

Now, your honor, we are supported in this position by a very distinguished man indeed, no less a man than Buckle, the author of "The History of Civilization." He states that there have been two opposing elements to the progress of civilization of man. The first of these two is the Church; the Church which commands what a man shall believe. And the other is the State, which commands him what to do. Now, sir, Buckle says that the only good laws passed in the last three or four hundred years have been laws that repealed other laws. That is the view exactly of Anarchists. Our belief is that all these laws should be repealed, and that is the only good legislation that could possibly take place.

Now, law is license, and consequently despotic. A legal enactment is simply something which authorizes somebody to do something to somebody else or for somebody else that he could not do were it not for the statute. Now, then, the statute is the divestment and the denial of the right of another, and we hold that to be wrong; we consider that the invasion of a man's natural right. Mark you, we do not object to all laws; the law which is in accordance with nature is good. The constitution of the United States, when it guarantees me the right of free speech, a free press, and of unmolested assemblage, and the right of self-defense, is good, because it sanctions it. Why? Because it is in conformity with natural law. It don't require any statute law to provide such a safeguard as that; that is inalienable, and it is a natural right, inherited by the very fact of my existence, and the mere fact that it is embraced in the constitution does not make it any more sacred at all. On the contrary it shows how foolish it is to do by constitution that which kind mother Nature has already freely and graciously done for us. The more we are governed the less we are free. I do not believe your honor will deny that.

The law-abiding citizen, especially if he is called upon to do something under a law that enslaves him, is an uncomplaining slave to the power that governs him. Imagine a chattel slave down south who was law-abiding, who was obedient; what does that mean? That means he did not have any objection; he did not have anything to say against the law that makes him another man's slave. Now, the workingman today in this country who says nothing, who makes no objection to any of these enactments, with no protest to make at all against these infamous things that are practiced by legislation, that workingman is a law-abiding, obedient workingman. He is a nice, quiet, peaceful, genteel citizen.

Anarchists are not that kind. We object to those laws. Now, whether the government consists of one over the million, or a million over one, an Anarchist is opposed to the rule of majorities as well as minorities. If a man has a right he has a right, whether that right is denied by a million or by one. Right is right, and the majority that sets itself up to dictate to minorities, simply transform itself into tyrants; they become usurpers; they deny the natural right of their fellow-men. Now, sir, this will put an end to the law factory business. What would become of your law makers? Why, a human law maker, your honor, in my humble judgment, is a human humbug. Yes, sir, just think of these law factories that we have throughout the country, the legislatures of our States and the Union, where they manufacture laws just as we go to a factory to manufacture a pair of boots! Why, your honor, the same pair of boots won't fit every man; how can you make a law that will apply to the individual cases of each one?

Now, your honor, I suppose that you would hold, like they did in the days of old—I don't know whether you will or not, but there are some men who would hold—that a man who would adhere to this kind of opinions ought to die; that this world has got no use for him. Well, that remains to be seen.

The natural and the imprescriptible right of all is the right of each to control oneself. Anarchy is a free society where there is no concentrated or centralized power, no State, no king, no emperor, no ruler, no president, no magistrate, no potentate of any character whatever. Law is the enslaving power of man. Blackstone defines the law to be a rule of action. I believe that is it. Colonel Foster, I would like to ask your opinion if that quotation is correct? Blackstone describes the law to be a rule of action, prescribing what is right and prohibiting what is wrong. Very true. Now, Anarchists hold that it is wrong for one person to prescribe what is the right action for another person, and then compel that person to obey that rule. Therefore, right action consists in each person attending to his business and allowing everybody else to do likewise. Whoever prescribes a rule of action for another to obey is a tyrant, a usurper, and an enemy of liberty. This is precisely what every statute does. Anarchy is the natural law, instead of the man made statute, and gives men leaders in the place of drivers and bosses. All political law, statute and common, gets its right to operate from the statute; therefore all political law is statute law. A statute law is a written scheme by which cunning takes advantage of the unsuspecting, and provides the inducement to do so, and protects the one who does it. In other words, a statute is the science of rascality or the law of usurpation. If a few sharks rob mankind of all the earth, turn them all out of house and home, make them ragged slaves and beggars, and freeze and starve them to death, still they are expected to obey the statute because it is sacred. This ridiculous nonsense that human laws are sacred and that if they are not respected and continued we cannot prosper, is the stupidest and most criminal nightmare of the age. Statutes are the last and greatest curse of man, and when destroyed the world will be free. The statute book is a book of laws by which one class of people can safely trespass upon another. Without this book one person would never dare to trespass upon the rights of another. Every statute law is always used to oppose some natural law. (I am reading a few extracts from an editorial in the *Alarm*). A statute is always used to oppose some natural law, or to sustain some other equally vicious statute. The statute is the great science of rascality by which some few trample upon and enslave the many. There are natural laws provided for every work of man. Natural laws for self-operating. They punish all who violate them, and reward all who obey them. They can not be repealed, amended, dodged, or bribed and it costs neither time, money, nor attention to apply them. It is time to stop legislating against them. We want to obey laws, not men, not the tricks of men. Statutes are human tricks. The law—the statute law—is the coward's weapon; the tool of the thief, and more: the shield and buckler of every gigantic villainy, and frightful parent of all crimes. Every great robbery that was ever perpetrated upon a people has been by virtue of and in the name of law. By this tool of thieves the great mass of the people who inhabit our planet have been robbed of their equal right to the use of the soil and of all other natural opportunities. In the name of this monster (statute law) large sections of our race have been bought and sold as chattels; by it the vast majority of the human race are today held in the industrial bondage of wage-slavery, and in its name our fair earth has been times without number deluged in human blood. By the instrumentality of this tool, cowards and thieves, tyrants and usurpers are robbing their fellows of their substance, despoiling them of their natural rights, and depriving them of liberty. Man's legal rights are everywhere in collision with man's natural rights; hence the deep-rooted and widespread unrest of modern civilization. The only sacred right of property is the natural right of the workingman to the product, which is the creation of his labor. The legal right of the capitalist to rent and interest and profit is the absolute denial of the natural right of labor. Free access to the means of production is the natural right of every man able and willing to work. It is the legal right of the capitalist to refuse such access to labor, and to take from the laborer all the wealth he creates over and above a bare subsistence for allowing him the privilege of working.

A laborer has the natural right to life, and as life is impossible without the means of production the equal right to life involves an equal right to the means of production. The legal right of the capitalist is virtually the assertion that one man has a greater right to life than another man, since it denies the equality of natural conditions. Our present social system, therefore, is based upon the legalization of robbery, slavery, and murder. The laborer who does not get more than a bare subsistence as the fruit of his toil is robbed. The laborer who is forced to beg for work and has to accept it on any terms or starve is a slave. The laborer who, being unable to get work, but who in turn has too much manhood to beg, steal, or become a pauper, is by the refined process of slow starvation murdered.

Laws—just laws—natural laws—are not made, they are discovered; law enacting is an insult to divine intelligence; and law enforcing is the impeachment of God's integrity and his power. I make, as an Anarchist, this declaration for the benefit of our Christian ministry, who, while professing loyalty to God's laws, never forget to pray and work for the supremacy of man's laws and man's government—those pious frauds who profess their faith in the "power" of God, while they employ the police, the militia, and other armed hirelings to enforce their man-made laws and maintain their "power" over their fellow-men. Oh, consistency, indeed thou art a jewel! These hypocrites always did, and do today, employ brute force to compel their fellow-men to obey and serve them, while they whine and snivel behind their sanctimonious masks about their "love of man and the power of God." I hope some of them will preach in their pulpits next Sunday morning on this topic.

The economic regulates and controls the social status of man; the mode and manner of procuring our livelihood affects our whole life; the all-pervading cause is economic, not political, moral, or religious, and social institutions of every kind and degree result from, grow out of, and are created by the economic or industrial regulations of society. Every human being, consciously or unconsciously, is affected and controlled by it in what they think, or say or do. There is no escape; no evasion from its consequences. It is logic. It is cause and effect. Evil exists on every hand; the well-disposed, philanthropic, and generous, and the good seek relief from these evil influences by moral suasion, by self-denial, by religion, by politics, etc., etc, but in vain, in vain! The evils remain, and not only remain, but grow worse and worse. Why, if the fountain is corrupt, can the stream be pure? If the cause remains, must not the effects follow? Jails, judges, and executioners, police, armies and navies, pestilence, misery and ignorance and debauchery, and evils of all kinds of high and low degree, all flow from one fountain; that flowing fountain of human woe is the economic or industrial subjection and enslavement of man to man. Every human ill is produced by the denial or the violation of man's natural rights or by the neglect or refusal of man to conform his life to the requirements of nature. Wickedness, wretchedness, ignorance, vice, crime, poverty are the penalties which nature inflicts upon her disobedient children. The natural man is a happy man. He is virtuous and right; truly so. Whoever violates the right of another, sooner or later punishes himself. Nature is inexorable. From her penalty there is no escape. But in a court of law—of so-called "justice"—if you are a member of the Citizens' Association, or if you have a big bank account, in other words, if you are a member of the propertied class, you crawl out of anything you want to, for law is for sale; that is to say, whoever can purchase the lawyers, stock the jury and bribe the court, can win. There is only one law for the poor—to wit: Obey the rich.

The existing economic system has placed on the market for sale man's natural rights. What are these rights? Well, among the many I will enumerate one or two. The right to live, for instance, is an inalienable right. So too, is the right to liberty and the pursuit of happiness. Now, how can I possess these rights and enjoy them, when the very condition and the means for their procurement is owned by and belong to another?

Shakespeare makes Shylock say at the bar of the Venetian court, "You do take my life when you take the means whereby I live." Now, the means of life are monopolized; the necessary means for the existence of all has been appropriated and monopolized by a few. The land, the implements of production and communication, the resources of life are now held as private property, and its owners exact tribute from the propertyless. In this way the privileged class become millionaires. They deny the equal right of every one to freely use our natural inheritance, the earth. The denial of that right is death to whom it is denied. The right to live is made a privilege by law, granted by law, which is granted or denied by the possessor to the dispossessed. Human rights are for sale. "If thou wilt not work, neither shalt thou eat," says the Scriptures. This finds immunity among those who can pay for it. Those who work eat not; and those who eat work not. They do not have to; they hire some hungry, poor devil to do the work for them. The hired man whom the capitalist press gloats on the idea of, and whom the pious frauds declare is the dispensation of divine providence, whom we will always have among us as a social fungus, the outgrowth of a rotten, corrupt industrial regime.

In conclusion I will say, compulsion is slavery, and those disinherited of their natural rights must hire out and serve and obey the oppressing class or starve. There is no other alternative. Some things are priceless, chief among which is life and liberty. A freeman is not for sale or hire.

You accuse the Anarchists of using or advising the use of force; it is false. "Out of your own mouth you stand condemned." The present existing state of society is based upon and maintained by and perpetuated by force. This capitalistic system that we have today would not exist twenty-four hours if it were not held together by the bayonets and the clubs of the militia and police. No, sir, it would not! Now, sir, we object to this. We protest against it. But you accuse us, or the prosecution here accuses us, of that very thing which they themselves are guilty of. It is the old, old story of Aesop's fable, the lamb standing in the water and the wolf above him; he looks up; the water has run down, the wolf stands above him; he looks down there toward the lamb, and says, "Ho, there! you are making the water muddy." The lamb observes, "My friend, I am below you in the stream." "That don't matter; you are my meat, anyhow." And he goes for him and eats him up. That is just the way of the capitalist toward the Anarchist. You are doing the very thing you accuse us of, and against which we protest. Now, any institution that is based upon force is self-condemned; it does not need any argument, in my opinion, to prove it.

The political economy that prevails was written to justify the taking of something for nothing; it was written to hide the blushes of the rich when they look into the faces of the poor. These are they who brand Anarchy as a compound of "incendiarism, robbery and murder"; these are they who despoil the people; they who love power and hate equality; they who dominate, degrade and exploit their fellow-men, they who employ brute force, violence and wholesale murder, to perpetuate and maintain their privileges.

On July 14, Juryman Hamill took his seat in the box here, and the question was asked him:

Q. "Do you believe in Socialism, Anarchism or Communism?"

A. "Some of the principles I believe in."

Lawyer Ingham will remember the juryman said that.

Q. "Do you believe in capital punishment, or hanging for murder?"

A. "I do not."

Q. "Do you believe in self-defense?"

A. "Yes, sir."

Q. "Then, don't you believe that society has a right to protect itself?"

A. "Not to take life."

Challenged for cause by Mr. Ingham.

Now, you see that this is positive proof that the capitalistic system is upheld by force, is perpetuated by force. Lawyer Ingham calls it in a generic term, society. What do you mean by "society?" What is "society?" Why, a wage worker is no part of society, except to build the palaces for the fellows who run society, to live in, and furnish them with fine clothes and nice wines, with luxury and ease, and so on. They—the workers—are no more part of that society than the slave was of the plantation in the south. They are part of the society as the mud-sills who do the work, but have no part of the benefits. That is the society to which my friend Ingham refers.

Now, we do not want to obey—we Anarchists; we do not want to obey this society—this generic society. What is Vanderbilt, Gould, Mr. Phil Armour, and a lot of that kind? They are the parasites, the leeches, who take all and cry for more. That is society. That constitutes the present society. Now, we do not like those fellows; we do not want to obey them. We do not want to serve them; we do not want to be slaves to them, and by golly, they are going to take our lives because we do not want to obey them; because we are Anarchists, for Anarchy simply means disobedience. Now is that not infamous—is that not ridiculous? The present society is the slavery of labor.

Now, every juryman was asked these questions by, I believe, Mr. Grinnell—or Mr. Ingham—one or the other:

"Do you believe in the enforcement of the law?"

"Do you believe that society has a right to protect itself by law?"

"Have you any sympathy for any person or class whose object is the overthrow of the law, or whose object is to overthrow law and government by violence?"

Now, your honor, what is government but violence? What is it? Force. The last resort of every law is force. They have in reserve, always in reserve, you understand, the police and the militia, always; as long as nobody questions the law, of course, nothing is said about the club or the bayonet. But let a strike take place; let the working class object to overwork, starvation wages, or compulsory idleness, then out come the police, the militia, and the Pinkerton army to preserve "law and order," to force, to drive the workers into submission, and "protect" society. Thus labor is enslaved by law. Oh, you sly rogues! Oh, you sly fellows! Why it is you who cause the workingman—especially if he is an Anarchist like me—to occupy this position. He is damned if he does, and he is damned if he doesn't. So it is tweedle-dee and tweedle-dum, whichever position you take with these gentlemen upon that question.

Now, Juryman Ames, on July 8, said he was a hat and cap merchant. He took a seat in the box. In reply to the question whether he held any prejudice against Anarchists, Communists, and Socialists, he said: "Well, my early education and bringing-up is entirely against anything of this kind."

State's Attorney Grinnell then rose and objected to asking jurors as to their prejudice against Anarchy, Communism, and Socialism. You see Mr. Grinnell thought if he could only get that man—that kind of a fellow—on the jury, wouldn't it be a fine thing? He don't want that kind of a man asked the question. A fellow that was against all this sort of stuff and this kind of thing—he knew that that kind of a man would be solid for hanging a man that held such ideas. I suppose that was his idea; I don't know what else he could have objected for. Mr. Grinnell said in that connection: "This is a charge of murder. This question of Anarchy is here too much." You remember this, gentlemen. "We are here to try these men for murder, and not because they are Anarchists." This was the second day of the trial, mind you. That was Mr. Grinnell; but he was careful to ask every one of the jurymen if they had any sympathy, to ask them if they were in favor of the labor movement; if they were members of a labor union; if they were members of a trades union—he was very particular to find that out—and in arguing the case before the jury he and his assistants finally declared that Anarchy was on trial, and that was the thing we must be convicted of.

H. E. Graves was a railroad superintendent.

Q. "Are you opposed to labor unions or prejudiced against members of labor organizations?"

A. "I am; I am opposed to labor organizations of any and all descriptions."

Judge Gary inquired of him as follows:

Q. "You believe in individualism—that is, every one, whether a capitalist or a laborer, acting for himself, do you—you are opposed to combination?"

A. "Yes, sir."

Attorney Foster—"Do you believe in railroad pools?"

A. "Yes, sir."

He was laughed out of the court room. Now, Judge Gary, in his questions to this man, teaches us individualism. Now, that is Anarchy, pure and simple.

The Court—Do you take that from any short-hand report?

Mr. Parsons—Yes sir.

Mr. Foster—That is true, so far as the answer of the witness is concerned.

The Court—It don't sound like anything that I would say.

Mr. Parsons—Do you believe in individualism: everyone, whether capitalist or laborer, acting for himself; do you? Your honor, I took that down at the time you said it. I did not take it from the short hand reports.

The Court—I don't care. Go on.

Mr. Foster—What I have reference to is what the juror answered.

The Court—My own language is cited there. I don't remember it now, but it is of no consequence. Go on.

Mr. Parsons—If every one acted for himself, as the judge says, that would be liberty. And liberty is the end of authority, of government and of statute laws.

July 13.—Juryman Reed, a State street music dealer. Attorney Ingham says: "If the prisoners are guilty you want them convicted; and if they are innocent, you want them acquitted, do you not?" Then, "can't you listen to the testimony fairly and impartially and decide whether they are guilty or innocent?"

Juryman Reed said:

A. "When they do not teach a doctrine that undermines the law, that don't break the law, then there is no objection to the labor organizations. There could not be any. I have a prejudice against any man who seeks to undermine the social and political laws of the country. I am a Freethinker."

Now, this man condemned us to death, because we seek to

undermine the social and political laws of the country. He is a Freethinker; we accepted him for that reason, because we thought that, as he claimed the right of free thought on religious matters, he would certainly be consistent and give us the right of free thought on political and social questions. But alas! Juryman Reed is a Boston man. That is the country where they used to burn witches and condemn religious heretics to death. The right to free thought has been acquired after a century of bloodshed and struggle, and now, because we, the Anarchists, are social and political heretics, he strangles us on the gibbet. Juryman Reed concedes the right of free thought while he denies us the right of free action. What is one worth without the other? What a mockery to say to the slave, "you are free to think you ought to be free, but you have no right to be free." To compel me to work and to suffer for your benefit, and then console me with the assurance that I am free to think what I please about it, is the very mockery of liberty. This is the fruit of authority, of force, of government. Juror Reed would have been hung one hundred years ago. He hangs me today. Do you wonder that I am an Anarchist?

I will read from the *Alarm* an article headed "White Slaves—The Bitter Cry of the Poor Working Girls—A True Picture of Civilization Under the Infamies of Capitalism—Life, Liberty, and Happiness in America—Facts for Fathers and Mothers to Consider." Then follows a two-column article in the New York *Evening Telegram*, a capitalistic newspaper, descriptive of the life of the sewing girls in New York city—American girls—the future mothers of American citizens. I will not take up the time of the court in reading it in full. I will read a short extract as follows:

"It must be confessed that the outlook for labor in all its branches of industry is most discouraging, and revives the idea of that terrible story in Blackwood, where a prison of iron has been so constructed as to gradually contract until it becomes an iron shroud that crushes the prisoner within to a shapeless pulp. Labor is encircled by an iron shroud made of two factions, the tendency of capital to concentrate itself in few hands and the undeniable fact that the number of laborers will always increase in greater ratio than the amount of employment for them. These items alone would, if not counteracted by some system that is vital, reduce the working class in time to a condition far worse than slavery. In fact, slavery has been in all past ages the one remedy for the overpowering woes of labor, but a remedy that undermined and ruined each civilization in its turn. In the meantime, it is to be hoped that the women of America will take up the cause of their sex and publicly denounce the monsters who propose to young girls to work sixty hours a week for less than will feed and clothe them. Young as is the American nationality, it stands front to front today with the wonderful problem of civilization. The cause of the striking girls at Wallack's shirt factory is not only the cause of womanhood throughout the world; it is also the entering wedge for the great problem, 'What are rights of labor?' It must be obvious to every senator and congressman and to every dabbler in political economy that life is not worth living when honest girls cannot support themselves by sixty hours of intense labor. It is idle to prate about the great laws of supply and demand in the face of this present fact that an honest girl, who works ceaselessly throughout the week, has not enough wages to pay for her board and clothes. In America we change conditions and right wrong by inquiry. In Europe a social revolution is brewing, however, before which the great revolution of France will pale."

I merely quote this article in order to show that class of people who are crying out that our grievances are imaginary—that these grievances are facts—not imaginary.

Well, now, I come to consider our city of Chicago. Take the management of the political affairs of the city, your honor. They are noted for their political corruption.

Take these policemen—now I do not abuse the policemen; the policeman is a workingman the same as I am. Now, a man's standing on the police force, it is notorious, depends entirely upon his ability and his willingness to club, and club often—hit everything that comes along and drag it in. The policemen have to get their positions through the aldermen. It is notorious that they have to use corrupt methods to do it, and when a man is once on the force, imagine how subject he is to his higher officials. Whatever his superior hands him to do he must do. He must obey. He must do it or he will lose his job. I do not blame the police. It is not the individuals that I blame at all. I say here, as I said at the Haymarket—it is not individuals, it is not against the man, but it is against the system that produces these things that we contend. We object to that.

The charge is made that we are "foreigners," as though it were a crime to be born in some other country.

My ancestors came to this country a good while ago. My friend Neebe here is the descendant of a Pennsylvania Dutchman. He and I are the only two who had the fortune, or the misfortune, as some people may look at it—I don't know and I don't care—to be born in this country. My ancestors had a hand in drawing up and maintaining the Declaration of Independence. My great great grand-uncle lost a hand at the Battle of Bunker Hill. I had a great great grand-uncle with Washington at Brandywine, Monmouth and Valley Forge. I have been here long enough, I think, to have rights guaranteed, at least in the constitution of the country. I am also an internationalist.

My patriotism covers more than the boundary lines of a single state; the world is my country, all mankind my countrymen. That is what the emblem of the red flag signifies; it is the symbol of free, of emancipated labor. The workers are without a country. In all lands they are disinherited, and America is no exception. The wage-slaves are the dependent hirelings of the rich in every land. They are everywhere social pariahs without home or country. As they create all wealth, so also they fight every battle, not for themselves but for their masters. In the future labor will fight only in self defense and work for itself and not for another. Every government is a conspiracy to enslave the laborer.

Take the morality of the capitalistic system and look at it. In the morality of the capitalistic system, everything is for sale. Love, honor, liberty, everything for sale; everything has its price, under this modern system of commercialism; profit and loss; *meum et teum*, and this trains every man to be a liar and hypocrite. Men are taught to be hypocrites, to carry a mask on their face, to lie, to misrepresent everything. No man can be honest and succeed in business or make money. It is impossible. Honesty is punished with poverty, while dishonesty revels in every luxury.

Now, sir, is it fair to try a man by a class jury for disloyalty to that class? A verdict of guilty from such a source is a foregone conclusion. Do you call such a trial as that a fair, impartial, or unprejudiced trial?

Nonsense. I believe if there had been some workingmen on that jury they would have understood something about this question; they would have considered the matter quite differently. They would, at least, have given our side a fair chance.

The coal monopoly has been touched upon. Why, the capitalistic papers of Chicago say "strangle it." That is what Fielden said on the Haymarket. The trouble is that the moment this thing is touched you sling open the door of Socialism and in they pile pell-mell. It is no use talking. Three coal kings met in the parlor of a New York hotel—this was done last year—they advanced the price of coal, which is a free gift of nature to all her children as much as air and fire and water and mind are; it belongs to the people alone, as Socialism maintains and will consummate, even if this court should carry out and baptize in blood an attempt on the part of the people, peaceably and lawfully and constitutionally, to do and to accomplish this result. I say these coal monopolists advanced the rate of coal fifty cents a ton, the equivalent of an advance of $30,000,000 from the needy people of the United States.

But a few days ago the same coal monopoly met again and advanced the price of anthracite fifteen cents per ton, and by limiting the output they still farther advanced the price of what remains on their hands in the market, and practically put a tax for this prime necessity of life upon the people, west and east, and turned the hundred thousand miners out to freeze and starve.

Last year I was in the west. I was sent for by the Knights of Labor in Kansas on the 4th day of July, last July a year ago, to address them. While traveling that section I went throughout Kansas, Nebraska, Iowa, and Missouri, and among the places I visited were the coal mines. I went down into the mines. I saw the manner in which this coal business was carried on. They dig up the coal out of the ground; they bring it up to a place which they call the screening. There are several kinds of coal, three kinds, the lump, the nut, and the screenings. Now, the screenings is the portion of the coal which falls through a certain sifter, or sieve, and among it is the dust, little lumps of coal an inch and a half to three inches in diameter. This coal constitutes, the miners tell me, about one-fourth of a ton to each ton. Well, the miner receives nothing for that at all, he doesn't get a cent; it is not paid for. Last Fourth of July I witnessed these things traveling throughout the States, and when I returned home, I was hard up. I did not have money enough to buy a ton of coal at once. I had to buy my coal by the scuttle, and I paid 10 cents a scuttle for coal that winter, and the coal that I bought was this screening coal which the miners did not get a cent for. It cost me $9 a ton, and the miners did not get a cent for it. And yet there are people here who say that these grievances are imaginary, and that there is nothing in them.

Well, now, here is a nice thing to be read in this country, in this age. A man was interviewed the other day in the Chicago papers. His name was Lord Shastakoff, a minister of the Russian navy, traveling in America for his health. This minister, this master of the czar's council, met the reporters. He says: "Have you hanged your Nihilists?" referring to the condemned Anarchists. On being told that all were condemned and in prison, but they were not yet hanged, he expressed the hope that the execution would take place at an early day, and strongly discountenanced any delay in the matter. Talk about foreigners—you fellows that are talking about foreigners; I think that is a pretty good one. You are going to hang these men on this theory, because they are foreigners. Actually it was made a point to the jury—urged upon the jury by the State's attorney—that we were foreigners, and that we were hostile to the great and glorious institutions of our America. "They were not born here"; and they actually tried to make the jury believe that none of us were born here—that all of us were imported; and it did sway that jury; it did have its effect upon that jury. Now, here comes this fellow from the czar's dominions.

He says, "Gentlemen, that has been a good job; carry it out; don't give them any show at all."

Now, I denounce this thing. But you say we are revolutionists. Well, if we are, who made us such? Are not the labor exploiters, the monopolists, the mine, factory and workshop czars creating a revolution? They are the revolutionists.

I am only a "kicker." I object, I say "No! take your yoke off my neck, take it off, I will not have it on there," and they reply, "You stand still, now, and let me put in this coupling pin, and you'll carry that yoke well enough—if you don't I will have you carried off to the police station; if you make any noise about it, I will have you hung!" Sir, our execution will be a legal notification to the American workingmen to be warned by our fate that they must not expect to have any of their "imaginary" grievances, as it were, remedied or rectified.

Now, your honor, I have gone into this matter for the reason that you said that there was nothing in extenuation for these utterances and this kind of an organization. I believe you used language something like that. I have gone into this matter as extensively as I have for the purpose of showing that, if your honor was laboring under a misapprehension, I wanted to remove that misapprehension; that has been the object of what I have said or had to say outside of the matter or mere record of the trial. Now, before I conclude on this point of extenuation, I want to read an editorial in the Chicago *Daily News* of September 25. What is this? Is it October?*

General Parson—Yes, the 9th of October.

Mr. Parsons—Yes. It is concerning this workingman's movement: "The strong probability of Mr. George's election in New York has also a meaning for the so-called capitalistic class of this community. A brief summary of the inception and progress of the Anarchists' movement, which terminated at the Haymarket on the 4th of May last, will make this clear.

"Following the great railroad strikes of 1877 came the failures of savings banks; the unpunished defalcations of the trustees of the poor, and the enormous immigration, increasing competition for work and bringing with it a large element of the victims of Bismarck and of Bismarck's severity, soured with life and ready for desperate deeds. Under such inauspicious circumstances workingmen's parties were formed and tickets put in the field; some were captured, others disorganized, some fell into the hands of the Socialists, who found time to form a party which elected Frank Stauber to the city council from the fourteenth ward." I was a prominent actor, your honor, in all of this matter that has been related here in the *News*.

* [NOTE.—I was greatly exhausted from physical and mental exertions, having spoken two hours the day before and over four hours consecutively that day, the judge denying me a short respite at noon. At many times during the speech the judge had indicated his impatience by his actions and looks, to the discomfiture of the speaker. When I asked this question I felt my memory fail me.]

"Stauber was subsequently re-enforced by the election of Alpeter in the sixth ward and another one in the Fourteenth and Chris Mayer in the fifteenth, while the Socialistic labor candidates for the fifth and seventh wards were only defeated by a mere majority. Alpeter and Stauber and his colleagues refused all overtures from the ring which then as now controlled these politics. They were proof alike against bribery and intimidation and the party which they faithfully and honorably represented was becoming powerful and troublesome as an opponent to the ring. At the city election following, a flagrant violation of the ballot box was perpetrated in the sixth ward by 'Cabbage' Ryan, through which Alpeter was defrauded of a seat, and the offender was sheltered from punishment, his case being dismissed without a hearing in some manner. This was followed the next year by the breaking open of the box in the second precinct of the fourteenth ward, and the fraud and perjury by which Stauber was kept out of his seat for twenty-three months, fraud and perjury which were condoned by the courts. It was upon the same day and at the same election that Cullerton succeeded by a suspicious majority of not over twenty votes over a Socialist by the name of Bauman, and the council practically denied the contestant an opportunity to present his rights. One of these frauds was perpetrated in the interest of the Republican party, the other in the interest of the Democratic. The record needs no comment, but it is no small wonder that the party was driven from the field, unable to cope with the rascals of both the other parties."

Then he goes on to show that it was such things as this that brought about Anarchy and produced the Haymarket affair; brought that affair about—that is, he is assuming, your honor, that we, the men alleged, the men convicted by the jury, are guilty of that thing which we specifically now and here deny. But even if true, the editor of this *News* alleges, that there were extenuating circumstances: that there was some one else connected with the moral responsibility, even though we were personally guilty of the offense. Now, on the idea of extenuation, Mayor Harrison, about three weeks ago, was asked: "How do you like the verdict in the Anarchist case?" "Well, I don't care to talk about it. We have punished these people who violated the law, and now it remains for us to cure the disease." What does this mean, your honor? Why, that we are an effect; Mayor Harrison says we are an effect. Now it is a funny doctor that would go to work to cure the effect of a disease. You would never get rid of the disease, would you? You never would touch the cause. The mayor of the city of Chicago says we are the effect. I submit this here as an extenuating circumstance, and as a part of my plea for a new trial. The mayor said: "There is a wide discontent among the working people—there is no doubt about it; it can not be cured with bullets or policemen's clubs. We have got to remove the cause. That is the task that is before the thinking men, the law makers today. There is no doubt but that the working people have reason to be discontented all over the country. Legislation in the interest of the big corporations and the monopolies is the fact, and no law making for the laboring classes. That is what makes the laboring man discontented. You must change all that, and legislators must be elected who can not be bought by the corporations, or what will happen? The people will rise up in mobs, some day, and will have to be subdued with the bullet, and that would be the end of free government." Why, your honor, that is precisely what I have said a hundred, and perhaps a thousand times. That is all I have ever said—go and fetch Harrison—bring him here. He is as much legally guilty on those words as I am this afternoon. I offer that as showing that there are extenuating circumstances, even though we be guilty as charged, which we deny. Mayor Harrison says there is "wide discontent among the working people which can not be cured with bullets and policeman's clubs." Now, I want to ask this court if it thinks that that discontent can be cured by hanging us?

Take the governor of this State—Governor Oglesby. He made a speech not long ago on monopoly. He said that we stood upon a social volcano. What did he mean? If he had made that remark at the Haymarket he would be in this box here today, and turned over to the hangman. If he had happened to be at the Haymarket meeting and made that remark—if there had been a conjunction of circumstances which would have brought him to the Haymarket and had he been a workingman, such would have been his fate.

None of the men were ever arrested before, not one of us; and I never was arrested. I came to the court of my own accord. The other seven were never arrested before, never were drunk, never were disorderly. Sober, steady, industrious, intelligent, upright, honorable, decent workingmen; there is not a spot, a blemish, nor a single stain against any of the eight.

Now as to this Gilmer and Burnett matter. I, as a man here on trial wishing to know what your decision is to be with reference to my having a chance to prove my innocence, being convicted upon the testimony of a man like Gilmer, offered the man Burnett as an offset to Gilmer. He was unimpeached. No one questioned his veracity. He stood here as an honest man. Gilmer did not. The State's attorney, in his eagerness to produce this result—and, by the way, right here I want to say, it is no particular credit for the prosecution to bring about this verdict. All the rules of evidence and procedure were reversed on this trial. Instead of being considered innocent until our guilt was established, we have been held guilty unless we could establish our innocence. Why, the whole capitalistic press, the whole of the police, the bankers, millionaires, etc., everything was against these poor men. We had no money, influence, or friends. It was not difficult to bring that about at all, and if they did not have a case they could make one easily. That was an easy matter for them to do—a very, very easy thing for them to do. Now, Mr. Grinnell, he must have known that Gilmer's testimony was false. I don't know whether he did or not. But it seems to me he ought to have known it, because it was clearly demonstrated by the witness Burnett, who stood upon the stand, and whose testimony is unimpeached, that he called upon and had talks with Attorney Grinnell as early as May 6, and had a number of interviews with him for the express purpose of having him identify Schnaubelt's picture and fasten the deed upon Schnaubelt. Burnett refused to do that. He said: "No, no; that ain't the man. Besides, it was not that way. He was further down. It was not up at the alley." Now, Burnett's testimony contradicted every statement of Gilmer, and Burnett is unimpeached and Gilmer is impeached. If the district attorney knew of this fact, if he knew the fact that Burnett was an honest man, and called at his office and refused to identify Schnaubelt, your honor, did not the district attorney lend himself to a very bloody piece of work? I do not see how he is going to get clear of that. It may be he will, but it seems to me that if this verdict is to be carried out then our blood will be on his head for subornation of perjury. I may be mistaken, your honor; I do not impugn any man's motives. I don't know, but it seems to me it is the only construction which could be put upon this testimony.

Two witnesses, since this verdict was made, came forward voluntarily and made an affidavit that they had been in Gilmer's company the night of May 4, at another place, and that Gilmer was not at the Haymarket. Then Mr. Bonfield, the chief of detectives, who is Mr. Grinnell's right hand man—he takes these two men in his charge, and by bribery or intimidation, or by some other means, I don't know what, he induces them to retract their sworn statement. Wasn't that a scaly transaction, worthy of the villainy and corruption of the detective department?

Your honor, I have got what would take me an hour and a half, possibly two hours, at least, to say. I am used to an active, outdoor life, and until my incarceration here I have never been deprived of personal activity, and the close confinement in a gloomy cell—I only have about two hours and a half exercise each day, practically about two hours of the twenty-four—and of course it has deteriorated my physical system somewhat; and then, the long mental strain of this trial in addition to it. I thought if your honor could possibly give me a little rest for lunch, if we could adjourn until two o'clock—it is now one o'clock—I don't think I could get through under two hours. Still, if your honor insists, I am ready to proceed.

The Court—I do not think I am under any obligation to have repeated adjournments of the court for the purpose of listening to the reading of newspapers or disquisitious upon political economy, the question only being in this case, whether the defendants killed Matthias Degan. That is the only question in the case.

Mr. Parsons—Yes, sir; of course.

The Court—Not whether they did it with their own hands, but whether they set causes at work which did end in his death.

Mr. Parsons—Well, your honor, I am proposing to show you here that by a new trial, by a suspension of the judgment and sentence of death, we can establish our innocence; that is what I am proposing here to do; that is why I am offering this. You quoted our speeches and read many articles from our labor papers to prove that we "set causes at work which did end in his (Degan's) death." Now, sir, I am showing you by the very same kind of testimony taken from the speeches and newspapers of monopolists that they and not we "set causes at work which did end in his death." And, sir, I leave the world to judge if our testimony against them is not as strong or stronger than is your testimony against us. Of course it is not sworn to; it can not be. I can not get witnesses in here to swear to them. I can not swear to it myself; that is the purpose I have in view. But you did not have our speeches and newspaper articles sworn to. You took them for granted. Now, sir, against these I put the utterances and newspaper articles of the monopolists. Now, my long review of the labor question was made for the express purpose of having your honor understand the motives that were actuating us in this labor movement; that you might see that labor had grievances; that it had reasons for organizing; that it was not a matter of mere peevish discontent, as we are charged by some unthinking people, or that the grievances of the workingmen are imaginary, as alleged by those people who do not feel any interest in this matter.

In overruling the motion for a new trial, your honor used this language: "Whether these defendants, or any of them, did participate or expect the throwing of the bomb on the night of the 4th of May is not a question which I need to consider, because the instructions did not go upon that ground. The jury were not instructed to find them guilty if they believed that they participated in the throwing of the bomb, or encouraged or advised the throwing of that bomb, or had knowledge that it was to be thrown, or anything of that sort. The conviction has not gone upon the ground that they did have any actual participation in the act which caused the death of Degan, but upon the ground, under the instructions, that they had generally, by speech and print, advised a large class to commit murder, and had left the occasion, time and place to the individual will, whim and caprice of the individuals so advised; and that in consequence of that advice and in pursuance of it, and influenced by it, somebody not known did throw the bomb that caused Degan's death. Now, if that is not a correct principle of law, then the defendants are entitled to a new trial. This case is without precedent. There is no example in the law books of a case of this sort. No such occurrence has ever happened before in the history of the world."

Now, your honor, you, by these words, frankly admit that we have not been convicted for any act done, but simply because of speeches made and of opinions expressed. I am, therefore, showing you that that bomb was hurled by labor's enemies at the instigation of the monopolists, and not by us. Their speeches, their utterances, their newspapers openly counseled and advised by "speech and print" just such things. Did they not? Then are they not the guilty perpetrators? The question, to use your honor's language, is "not whether they did it with their own hands, but whether they (the monopolists) set causes at work which did end in the Haymarket tragedy?" By their own proposals I have shown you that they did.

Socialism, your honor, means the abolition of wage slavery, because it allows the people to carry on production and consumption by means of a system of universal co-operation. That is what I said at the Haymarket. I pointed out at the Haymarket the fact that the workingmen were being deprived, according to Colonel Wright, the commissioner of the Bureau of Labor Statistics of the United States. He proves by the statistics that they were producing values to the extent of $10 a day, and receiving $1.15; that they were deprived of $8.85. Now, I said to them: "Here," said I, "Socialism will give you that $8.85; under Socialism you would get that whole $10, whereas under the wage system you receive $1.15 of it. But that is not all: Socialism will make labor saving machinery a blessing instead of a curse to you; by it wealth will be increased, and drudgery diminished indefinitely. Socialism is simple justice, because wealth is a social, not an individual product, and its appropriation by a few members of society creates a privileged class—a class who monopolize all the benefits of society by enslaving the producing class." Now, your honor, this is what makes the monopolists mad at the Anarchists. This angers the corporation men. See what they say. The result is that a verdict must be brought against Socialism; because, as the district attorney states here, the law, and the government, and Anarchy are upon trial. That is the reason. Not for what I did, but it is for what I believe. It is what I say that these men object to. The verdict was against Socialism, as said by the Chicago *Times* the day after the verdict.

"In the opinion of many thoughtful men, the labor question has reached a point where blood-letting has become necessary," says the Chicago *Iron-Monger*.

"The execution of the death penalty upon the Socialist malefactors in Chicago will be in its effect the execution of the death penalty upon the Socialistic propaganda in this country.

"The verdict of death pronounced by a Chicago jury and court against these Socialist malefactors is the verdict of the American people against the crime called Socialism," says the Chicago *Times*. By the American people the *Times* means the monopolists.

In more familiar words, as used heretofore by the *Times*, "other workingmen will take warning from their fate, and learn a valuable lesson." The *Times* in 1878 advised that "hand grenades (bombs) should be thrown among the striking sailors," who were striving to obtain higher wages, "as by such treatment they would be taught a valuable lesson, and other strikers would take warning from their fate."

So it seems, "hand grenades for strikers," and "the gallows for Socialists," are recommended by the organ of monopoly, as a terror to both.

Socialism aims not at the lives of individuals but at the system which makes paupers and millionaires possible. Socialism aims at the death of no man nor the destruction of property, and the capitalistic press lies, and they know it, when they make such charges against Socialists. They lie about us in order to deceive the people; but the people will not be deceived much longer. No, they will not. The monopolist organs of our cities have advised hand grenades, strychnine, arsenic and lead instead of bread, for the unemployed and those seeking to better their condition, long enough. It is time for this to stop. When will it stop? In the sermon on the mount Christ said: "What man is there of you who, if his son shall ask him for bread, will give him a stone, or if he shall ask for fish will give him a serpent? All things, therefore, whatsoever ye would that men should do unto you, even so do ye even so unto them." It was, however, reserved for the close of the nineteenth century, of the

Christian era, in the city of Chicago, and by the editor and proprietor of the Chicago *Tribune*, to permit to be said, unrebuked, in his paper: "When a tramp"—an unemployed and starving laboring man—"asks you for bread put strychnine or arsenic on it and he will not trouble you any more, and others will keep out of the neighborhood." I suppose, your honor, this was said by a law-and-order pharisee.

This verdict, as it now stands, proclaims to the world that he who throws a bomb and kills a score of people is safe, while he who speaks or writes or works to organize labor and peaceably remove—because I deny the charge of any organization to attack anybody, the proof does not show it, nor sustain it, nor maintain it—to peaceably remove the cause of the people's discontent is in danger of dungeons and of the scaffold.

Every man called upon to act upon the jury, swore that he was an enemy to the labor movement, was prejudiced against the idea of Socialism or free labor. Not satisfied with such a jury, the enemies of free rights resorted to perjury and other inhuman acts to bring about a conviction. A few days ago, in an interview in the New York *World* and copied in the Chicago papers, Mayor Harrison said: "Right here I would like to say there has been the heartiest co-operation between Mr. Grinnell and myself from first to last, for without me he would never have been able to get certain evidence to obtain which I did that which, if it had been done in the city of London, would upset the throne of Victoria, that which could be done in no monarchical country with safety was done here; because in full sympathy with the people and as a servant of the people I did precisely what I knew the people wanted done and would sustain, something which, if wrong, they could easily rectify." Now, your honor, there were wrongs done here. The mayor says so. You can rectify them. Suspend your sentence. Give us a chance in a new trial. Now, here is the officer highest in the city, who frankly admits that he employed unlawful means in order to arrest us, because the people wanted him to do it. Has this court, has the States attorney and the police done the same thing in order to convict us? Mayor Harrison refers to the arrest of persons, the seizure of property, the searches of homes and places of business without warrant, and in admitted disregard of constitutional and legal guarantees of personal liberty and right, which was done by the city police immediately after the meeting of May 4, 1886. As proof of what he said, there followed that night in this city an era of official lawlessness in these respects, which according to Mayor Harrison, would not have been tolerated in any other civilized country in the world, and which if done in the city of London would have upset the throne of Victoria, and which the Mayor said could not have been done in any monarchical country with safety. The Mayor's confession is charmingly frank, and is significant. Is it then true that in this land, which boasts its liberty, private right can be more safely disregarded in obedience to public clamor than in any other civilized country? Is it true that the ruling, the moneyed class can set aside the law with impunity? Is it true that we are in an era when only property is sacred, and not the liberty or right of the common citizen; when the poor man may be arrested, or a hated minority hung with impunity, but to touch the institution of property is sacrilege? Is it true that the processes which resulted in this verdict were as illegal as those original proceedings against us were high-handed, unauthorized, and unconstitutional, as confessed by the Mayor? Is it true that the verdict itself is the result of the same public sentiment which sustained the unauthorized, unlawful conduct spoken of by Mayor Harrison? Can these things be true? See the methods employed to cook up testimony against us. On the 22nd day of August, 1886, the day following the verdict, at the conclusion of the trial, Captain Michael Schaack, who is credited with manipulating the evidence against us, made a statement which was sent out by the Associated Press as follows: He was asked if the police were now through with their labors. "Through," said he, "why, they have barely commenced. We mean to have others who are liable to the same charge indicted. I tell you the Anarchist business in Chicago is only commenced and before it is through we will have them all in jail, hanged or driven out of the city." "Did you place any men under arrest yesterday?" "That I do not wish to state." "The report is made that there are warrants out for a large number of persons." "If you think a moment you will see how foolish the idea would be. We have no room for a large number of persons in the jail, and it would be a needless expense to arrest many at once. We can get them as fast as we want them. We don't need to arrest them now. They may try to leave the city. Time enough to arrest them when they do." "Will any women be arrested?" "Why not? Some of them are a mighty sight worse than the men." "Do you think," said the Captain, continuing, "that if I had told the newspapers what I was doing when the Anarchist trial was going on that the jury would have brought in the verdict of yesterday? No, sir, a thousand times, no! Every prisoner would have gone free. Every reporter who came to me got nothing. I was making up the evidence, piece by piece, little by little, putting it where it belonged. If I had told all I knew as fast as I got the points the defense would have known what evidence was to be brought against them, and would have been prepared to meet it."

Now, your honor, it was claimed throughout this trial—the State's attorney claimed throughout the trial that he relied confidently on a verdict of guilty. They maintained that there was no doubt about it. I wish to call your attention to the declaration of Schaack: "No, sir, a thousand times no! Every prisoner would have gone free had I told all I knew as fast as I got the points. The defense would have known what evidence was to be brought against them, and would be prepared to meet it." This is equivalent to a declaration that if the accused persons had known what evidence was to be brought against them they would have brought evidence that would have been sufficient to acquit them "a thousand times" over. Here, then, is an explicit confession that we were condemned to death by evidence that was kept secret from both us and the public, and finally sprung upon us at the trial. See how Gilmer was sprung upon us. The district attorney, when he opened his case, said that he had nothing to conceal; he was going to be fair, and square, and honest about the thing; going to tell us what he was going to prove, and in the middle of the trial he brings up this man Gilmer, a wholly unexpected thing to us, and that was the hair upon which hung the thread which connected us with Matthias Degan, and the instrumentality by which the verdict was brought about. The States Attorney said he was not going to conceal anything and then concealed the very thing that was material.

Now, your honor, this confession that certain testimony was sprung upon us at the trial, this Gilmer matter, for instance, when no earthly opportunity was given us to meet it, and that we would have been acquitted a thousand times over, Captain Schaack's admission if we had known this evidence and then been permitted to contradict it and explain it; this confession, says Boston *Liberty*, commenting upon this infamous proceeding, is equivalent to a confession that we were innocent and that Captain Schaack knew we were innocent, or what is the same thing, that he knew that there was evidence that would have acquitted us a thousand times over if we had been allowed to produce it; but he glories in the fact that he was too smart for us; that by keeping this evidence secret from us and the public he was enabled to bring us into the trap; a trap, your honor, a trap which he and one other man—I suppose he refers to the State's attorney—had prepared for us, and thus secured our conviction.

Now, if this is not a confession that Captain Schaack and one other man, an accomplice, set themselves deliberately to work to procure the judicial murder of seven innocent men, men who they declare themselves to be innocent men, known by him and his accomplice to be innocent, then what is it? Plainly, it is nothing else. Schaack's confession that our evidence was such that if permitted to be introduced it would have acquitted us a thousand times over is equivalent to a confession that it is true, and that to procure our conviction by the suppression of this evidence was to procure the judicial murder of innocent men. And this work, says Captain Schaack, is to go on until he has all the Anarchists in jail, hung, or driven out of the city.

Your honor, I would like to make a remark right here. What stronger evidence can be required to prove the infamous character of what are called our criminal courts? Evidently, the courts are criminal, whether the persons they convict are criminal or not. Under such a condition of things as this, manifestly, a trial can have no color of justice or reason or be anything else than a conspiracy to convict a man, whether he be innocent or guilty, unless he is permitted to know what it is that they propose to prove upon him. This would be just, but justice and law are quite different things.

Now, as a part of this foul conspiracy the district attorney sprung his witness, Gilmer, upon us when it was too late for us to prove him to be a suborned, perjured liar, and the confession of this man Schaack is one that concerns the American people. They are bound to take notice of it. This trial, your honor, is not simply the trial and condemnation of seven Anarchists, but is the trial of the government of the State of Illinois, as represented by the gentleman in this prosecution, and the government of the United States itself. The oppressions of which we complain is such as the government of the United States is responsible for, and such as many millions of people, in fact, nearly all the people in the United States, are crying out against. You need not think that we stand alone. Some are crying out in more desperate tones than others, but all in tones that it will not do for any government, much less a government—a pretended government of the people—can disregard.

Now, in this state of things a murder is committed by some one. Not by us, nor by any of us but by some one as yet unknown. We are confessed by the chief agent in procuring our conviction to be innocent, and have had abundant proof of our innocence, or if we had been permitted to do so we could have proved ourselves innocent "a thousand times over," says Captain Schaack. But the government which, in the opinion of the despairing millions, whose woes and whose miseries we voice here today—the government is responsible for their wrongs, but the government does not brook any forcible resistance by even so much as a single man. It regards this single man as a torch that may explode vast numbers of others. It, therefore, demands not only a victim, but victims. Victims they must have, whether they be innocent or whether they be guilty. The innocent will answer for examples as well as the guilty. "Away with them! Victims are what we want," says monopoly and corporations. So, being unable to discover the guilty man, the machinery is set to work to convict seven innocent ones in his stead.

Your honor, there has been a great deal said in the trial of this case about the "Board of Trade demonstration," and the red and black flags.

In your refusal to grant us a new trial you allege as one of the reasons why Oscar Neebe should be sent to the penitentiary for fifteen years is that he presided at mass meetings of workingmen and organized several Trades Unions. You say:

"As to Neebe's part, there is the evidence of witnesses that he presided at meetings called by the class of people from whom this combination was drawn, and that he called meetings of the people who were engaged in the movement. There is evidence that he marched in the Board of Trade procession, the object of which was said to be the demolition of that building."

Now sir, do you hold it to be a crime for a man to organize the working people to defend themselves against "rifle diet, police clubs, strychnine," etc., or to preside at mass meetings of workingmen? You say that the object of the Board of Trade demonstration was "the demolition of the building." Who told you so? Where did you get your information? There is no evidence before this court to that effect. Not a particle. You say that our purpose was "to sack the Board of Trade." Ridiculous! Where did your honor get such an idea from? There is no testimony here to that effect. What right has your honor to assume what our motives were to charge us with intentions contrary to the proof? Now, sir, I deny it. It is not true.

Your honor, you say, in overruling our motion for a new trial, that our purpose was "the demolition of the building," to "sack it." Where is the proof? The article I have just read giving an account of the demonstration says it was intended as a protest against the practices of these monopolists; that was all. It was intended as a manifestation of the working people's discontent with the existing order of things; a protest against the practices of the class which the Board of Trade represents. Now, sir, is this the kind of testimony upon which you intend to deprive us of our lives and liberty? Is this the great crime for which we must suffer death? Because we have held such meetings, and made such speeches, you claim that we are responsible for the action of the person who threw the bomb at the Haymarket. If this is law, then every dissatisfied workingman and woman in America could be convicted for the same reason.

Your honor, this was a class verdict. I will admit one thing: I believe the jury were to a large extent imposed upon. Now, when the State's attorney comes in and brings the gory garments of the police, clotted with blood and filled with holes, and exhibits these garments to the jury—nobody denies that these men were killed—what was that done for? To prove that the policemen had been killed? Nobody denies that, what was it done for? It was done to prejudice that jury, to inflame that jury, and, in the language of Mr. Grinnell when he closed his speech, he says: "Let these things steel your hearts against these miserable wretches and scoundrels."

Suppose this Indianapolis man, sent by monopolists, came here and threw the bomb, and these gory garments are to be thrown around here in the court room before the jury for the purpose of steeling their hearts to bring about the conviction of eight innocent men? I ask your honor—I ask you for another trial.

Lawyer Ingham with clenched fist, swollen neck and blood-shot eyes exclaimed to the jury: "The State of Illinois is strong enough to hang every one of these Anarchists!" Well, who said it was not? But who would believe it mean enough to do so just because it can? The burley brute rapes his helpless victim simply because he is mean enough and strong enough to do so. The bourgeoisie society is not itself, however, unless it commits wholesale outrages upon the proletariat and afterwards gloat over its victims.

The ballot. Your honor, you have heard of this Law and Order League in these United States. It has been organized in Chicago and called a conservators' league or association. It is an organization of big tax-payers, if you have heard of it, and they come out and openly declare that they do not intend to permit the Knights of Labor and the workingmen to come into power through the ballot box. That is their own declaration, made in the papers here at their meetings, in their reports. Of course I don't know anything further about it. But I want to ask you this question, viz: Don't you think a man who is not able to control his bread—and you know what I mean by that—has a poor chance to control his vote; not a very good chance to control his vote? In other words, don't you think those who control the industries of the country can and do control the votes of that country? Don't you think that a man who must sell his labor or starve will sell his vote when the same alternative is presented? Does politics control wealth or wealth politics? Are the economically enslaved politically free? Your honor, political liberty without economic freedom is an empty phrase. The wage slave is a political freeman; yes, he is free to choose from among his economic masters the one who shall rule and govern him. A choice of masters, that is all. So this "Law and Order" League proposes to control the ballots of their wage slaves.

Now, then, the Haymarket, what of it? I had been away to Cincinnati. I went to Cincinnati Saturday night, May 1. I spoke there Sunday morning or during the day, at a great labor demonstration; an eight hour demonstration, a picnic of the workingmen at Cincinnati. They sent for me to come down. I stayed there Sunday. I went to their grove Sunday night, and I started back to Chicago Monday night, reached here Tuesday morning, May 4, and went home about eight o'clock and saw my wife. I took a nap on the lounge. About ten o'clock she woke me, then she says to me, "We had a very interesting meeting last Sunday of the tailor girls, the sewing girls of Chicago, a large mass meeting. I spoke to them, addressed the meeting; they were anxious to organize and I think we ought to do something to help those sewing women to organize and join the eight hour movement, because they work harder than anybody; these great tailor machines are very hard to work." So ended the conversation. She showed me the importance of having a meeting called at once and doing something for the eight hour movement for the girls. Well, I went on my way down town and I went to Greif's Hall. All the halls were occupied; this was during the eight hour strike. All the halls were occupied. A great many meetings were being held. I could get a hall nowhere else and the meeting was to be a business meeting anyway. It was not to be a general meeting, merely to appropriate money and take action and appoint a committee to get up hand bills and go and get some hall and so forth. That was all, so it did not require much; any ordinary room, any little room, anywhere, would have done for that, and the offices of the *Arbeiter-Zeitung*, at 107 Fifth avenue, suited that purpose; so I announced it in the *News* about twelve o'clock, I believe, and it was in the *News* in the afternoon of that day, not stating what the meeting was for, only it was important business. So at eight o'clock or about half-past seven that night—my wife and Mrs. Holmes left my home at No. 245 West Indiana street, accompanied by my two little babes—you have seen them here, a little girl of five and a boy of seven, you have seen them in the court room often. It was a nice evening and we walked down town; we walked until we got to Randolph and Halsted streets—however, in the afternoon, late in the afternoon, at the office of the *Arbeiter-Zeitung*, I learned that there was going to be a meeting at the Haymarket. But the meeting at No 107 Fifth avenue had already been called, and I could not attend it: I could not go over there. At half-past seven I left home with my wife, Mrs. Holmes and the children. We got to Halsted street. Two reporters, seeing me, thought there was a chance to get an item and came over to me—the *Times* man and the *Tribune* man; I forget their names.

"Hello, Parsons, what is the news?" says one.

"I don't know anything."

"Going to be a meeting here tonight?"

"Yes, I guess so."

"Going to speak?"

"No."

"Where are you going?"

"I have got another meeting on hand tonight."

And some playful remark was made. I slapped one of them on the back. I was quite well acquainted with the men and we made one or two brief remarks, and as they testified on the stand, I got on the car right then and there with my wife and two children, in company with Mrs. Holmes, and they saw that. I went down to fifth avenue.

When I got down there I found four or five other ladies there and about—well, probably, twelve or fifteen men. It was about 8:30 o'clock when we opened—I guess it was. We stayed there about half an hour. We settled the business. About the time we were through with it a committee came from the Haymarket, saying: "Nobody is over there but Spies. There is an awful big crowd, 3,000 or 4,000 people. For God's sake send somebody over. Come over, Parsons; come over, Fielden." Well, we went there. The meeting was adjourned and we all went over there together—all of us; my wife, Mrs. Holmes, two other ladies, and my two little children, went over to the Haymarket meeting. And these ladies sat ten feet behind the wagon from which I spoke.

Your honor, is it possible that a man would go into the dynamite-bomb business under those conditions and those circumstances? It is incredible. It is beyond human nature to believe such a thing possible, absolutely.

Well, the next day—I related on the witness stand all that I saw—the next day I saw that they were dragging these men to prison, treating them in a shameful manner. I left the city. I went to Geneva, Ill., for a couple of days; stayed there with friend Holmes. Then I went to Elgin, Ill.; stayed there a couple of days. Then I left there and went to Waukesha, Wis., where I obtained employment as a carpenter and afterward as a painter, and remained for over seven weeks in Waukesha. My health was debilitated, and I went to the springs when I was thirsty. The house I was working on was only half a block from the springs, and I needed the recreation and the rest, the pure air, and the water besides. When I saw the day fixed for the opening of this trial, knowing I was an innocent man, and also feeling that it was my duty to come forward and share whatever fate had in store for my comrades, and also to stand, if need be, on the scaffold, and vindicate the rights of labor, the cause of liberty, and the relief of the oppressed, I returned. How did I return? It is interesting, but it will take time to relate it, and I will not state it. I ran the gauntlet. I went from Waukesha to Milwaukee. I took the St. Paul train in the morning at the Milwaukee depot and came to Chicago; arrived here at 8:30, I suppose, in the morning. Went to the house of my friend, Mrs. Ames, on Morgan street. Sent for my wife and had a talk with her. I sent word to Captain Black that I was here and prepared to surrender. He sent word back to me that he was ready to receive me. I met him at the threshold of this building and we came up here together. I stood in the presence of this court. I have nothing, not even now, to regret.

APPENDIX

The Eleventh of November, 1887

Memorial Oration, delivered on November 11, 1901, in Chicago, by Voltairine de Cleyre

LET me begin my address with a confession. I make it sorrowfully and with self-disgust; but in the presence of great sacrifice we learn humility, and if my comrades could give their lives for their belief, why, let me give my pride. Yet I would not give it, for personal utterance is of trifling importance, were it not that I think at this particular season it will encourage those of our sympathizers whom the recent outburst of savagery may have disheartened, and perhaps lead some who are standing where I once stood to do as I did later.

This is my confession: Fifteen years ago last May when the echoes of the Haymarket bomb rolled through the little Michigan village where I then lived, I, like the rest of the credulous and brutal, read one lying newspaper headline, "Anarchists throw a bomb in a crowd in the Haymarket in Chicago," and immediately cried out, "They ought to be hung."—This, though I had never believed in capital punishment for ordinary criminals. For that ignorant, outrageous, blood-thirsty sentence I shall never forgive myself, though I know the dead men would have forgiven me, though I know those who loved them forgive me. But my own voice, as it sounded that night, will sound so in my ears till I die,—a bitter reproach and shame. What had I done? Credited the first wild rumor of an event of which I knew nothing, and, in my mind, sent men to the gallows without asking one word of defense! In one wild, unbalanced moment threw away the sympathies of a lifetime, and became an executioner at heart. And what I did that night millions did, and what I said millions said. I have only one word of extenuation for myself and all those people—ignorance. I did not know what Anarchism was. I had never seen it used save in histories, and there it was always synonymous with social confusion and murder. I believed the newspapers. I thought these men had thrown that bomb, unprovoked, into a mass of men and women, from a wicked delight in killing. And so thought all those millions of others. But out of those millions there were some few thousand—I am glad I was one of them—who did not let the matter rest there.

I know not what resurrection of human decency first stirred within me after that,—whether it was an intellectual suspicion that may be I did not know all the truth of the case and could not believe the newspapers, or whether it was the old strong undercurrrent of sympathy which of ten prompts the heart to go out to the accused, without a reason; but this I do know that though I was no Anarchist at the time of the execution, it was long and long before that, that I came to the conclusion that the accusation was false, the trial a farce, that there was no warrant either in justice or in law for their conviction; and that the hanging, if hanging there should be, would be the act of a society composed of people who had said what I said on the first night, and who had kept their eyes and ears fast shut ever since, determined to see nothing and to know nothing but rage and vengeance. Till the very end I hoped that mercy might intervene, though justice did not; and from the hour I knew neither would nor ever could again, I distrusted law and lawyers, judges and governors alike. And my whole being cried out to know what it was these men had stood for, and why they were hanged, seeing it was not proven they knew anything about the throwing of the bomb.

Little by little, here and there, I came to know that what they had stood for was a very high and noble ideal of human life, and what they were hanged for was preaching it to the common people,—the common people who were as ready to hang them, in their ignorance, as the court and the prosecutor were in their malice! Little by little I came to know that these were men who had a clearer vision of human right than most of their fellows; and who, being moved by deep social sympathies, wished to share their vision with their fellows, and so proclaimed it in the market-place. Little by little I realized that the misery, the pathetic submission, the awful degradation of the workers, which from the time I was old enough to begin to think had borne heavily upon my heart, (as they must bear upon all who have hearts to feel at all), had smitten theirs more deeply still,—so deeply that they knew no rest save in seeking a way out,—and that was more than I had ever had the sense to conceive. For me there had never been a hope there should be no more rich and poor; but a vague idea that there might not be so rich and so poor, if the workingmen by combining could exact a little better wages, and make their hours a little shorter. It was the message of these men, (and their death swept that message far out into ears that would never have heard their living voices), that all such little dreams are folly. That not in demanding little, not in striking for an hour less, not in mountain labor to bring forth mice, can any lasting alleviation come; but in demanding, much,—all,—in a bold self-assertion of the worker to toil any hours he finds sufficient, not that another finds for him,—here is where the way out lies. That message, and the message of others, whose works, associated with theirs, their death drew to my notice, took me up, as it were, upon a mighty hill, wherefrom I saw the roofs of the workshops of the little world. I saw the machines, the things that men had made to ease their burden, the wonderful things, the iron genii, I saw them set their iron teeth in the living flesh of the men who made them; I saw the maimed and crippled stumps of men go limping away into the night that engulfs the poor, perhaps to be thrown up in the flotsam and jetsam of beggary for a time, perhaps to suicide in some dim corner where the black surge throws its slime.

I saw the rose fire of the furnace shining on the blanched face of the man who tended it, and knew surely as I knew anything in life, that never would a free man feed his blood to the fire like that.

I saw swart bodies, all mangled and crushed, borne from the mouths of the mines to be stowed away in a grave hardly less narrow and dark than that in which the living form had crouched ten, twelve, fourteen hours a day; and I knew that in order that I might be warm—I, and you, and those others who never do any dirty work—those men had slaved away in those black graves, and been crushed to death at last.

I saw beside city streets great heaps of horrible colored earth, and down at the bottom of the trench from which it was thrown, so far down that nothing else was visible, bright gleaming eyes, like a wild animal's hunted into its hole. And I knew that free men never chose to labor there, with pick and shovel in that foul, sewage-soaked earth, in that narrow trench, in that deadly sewer gas ten, eight, even six hours a day. Only slaves would do it.

I saw deep down in the hull of the ocean liner the men who shoveled the coal—burned and seared like paper before the grate; and I knew that "the record" of the beautiful monster, and the pleasure of the ladies who laughed on the deck, were paid for with these withered bodies and souls.

I saw the scavenger carts go up and down, drawn by sad brutes driven by sadder ones; for never a man, a man in full possession of his self-hood, would freely choose to spend all his days in the nauseating stench that forces him to swill alcohol to neutralize it.

And I saw in the lead works how men were poisoned, and in the sugar refineries how they went insane; and in the factories how they lost their decency; and in the stores how they learned to lie; and I knew it was slavery made them do all this. I knew the Anarchists were right,—the whole thing must be changed, the whole thing was wrong,—the whole system of production and distribution, the whole ideal of life.

And I questioned the government then; they had taught me to question it. What have you done—you the keepers of the Declaration and the Constitution—what have you done about all this? What have you done to preserve the conditions of freedom to the people?

Lied, deceived, fooled, tricked, bought and sold and got gain! You have sold away the land, that you had no right to sell. You have murdered the aboriginal people, that you might seize the land in the name of the white race, and then steal it away from them again, to be again sold by a second and a third robber. And that buying and selling of the land has driven the people off the healthy earth and away from the clean air into these rot-heaps of humanity called cities, where every filthy thing is done, and filthy labor breeds filthy bodies and filthy souls. Our boys are decayed with vice before they come to manhood; our girls—ah, well might John Harvey write:

"Another begetteth a daughter white and gold,
    She looks into the meadow land water, and the world
Knows her no more; they have sought her field and fold

But the City, the City hath bought her,
It hath sold
Her piecemeal, to students, rats, and reek of the graveyard mould."

You have done this thing, gentlemen who engineer the government; and not only have you caused this ruin to come upon others; you yourselves are rotten with this debauchery. You exist for the purpose of granting privileges to whoever can pay most for you, and so limiting the freedom of men to employ themselves that they must sell themselves into this frightful slavery or become tramps, beggars, thieves, prostitutes, and murderers. And when you have done all this, what then do you do to them, these creatures of your own making? You, who have set them the example in every villainy? Do you then relent, and remembering the words of the great religious teacher to whom most of you offer lip service on the officially religious day, do you go to these poor, broken, wretched creatures and love them? Love them and help them, to teach them to be better? No: you build prisons high and strong, and there you beat, and starve, and hang, finding by the working of your system human beings so unutterably degraded that they are willing to kill whomsoever they are told to kill at so much monthly salary.

This is what the government is, has always been, the creator and defender of privilege; the organization of oppression and revenge. To hope that it can ever become anything else is the vainest of delusions. They tell you that Anarchy, the dream of social order without government, is a wild fancy. The wildest dream that ever entered the heart of man is the dream that mankind can ever help itself through an appeal to law, or to come to any order that will not result in slavery wherein there is any excuse for government.

It was for telling the people this that these five men were killed. For telling the people that the only way to get out of their misery was first to learn what their rights upon this earth were;—freedom to use the land and all within it and all the tools of production—and then to stand all together and take them, themselves, and not to appeal to the jugglers of the law. Abolish the law—that is abolish privilege,—and crime will abolish itself.

They will tell you these men were hanged for advocating force. What! These creatures who drill men in the science of killing, who put guns and clubs in hands they train to shoot and strike, who hail with delight the latest inventions in explosives, who exult in the machine that can kill the most with the least expenditure of energy, who declare a war of extermination upon people who do not want their civilization, who ravish, and burn, and garotte and guillotine, and hang, and electrocute, they have the impertinence to talk about the unrighteousness of force! True, these men did advocate the right to resist invasion by force. You will find scarcely one in a thousand who does not believe in that right. The one will be either a real Christian or a non-resistant Anarchist. It will not be a believer in the State. No, no; it was not for advocating forcible resistance on principle, but for advocating forcible resistance to their tyrannies, and for advocating a society which would forever make an end of riches and poverty, of governors and governed.

The spirit of revenge, which is always stupid, accomplished its brutal act. Had it lifted its eyes from its work, it might have seen in the background of the scaffold that bleak November morning the dawn-light of Anarchy whiten across the world.

So it came first,—a gleam of hope to the proletaire, a summons to rise and shake off his material bondage. But steadily, steadily the light has grown, as year by year the scientist, the literary genius, the artist, and the moral teacher, have brought to it the tribute of their best work, their unpaid work, the work they did for love. To-day it means not only material emancipation, too; it comes as the summing up of all those lines of thought and action which for three hundred years have been making towards freedom; it means fulness of being, the free life.

And I say it boldly, notwithstanding the recent outburst of condemnation, notwithstanding the cry of lynch, burn, shoot, imprison, deport, and the Scarlet Letter A to be branded low down upon the forehead, and the latest excuse for that fond esthetic decoration "the button," that for two thousand years no idea has so stirred the world as this,—none which had such living power to break down barriers of race and degree, to attract prince and proletaire, poet and mechanic, Quaker and Revolutionist. No other ideal but the free life is strong enough to touch the man whose infinite pity and understanding goes alike to the hypocrite priest and the victim of Siberian whips; the loving rebel who stepped from his title and his wealth to labor with all the laboring earth; the sweet strong singer who sang

No Master, high or low;

the lover who does not measure his love nor reckon on return; the self-centered one who "will not rule, but also will not ruled be"; the philosopher who chanted the Over-man; the devoted woman of the people; ay, and these too,—these rebellious flashes from the vast cloud-hung ominous obscurity of the anonymous, these souls whom governmental and capitalistic brutality has whipped and goaded and stung to blind rage and bitterness, these mad young lions of revolt, these Winkelrieds who offer their hearts to the spears.

About the contributors

Lucy Parsons (1851–1942) was a labor organizer, writer, public speaker, and cofounder of the Industrial Workers of the World. She was of Black, Mexican and, likely, Native American ancestry. Parsons published *Life of Albert R. Parsons* in 1889 and a collection of her writings, *Lucy Parsons: Freedom, Equality and Solidarity – Writings and Speeches, 1878–1937*, was published in 2004.

David R. Roediger teaches American Studies at University of Kansas. He is the author of *An Ordinary White: My Antiracist Education* and the co-editor, with Franklin Rosemont, of *Haymarket Scrapbook*.

Voltairine de Cleyre (1866–1912) was the first prominent American-born anarchist. From her writings and speeches, through the illnesses that plagued her, the assassination attempt that left her clinging to life, to her early death at forty-five, she worked tirelessly to promote anarchism.

August Spies (1855–1887) was a German-born anarchist, editor of the *Arbeiter-Zeitung*, labor activist, and upholsterer by trade. He was hanged on November 11, 1887.

Michael Schwab (1853–1898), born in Germany, was a bookbinder by trade and associate editor of the *Arbeiter-Zeitung*, and was later pardoned by Illinois governor John Altgeld.

Oscar Neebe (1850–1916) was born in New York City, and settled in Chicago in 1877 with his family, was office manager of the *Arbeiter-Zeitung*, and was later pardoned by Illinois governor John Altgeld.

Adolph Fischer (1858–1887) was born in Germany and immigrated to the US at the age of fifteen. He was a member of the International

Working People's Association, a typesetter for the *Arbeiter-Zeitung*, and was hanged on November 11, 1887.

Louis Lingg (1864–1887) was born in Germany, apprenticed as a carpenter, and was active in his union. He died on November 10, 1887, after ingesting a blasting cap smuggled into his cell by Dyer D. Lum.

George Engel (1836–1887) emigrated to the US from Germany in 1873, moving to Chicago in 1876 where he operated a toy shop. Engel was a member of the International Working People's Association and was hanged on November 11, 1887.

Samuel Fielden (1847–1922) was born in England and settled in Chicago in 1869. Engel was a Methodist pastor, worked as a teamster, treasurer for the International Working People's Association, and was a labor activist. He served six years of his fifteen year sentence before being pardoned by Illinois governor John Altgeld.

Albert R. Parsons (1848–1887) moved from Texas to Chicago with wife Lucy in 1873, was a typesetter, labor leader, editor of *The Alarm*, member of the Knights of Labor, and in 1883 helped establish the International Working People's Association. He was hanged on November 11, 1887.

AK PRESS is small, in terms of staff and resources, but we also manage to be one of the world's most productive anarchist publishing houses. We publish close to twenty books every year, and distribute thousands of other titles published by like-minded independent presses and projects from around the globe. We're entirely worker-run and democratically managed. We operate without a corporate structure—no boss, no managers, no bullshit.

The **FRIENDS OF AK PRESS** program is a way you can directly contribute to the continued existence of AK Press, and ensure that we're able to keep publishing books like this one! Friends pay $25 a month directly into our publishing account ($30 for Canada, $35 for international), and receive a copy of every book AK Press publishes for the duration of their membership! Friends also receive a discount on anything they order from our website or buy at a table: 50% on AK titles, and 30% on everything else. We have a Friends of AK ebook program as well: $15 a month gets you an electronic copy of every book we publish for the duration of your membership. *You can even sponsor a very discounted membership for someone in prison.*

Email **friendsofak@akpress.org** for more info, or visit the website: **https://www.akpress.org/friends.html**.

There are always great book projects in the works—so sign up now to become a Friend of AK Press, and let the presses roll!

FRIENDS OF AK PRESS